The Women's Suffrage Movement and Irish Society in the Early Twentieth Century

Cliona Murphy

Lecturer in History
California State University at Bakersfield

HARVESTER WHEATSHEAF

NEW YORK   LONDON   TORONTO   SYDNEY   TOKYO

First published 1989 by
Harvester Wheatsheaf
66 Wood Lane End, Hemel Hempstead
Hertfordshire HP2 4RG
A division of
Simon & Schuster International Group

© Cliona Murphy 1989

Printed and bound in Great Britain
by Billing & Sons Ltd, Worcester

British Library Cataloguing in Publication Data

Murphy, Cliona
The women's suffrage movement and Irish
society in the early twentieth century.
1. Ireland (Republic). Women's suffrage
movements, to 1922
I. Title
324.6'23'09417
ISBN 0-7108-1219-1

---

1 2 3 4 5 93 92 91 90 89

For a very new Irish woman Victoria Rachel
and for her grandparents Cita and John

Contents

Contents

Acknowledgements

Finally I can sit down and write the acknowledgements. A number of people in four different countries have helped in the composition of this book. Firstly, I would like to thank Dr Tom Dunne of the Irish History Department, University College, Cork, Ireland for reading drafts of the chapters while I was doing my Ph.D. My thanks also to Professor W. Warren Wagar of the History Department, SUNY Binghamton, chairman of my Ph.D. committee, for reading and commenting on my draft chapters and coordinating the operation from the American side. Professors Africa, Hertz and Henke of Binghamton must be thanked for being on my committee. Dr Ged Martin of the Centre for Canadian Studies, Edinburgh, Scotland, encouraged me as a graduate student. My Master's work on H.G. Wells, oddly enough (and probably to H.G.'s delight!), led me to this study on Irish women. My late childhood friend Claire Barker of Cork, Ireland drew my attention to new publications which I might otherwise have missed while in the United States and London. The most helpful librarian at the Fawcett Library, London, David Doughan, was of invaluable assistance in pointing me in the right direction on a number of occasions. The friendship and help of Rosaleen Crowley, Una Fahy, Eileen Magner, Maria Luddy and Fiona Coleman is much appreciated. Thanks also to Nancy Clarke Budd of Surrey, England and Janet Carter of London, England.

Abbreviations

AOH	Ancient Order of Hibernians
IPP	Irish Parliamentary Party (also known as the Irish Party and Irish Nationalist Party)
IWFL	Irish Women's Franchise League (militant Irish suffrage movement
IWSLGA	Irish Women's Suffrage and Local Government Association
IRL	Irishwomen's Reform League
ISF	Irishwomen's Suffrage Federation
IWSS	Irish Women's Suffrage Society
IWWU	Irish Women's Workers Union
MWFL	Munster Women's Franchise League
NUWSS	National Union of Women's Suffrage Societies (English non-militant movement led by Mrs Fawcett)
UIL	United Irish League
WSPU	Women's Social and Political Union (English militant movement led by the Pankhursts)

· 1 ·

Placing Suffragist Women in Irish History:
Historiography and Goals

Although the movements for women's suffrage have long enjoyed a privileged position in women's history, the Irish women's suffrage movement has almost entirely escaped the attention of Irish and women's historians alike. At least until recently, Irish history has emphasised nationalism and shown very little interest in broader social issues. Yet the few historians who have even noticed it in passing have dismissed any call for further investigation on the grounds that it constituted little more than a shadow of the British movement, or conversely, a weak extension of the Irish Nationalist movement.

Where there has been historiographical emphasis on women it has concentrated on movements such as the Ladies Land League and Cumann na mBan; movements which existed in the case of the former to carry on the work of the imprisoned male Land League (1880–1) and in the case of the latter to act as a support group to the nationalist separatists. The reasons for this focus are fairly obvious. After the foundation of the state (1921) those women who put nationalism before suffrage, who aided the revolutionaries, carrying out dangerous missions such as smuggling guns or bombs, drew great praise from the revolutionaries and the new Irish state and thus, almost immediately, acquired a revered place in the sphere of folk history as heroines comparable only to ancient Gaelic Queens.

In contrast the suffragists[1] were viewed by their contemporaries and the next generation as unnationalistic, if not traitors, for putting another issue before the sacred cause of

1

nationalism. In the decades after independence they were on the whole forgotten, although one or two like Hanna Sheehy Skeffington and Louie Bennett were still active in political and trade union circles. The Ireland that gradually evolved after independence was imbued with a Catholic ethos, glorifying the family and the institution of marriage, and though it considered it had elevated women to a revered position it had no time for remembering the women who strode a very independent path. Rather it told them their place was in the home as wife and mother.[2] This idea was embodied in de Valera's 1937 constitution which created conditions whereby Ireland was to become a Catholic rather than a secular state, a state controlled by men.[3] "Ireland, more than most, is a man's country, . . . Women sit in the Dail [Parliament], it is true, but usually widows, or descendants of noted patriots." Thus wrote Elizabeth Coxhead in her book *Daughters of Eirin*, yet despite this insight she too made the mistake of ignoring the suffragist women.[4]

It is not only Irish historians who have ignored this side of Irish life in the early twentieth century, but women's historians too have neglected an examination of the movement in Ireland. Among the many studies of the suffrage movement in the United Kingdom, which after all included Ireland, few have concentrated specifically on the phenomenon in Ireland. Where reference is made, the impression is generally conveyed that Ireland provided little more than a branch of one of the English movements. Even Richard J. Evans's comparative study of feminist movements, *The Feminists* (1977), completely ignores the Irish case. This is despite the fact that he discusses movements just as small or even smaller in countries such as Finland and Iceland. A large part of his thesis has to do with suffrage movements being more successful in Protestant countries than Catholic and he looks at France, Belgium and Italy to illustrate his point. One wonders why he neglected Ireland. Perhaps he would have found a few points which would have contradicted his argument, perhaps he made the common mistake in regarding it as no different from the rest of the United Kingdom?[5]

Despite all this neglect there has been a steady trickle of publications on individual Irish women. This work has been carried out, until recently, for the most part by interested individuals rather than academic historians. It has not been specifically about feminist women, but nevertheless it shows a searching for some type of history of Irish women. R.M. Fox has contributed two books on the subject, *Rebel Irish Women* (1935) which has very interesting studies of Mary McSwiney, Hanna Sheehy Skeffington, Maud Gonne and others, but it is written with a certain condescension which indicates that these women were the exception, quaint in their unusualness but not the desired norm. Nevertheless it makes particularly interesting reading as the author personally knew many of the women concerned.[6]

His biography of the trade unionist Louie Bennett twenty-two years later is very informative despite the fact that he has written it with the jaundiced eye of a middle class Catholic nationalist.[7] He examines the forces which from her early adolescence influenced her towards a feminism of an all-embracing type. It is a pity he or someone else did not do a few more full length biographies of women of this period. Elizabeth Coxhead's study *Daughters of Eirin: Five Women of the Irish Renaissance* (1969) added substantially to the existing material, but made no effort to link the five women to each other or to a specific ideology which made them different.[8] There have been a number of interesting biographies of women like Maud Gonne and Countess Markievicz, but these women are firmly planted in the nationalist camp.[9] The recent Virago publication of Markievicz's prison letters provides glimpses of the tensions experienced between the nationalist and suffragist women.[10]

Autobiographical accounts of the period are valuable manuscripts in an area where secondary material is sparse. One of the leaders of the suffragist movement in Ireland, Hanna Sheehy Skeffington has written a number of lucid articles with her account of the movement—some were written with hindsight and others at the time of the movement itself, indeed one was writen on the eve of going into gaol.[11] She was always conscious of playing a role within a historical context and she saw herself in a line of succession of Irish feminists. However she believed she represented a new type of more determined woman who would not be put off by shallow, feeble promises. Thus all her writings are of great benefit in providing an insight into what was going on in the period under study and putting it in its context.

The fairly sizeable autobiography of James and Margaret Cousins, *We Two Together* (1950), is excellent for the historian interested in the inner workings of the suffrage organisation and the *raison d'être* of the movement. It recreates the atmosphere of the early twentieth century and the Irish Renaissance in Dublin, and recaptures the intellectual excitement many felt in the company of the great poets, playwrights and writers. It reveals the rather bizarre connections the suffragists had with mysticism, theosophy and spiritualism. It provides a factual account of the movement in Ireland and England, and gives details of the setting up of the Irish Women's Franchise League and of their subsequent demonstrations and militant activities. However it does have the defect of being written at a distance both in time and in space, in India in the late 1940s. This flaw is particularly noticeable when one compares the Cousins's recall of events with contemporary documents.[12]

In the 1960s Alan Denson compiled a bibliographical survey of the works of both James and Margaret Cousins and it is detailed to such an extent as to refer to every letter they wrote to the newspapers. Denson's work is invaluable and provides a very solid basis for a biography of this couple.[13]

By the mid 1970s a few establishment historians began to take an interest in this neglected area of Irish History thus reflecting the general trend of what was happening in the United States and Britain. (However it must be admitted that progress has been slower and the academic acceptability of a women's history considerably less.)

The first sign of the new approach was the O'Corrain and MacCurtain book, *Women in Irish Society* (1978).[14] In this collection of articles women are examined in Irish society from the coming of Christianity to the 1960s. Its articles by Lee on women and the church in nineteenth-century Ireland and MacCurtain on the suffrage movement are of particular interest to this history. A special issue of the *Crane Bag* in 1980 contained useful articles on women's higher education by Breathnach and on religion and women by MacCurtain.[15]

Other interesting articles appeared in *Eire/Ireland* by McKillen on the struggle between nationalism and feminism from 1914 to 1923. Both McKillen and MacCurtain ponder over the question whether nationalism damaged the feminist cause and divided people's loyalties. McKillen disputes MacCurtain's argument that the nationalist movement damaged the feminist movement, rather she argues that the nationalist and feminist movements had a reciprocal effect on each other with the nationalist movement becoming more feminist and the feminist movement becoming more nationalist as time went on.[16] This concentration on nationalism versus feminism has been the main focus of study in examinations of the Irish suffrage movement to the detriment of other equally interesting aspects of the movement.

The 1970s and 1980s have seen an acceleration of publications in women's studies area in Ireland, as elsewhere, no doubt brought about by the growing confidence of Irish feminist publishing houses established over the last decade or so.[17] A few interesting biographies have also appeared that shed light on the personalities involved in the suffrage movement. *Tom Kettle, An Enigma* is a portrait of an Irish Nationalist MP who for a multitude of reasons had turned his back on his former friends, the women suffragists. This book provides an insight into the way the suffrage question was viewed by the Irish Parliamentary Party. Indeed Kettle's dilemma on the question is but an individual example of what was happening to a whole party.[18] His ultimate defection from the suffragist camp illustrated that there was little hope of getting any Home Ruler to support women's suffrage seriously in either a Home Rule Bill or as an independent women's suffrage Bill in Parliament.

In *With Wooden Sword*, a portrait of the pacifist and suffragist Frank Sheehy Skeffington, there is a wealth of detail on the reasons behind the formation of the Irish Women's Franchise League. The book is good too on the IWFL's relationship with the Irish Parliamentary Party.[19] The comprehensive biography of Hanna Sheehy Skeffington by the same author, Leah Levenson, further adds to our knowledge of this unusual couple.[20] Charlotte Fallon's biography of Mary McSwiney, *Soul of Fire*, is a detailed account of this Cork woman's life.[21] First a suffragist and later caught up with the nationalist struggle McSwiney illustrates yet again the tensions between these two similar but conflicting ideologies. The first chapter of Fallon's book is particularly useful in providing an understanding of why one woman abandoned the struggle of her sex for the struggle of her countrymen. However it is all too obvious that there is a dearth of serious biographies on the many significant women who are mentioned time and again in this book. This is just another example of how neglected the area is. Two bibliographical compilations of women in Irish history are also worth noting. Though a little sparse in detail, content and size, *Missing Pieces* and *More Missing Pieces* have broken new ground in the attempt to establish the basis for a bibliographical dictionary of Irish women.[22]

In 1983 a pioneering study by Belfast feminist Margaret Ward, *Unmanageable Revolutionaries*, appeared. She has looked at the emergence of women's movements in the national and land context from their beginnings as relatively autonomous organisations to their eventual absorption into the male movements. However, while this book examines the movements thoroughly it does not put them into context in the wider area of women's history and tends to exaggerate the uniqueness of the Irish situation. For example the struggle between feminism and socialism was just as intense. The questions of priorities did not apply to Ireland alone.[23]

But largely what has been wrong with the current historiography is an excessive preoccupation with the political women, or to be more accurate the auxiliary women, those who were in various ways anxious to support the male nationalist organisations. However, Rosemary Cullen Owen's book (1984) based on her MA thesis, is one of the first attempts at a detailed study of the suffragists themselves. *Smashing Times* is a slim volume looking at the movement's internal actions in Ireland up until 1918. It is a good introductory work. It examines the nineteenth-century background and the reasons for the new revolutionary approach of the movement in the early twentieth century. It is particularly good on the movement's link with the Labour movement. While it briefly refers to reactions of Irish Party members and the churches, and touches on the women's experiences in gaol it does not do so in any great detail, devoting no more than a few pages to all three. It does not look specifically at public and press reaction nor does it give any attention to the movement in a world context. It is a study of the women's suffrage movement in Ireland in the very narrow sense with specific concentration on the militant IWFL. The present work attempts to deal with these shortcomings.[24]

One of the movement's most prominent leaders, Hanna Sheehy Skeffington, collected credible statistics which indicated that the suffrage movement in Ireland was proportionately as large as it was in Britain. Rather than the movement's membership being confined to the capital city, it was also drawn from many provincial towns and country districts. Rather than there being just one Irish suffrage organisation there were several ranging from left to right of the political spectrum, from Protestant to Catholic, from Nationalist to Unionist. Although the Irish movement for women's suffrage asserted solidarity with the aims—and often the means—of the British movement, and did receive verbal backing from London, its substantive connection to the British movement amounted to little more than its connections with the American or Australian movements. Proximity and a common government necessitated a certain amount of interaction between the Irish and British suffragists, but did not make them members of a single movement. The Irish Women's Franchise League had its own constitution, its own newspaper, and its own vision of a future in which Irish women would be enfranchised in a "Free Ireland".

While nationalism estranged the IWFL from the English suffragists, it did little to draw them closer to any section of the nationalists, the constitutionalist Irish Party, Republican Sinn Fein or the Ancient Order of Hibernians. For despite their intense consciousness of being Irish, their primary goal remained the attainment of women's suffrage: Home Rule came second, especially so long as the proposed Home Rule Bills promised to grant independence and control over women's future to Irish men alone. Under these conditions, claimed the sceptical women, instead of post-independence Ireland inaugurating Irish Home Rule, it would inaugurate "Irish Male Rule".

The situation was even more complicated. There were a number of suffragist groups in Ireland who while wishing to enfranchise women at the same time wished to remain in the Union with the United Kingdom. There were Unionists and Nationalists in the Munster Women's Franchise League and the Irish Women's Suffrage and Local Government Association, while the Irish Women's Suffrage Society tended towards Unionism. The Irish branch of Conservative and Unionist Women's Franchise Association under no account wished to leave the Union. Some Unionist women found themselves in the strange situation of advocating a women's suffrage amendment to a Home Rule Bill they did not want.

During the years 1908–14, the Irish suffragists faced a quandary. Until that point their history, which had begun in 1876, had been relatively quiet and unnoticed, doubtless as a result of their pacifism and the 'drawing room' nature of their movement. There was little they could do to force the hands of the legislators in another country. Beginning in 1908 a number of new factors changed the situation. A group of women formed the Irish Women's Franchise League which was willing to adopt militant methods when other methods failed. With a Liberal government in power, Home Rule seemed imminent, especially after 1911 when the Lords lost their veto. This created a situation where it was imperative that women's suffrage be included in a Home Rule Bill. The Irish Party held the balance of power and thus were responsible for the passing or blocking of Women's Suffrage Bills. During this time also the English Pankhurst movement, the Women's Social and Political Union, began to display imperialist designs on the Irish movement which were resisted by the IWFL and in a sense made them more independent.

At this stage the various suffrage groups in Ireland differed not only over nationalism, but over militancy, party affiliations, and even eligibility for suffrage. Yet this book will demonstrate that the history of the suffrage movement in Ireland cannot be reduced to a story of petty internal squabbles. The movement as a whole built up considerable strength and received recognition and support from the movements in the United States, Britain, South Africa, Australia, Norway and Finland. Women in these countries saw the Irish movement as distinct, solid and worthy of encouragement.

After 1914 the nature of the suffrage movement in Ireland changed considerably and therefore that period will to a large extent remain outside the scope of this study. Forces both in Irish and world politics necessitated philosophical adaptations to be made and affected the qualities that characterised the Irish suffrage movement in the years before 1914. The advent of the First World War had a number of consequences for women involved in the suffrage struggle. Some Irish women directed their efforts into voluntary work for the war, while others determined that a British war should have nothing to do with them both as women and as Irish people. They, nevertheless, found that it was impossible to ignore a war that was being fought on such a gigantic scale. It was difficult to go abroad to demonstrations and conferences and difficult to find an interested public. Their public was not only distracted by the war but also by the quickly accelerating nationalist movement in Ireland. The latter not only claimed the attention of the public but also of a number of suffragists and thus put a further strain upon the suffrage movement.

Many themes and questions recur throughout the book which have significance for the final conclusion about the place of the suffrage movement in modern Irish History. There were several tugs of loyalty experienced by the suffragists which meant that they could never concentrate on one issue alone. These tugs were between nationalism and suffragism, between Unionism and suffragism, between socialism and suffragism, and even between religion and suffragism. There was the tension between the Catholic and Protestant ideal of womanhood which emphasised motherhood and the picture the suffragists were putting forward of an educated, economically independent and internationally-minded woman. There was the tug between being concerned with all women or with a particular section of women and between being concerned with the suffrage alone or with other issues affecting women. These tensions shaped the movement, dictated its character and linked it to its society.

This brings us to the middle-class nature of the movement and the question of its narrow appeal. For whatever reasons, its concentration on a narrow suffrage demand was bound to alienate working-class women. Education, and especially higher education, which was becoming more widely available may have opened the world of feminism to the suffragists but it actually separated them further intellectually as well as socially from their fellow countrywomen. This becomes apparent again and again in the class-conscious speech of the suffragists. This image was not negated by the harsh experiences undergone by a minority of them in gaol and on the hungerstrike. For all along they were considered ladies, hence the horror and outrage at any indications that they were not being treated for what they were, educated middle-class women with a servant or two at home.

Should any movement be considered on its own and not in the context of its time and society, any concluding statements would be pointless. Hence the concentration of well over half of this book on the impact of the movement on Irish society and the reaction of Irish society to the suffragists. Indeed had the movement gone unnoticed in Ireland a detailed study of it would have little appeal. Since the movement was the embodiment of the idea that women should not be banned from having the vote because they are women, it obviously was part of the intellectual climate of the early twentieth-century Ireland. As with all ideas it did not remain between the pages of a book, or in the minds of one or two individuals. It was discussed, distributed by means of propaganda, pondered upon, debated, altered, extended, rejected and accepted by different parts of society. This process meant that the idea was alive, vibrant and significant in Irish society just as it was in many other societies throughout the world at this time. As such it is of interest that a number of Irish intellectuals considered it worthy of support. However, the idea did not remain within the limited circle of intellectuals, and it gradually filtered down through society and was reacted to in varying manners. The proponents of the idea proselytised throughout the country and were rewarded by the judgements of the press and the general public. In a sense it was a mirror image of another idea at the forefront of the people's minds in Ireland—that of the right of a nation to sovereignty. As shall be seen, this comparison was repeatedly being made.

One area of Irish society which was most concerned was the institutionalised churches, particularly the majority Catholic Church. From the pulpit, to the meeting hall, to the printed word, clergymen let it be known what they thought of this idea and how it could or could not be incorporated with the church's teachings on the position of women. Such an important source of power and influence in Ireland cannot be dismissed lightly in studying any social movement. Any challenge to their concepts had to be met head on.

Another body of men who could hardly avoid reacting were the Nationalists in the Irish Party who were bombarded with petitions, bags of flour and heckling to ensure that women's suffrage would be part of any Home Rule settlement. They were constantly reminded of the similarity of their demands with the women's demands and the irony of them failing to empathise with the women. If the women were to attain the suffrage either within the context of the United Kingdom or an independent Ireland they needed the help of the men.

From all accounts it would appear that at some stage most Irish towns received a visit from the suffragists and the Irish people had an opportunity to listen to the women at the public meetings. Their newspapers reported on the suffragists' activities. Therefore in their local papers, in their church and in the town square Irish people were confronted with the suffrage idea. And indeed they also had the opportunity of meeting a number of foreign suffragists who visited and toured Ireland. Their reactions are important for the historian desiring to assess the extent to which the idea became acceptable in Irish society. The interrelationship between Irish suffragists and those abroad is a further example of the idea being vibrant in Ireland. Therefore this study is not just concerned with a few years in the life of a women's suffrage movement but also with how that movement affected its society and challenged its views on the role of women. It will ask whether or not there was a receptive, ambivalent or hostile audience to the movement in Ireland. How was the movement seen by Nationalists, both constitutional and republican, men and women? Were there organised groups against women's suffrage? Did opponents within society and especially within the churches react not only against women getting the vote but to the very fact that they were outside in the streets and public parks campaigning for it? How did they react when women began smashing windows and going to gaol? How was the movement presented to the general public in the press? Were objections always on a moral basis, or were they sometimes based upon economic and political objections? What impression did the sporadic visits of foreign suffragists to Ireland have both on the Irish people and the Irish suffragists? How did going abroad shape the Irish movement? Why were the Irish Nationalist MPs so reluctant to agree to either a Women's Suffrage Amendment to the Home Rule Bill or a Women's Suffrage Bill? These and other questions will be examined in an effort in some small way to fill in a missing gap in Irish history.

Notes

1. In this study the word "suffragist" will be used to describe any woman involved in the fight for women's suffrage, be she in favour of or against militancy. The word "suffragette" coined by the *Daily Mail* in 1903 will only be used when it occurs in quotations.
2. Jenny Beale, *Women in Ireland—Voices of Change* (Gill and Macmillan, Dublin, 1986).
3. Basil Chubb, *The Government and Politics of Ireland* (Longman, London and New York, 1982).
4. Elizabeth Coxhead, *Daughters of Erin: Five Women of the Irish Renaissance* (Secker and Warburg, London, 1969), p. 13.
5. Richard Evans, *The Feminists* (Croom Helm, London, 1977).
6. R.M. Fox, *Rebel Irish Women* (Talbot Press, Dublin, 1935).
7. R.M. Fox, *Louie Bennett, Her Life and Times* (Talbot Press, Dublin, 1957).
8. Elizabeth Coxhead, *op. cit.*
9. A. Marreco, *Rebel Countess: The Life and Times of Countess Markievicz* (London, 1967), Jacqueline Van Vorris, *Countess Markievcz: In the Cause of Ireland* (Massachusetts University Press, Amherst, 1967),

Samuel Levenson, *Maud Gonne* (London, Cassell, 1977), Diana Norman, *Terrible Beauty: A Life of Constance Markievicz* (Hodder and Stoughton, London, 1987).

10. *Prison Letters of Countess Markievicz* (Virago Press, London, 1986).

11. Hanny Sheehy Skeffington, "Reminiscences" in *Irish Women's Struggle for the Vote*, A.D. Sheehy Skeffington and Rosemary Owens, "Women in Politics", *The Bell*, November 1943, *British Militarism as I Have Known it* (Donnelly Press), *Sinn Fein in America* (Davis, Dublin, 1919), *Irish Review*, July 1912. There is a radio transcript of an interview with Hanna Sheehy Skeffington in the National Library of Ireland.

12. James and Margaret Cousins, *We Two Together* (Ganesh, Madras, 1950).

13. Alan Denson, *James H. Cousins and Margaret E. Cousins. A Bio-Bibliographical Survey* (Kendal, Alan Denson, 1967).

14. Margaret MacCurtain and Donnacha O'Corrain (eds), *Women in Society: The Irish Dimension* (Arlen House, Dublin, 1978).

15. *Crane Bag*, 1980, Vol. 4, No. 1. The subject of women and higher education in Ireland is further tackled in Mary Cullen (ed.), *Girls Don't Do Honours: Irish Women in Education in the 19th and 20th Centuries* (Women's Education Bureau, Argus Press, Dublin, 1987).

16. Beth McKillen, "Irish Feminism and National Separatism 1914–1923", *Eire/Ireland* xvii: 3, Fall 1981, pp. 2–67, xvii: 4 Winter 1982, pp. 72–90.

17. These are Arlen House and Attic Press.

18. J.B. Lyons, *The Enigma of Tom Kettle—Irish Patriot, Essayist, Poet, British Soldier 1880–1916* (Glendale Press, Dublin, 1983).

19. Leah Levenson, *With Wooden Sword* (Gill and Macmillan, Dublin, 1983).

20. Leah Levenson and Jerry H. Natterstad, *Hanna Sheehy Skeffington: A Pioneering Irish Feminist* (Syracuse University Press, 1986).

21. Charlotte Fallon, *Soul of Fire* (The Mercier Press, Cork and Dublin, 1986).

22. *Missing Pieces: Women in Irish History* (Dublin: Irish Feminist Information Publications, 1983), *More Missing Pieces* (Attic Press, Dublin, 1985).

23. Margaret Ward, *Unmanageable Revolutionaries* (Brandon, Dingle, 1983).

24. Rosemary Cullen Owens, *Smashing Times* (Attic Press, Dublin, 1984).

· 2 ·

The Heterogeneity of the Irish Movement

The intensive period in the history of the women's suffrage movement in early twentieth-century Ireland was prefaced by almost forty years in which two to three generations of Irish grew accustomed to the idea of women in public life. The emergence of women into the public sphere occurred in a number of areas of Irish life and was usually accompanied or preceded by legislation and the formation of movements. A number of organisations were formed to help women, from bookbinding unions to sewing cooperatives. Organisations were set up to assist unmarried mothers and aid those who desired to emigrate.[1]

There were also changes in the education system. With the passing of the Intermediate Education Act (1878) and the Royal University Act (1879) a number of women had new doors opened to them.[2] There was much agitation among Irish women to be admitted into higher education on equal terms with men, and this was strengthened with the formation of the Irish Women's Graduate Association in 1902. Women involved in this Association like Hanna Sheehy Skeffington, Mary Hayden and Margaret Cousins were later to be involved in suffragist groups.[3]

In the late nineteenth century legislation was passed to enable women to sit on Poor Law Boards and on Local Government Councils. In 1896 women could become Poor Law Guardians and in 1898 they got the Local Government franchise. This served to portray women in public positions and was the first step towards full political participation. By 1899, 100,000 women in Ireland were qualified to be Poor

Law electors, eighty women had been elected to Poor Law Board Rural Councils and four women were sitting as Urban District Councillors.[4] These women helped break down stereotypes, but the fact that the majority of them were not Catholics posed an added problem. Mrs Dockrell of the Irish Women's Suffrage and Local Government Association explained to the International Congress of Women held in London in 1899:

> To properly appreciate the difficulties these women have to contend with, you must try to recollect the position of affairs in the sister country. Ireland is in a transition state. The governing power in local affairs has passed from the Unionists to the Nationalists, from Protestants to Catholics, from the educated, cultured, leisured classes to the trades, small farmers, and in many cases, even to the labourers; but the women who have been elected nearly all belong to the highly-educated class, and some of them are Unionists and Protestants. From this hasty sketch it will be seen that women who enter public life require a great deal of tact, patience and what I call a level-headed devotion to the public good; but I believe that this feminine element, particularly when allied with a certain masculinity of intellect and administrative ability, is destined to become a very potent factor in public life . . . I am a Unionist and a Protestant, about two thirds of the members of my council are Nationalists and Catholics, yet I was unanimously elected to be deputy vice-chairman, I have been placed upon many committees, including being made chairman of the Dwellings for the Very Poor.[5]

Similar sentiments can be found in *The Amazing Philanthropists*, a book written by Cork writer, suffragist and Poor Law Guardian, Susan Day. In this collection of imaginary letters, based upon her own experiences, Day emphasises difficulties she experienced both as a Protestant and as a woman in attempting to become a Poor Law Guardian. "He told me, by the way, that I would not have a chance of success as I am a Protestant." She also conveys the sympathy women in local government felt for women's suffrage. It is a delightful book, and not least because it is a study of the attitudes of people in a small town outside Cork to women's place in society. As Day shows, it was not unnatural that women who were seeking to better their interests in the industrial, educational and local government spheres should wish to extend it to the Parliamentary sphere.[6] In *Women in a New*

Ireland (1912), Day describes what the heritage of the last fifty years meant to Irish women.

> In profession after profession they have proved their merit. On County Councils, Boards of Guardians and Committees they have vindicated their public-spiritedness. But her position on administrative boards has only increased women's demands for the vote. In administering the law she has learned how to criticize it, and its weak spots stare up at her in helpless and hopeless and often tragic confusion.[7]

While women's participation in Local Government increased into the twentieth century it was deemed by most women to be unsatisfactory. Nevertheless, a report of the Executive Committee of the Irish Women's Suffrage and Local Government Association declared that women while waiting for the parliamentary franchise (which could only be "a question of years") must make, in the meantime, "the fullest use of the invaluable powers which our Local Government Act has already conferred upon Irish women".[8] Commenting on the good results for women in a Local Election in Wexford in 1912 the *Irish Citizen* wrote of the elected women "their best efforts are crippled until they can lay their hands on the legislative machine also, and take a share in framing the laws as well as administering them".[9]

There were two main organisations bent on obtaining the franchise for qualified women in the late nineteenth century. These were given impetus in their formation by John Stuart Mill's attempt to have women's franchise included in the 1867 Reform Bill. This attempt had been supported by a number of petitions from Ireland. One of the suffrage organisations was founded by the Haslams, a Quaker couple, in 1876. They were interested in agitating for women's rights in both local and national government. They founded the Dublin Suffrage Society which later became the Irish Women's Suffrage and Local Government Association. In 1874 they started a journal, *The Women's Advocate*, which gave details of their policies and outlined their actions, however it was shortlived and only ran to three issues. They also campaigned against the Contagious Diseases Acts which were being vigorously opposed by Josephine Butler and her followers in England[10] and which also applied to army camps in Ireland.

The fact that the Haslams and many of their followers were Quakers was not coincidental but fitted in with the Quaker belief in equality between the sexes which was evident also in suffrage movements abroad.

Dora Mellone, an Irish suffragist, wrote in 1913 that "The Quakers not only have a good record with regard to women's suffrage but are also fondly remembered in Ireland for their role in aiding Irish peasants through their soup kitchens during the Irish Famine." She continued that "the Society of Friends is as prominent in the history of suffrage in Ireland as it is in every other good work. Many have sought to help Ireland and have only earned the distrust of the Irish; to the Friends almost alone has it been given to win the trust and love of the Catholic South and the Protestant North, and so we find the name of Mrs Haslam in the list of suffrage work."[11] The Haslams devoted most of their life to the promotion of women in local and national government and travelled extensively. They were responsible for publishing material telling Irish women their rights in Local Government and advising them how to go about participating in Local Elections.[12] Their organisation became affiliated to the English National Union of Women's Suffrage Societies. They worked quietly but steadily and their numbers increased from a few dozen in the first years to over 500 before the war.[13] However, the very nature of their movement meant that the younger or more eager women of the early twentieth century found the need to form a totally different organisation.

The other suffrage centre was in Belfast mainly under the leadership of Isabella Tod. She founded the North of Ireland Women's Suffrage Society in 1873, also known as the Irish Women's Suffrage Society. She was a frequent contributor to the *Englishwoman's Review* and was involved in the temperance movement. She was a founder of Belfast Ladies Institute, was a major force behind the Ulster Head Schoolmistresses' Association[14] and wrote extensively on education for women.[15] At the fourteenth annual meeting of the Irish Women's Suffrage Society (1886) Isabella Tod told her audience that they had to prevail against "the greatest monopoly ever known—the monopoly which men held over educational and political rights . . . ."[16] This philosophy dictated her work. On her death in 1898 the Mayoress of Belfast paid tribute to Miss Tod. "She was one of the first to encourage the new movement of feminine emancipation which has developed so strikingly in our time; . . . In the political movement to which she devoted a great deal of time and energy—women's suffrage—she did not want the suffrage for its own sake, or for the sake of any political power that might accrue, but because she considered it, to quote her own words, 'the only practical means of redressing many wrongs'."[17] Tod provided a solid basis for a strong northern suffrage movement in the early twentieth century.[18] /

From contemporary accounts it would appear that women's suffrage was of interest to many, judging from the number of suffrage meetings held throughout the country in the late nineteenth century. In Cork in 1877 the Literary and Scientific Debating Society debated a paper by a Mr Morgan on 'Women's Franchise'.[19] In Limerick in 1881 a public meeting was held by the Catholic Literary Institute which proposed 'That the present social and political disabilities of women are unjust and impolitic'.[20] Suffragists in both the north and south of Ireland were genteel, and worked quietly away at attempting to achieve their goal. They held drawing-room meetings ('at homes'). When they were not talking about women's suffrage they discussed training for young girls and industrial conditions for women. Occasionally they invited a Member of Parliament to attend. Periodically they resorted to petitioning. Their method was persuasion. These were not very public organisations sticking as they did to restrictions of their class, religion and politics. Nevertheless, their meetings were reported methodically in the *Englishwoman* and *English-woman's Review*. Their actions were obviously influenced by what was happening on the parliamentary scene, who was in government and whether or not they had a supporter in Parliament. Apart from Mill's attempted amendment there was little of a constitutional nature that could offer hope to suffragists in the remainder of the nineteenth century. /

// While the IWSLGA and the Irish Women's Suffrage Society were old, respected and very middle-class organisations, it was obvious by the early 1900s that they were not catering to the needs of all those interested in women's suffrage. And there were some who believed they had outlived their usefulness as they were making little headway in attaining their objective. Such discontent is clear from the formation of a number of women's suffrage movements during these years.

In 1912 the *Irish Citizen* in its first issue reviewed all the existing suffrage groups in Ireland. It declared that for too long there had been much muddling of names and confusion over which group believed in what. It wished to set the record straight. First of all it declared that there were 3000 active women suffragists in Ireland and considering that "the population of Ireland is only one tenth of England, the figure shows an interest in the question quite comparable to that on the other side of the Irish Sea." It then went on to give details of the different groups.[21] Some were loose federations of many small groups like the Irishwomen's Suffrage Federation. Some placed more emphasis on the vote like the Irish Women's Franchise League, others, like the Irishwomen's Reform League, placed an equal emphasis on trade unionism. Some were breakaway groups from the Irish Women's Suffrage and Local Government Association. Others were vague talking shops for writers and society women, both nationalist and unionist, like the Munster Women's Franchise League. Militancy was seen as a necessary evil by some, it was totally condemned by others.

There were mixed feelings over what suffragists' relationship with nationalism should be. Some as their names imply were totally opposed to the formation of an Irish nation state. The Unionist Women's Franchise Association claimed to have 790 members in 1913.[22] It was anti-militancy and admitted putting the interests of the Unionist Party first.[23] Branches of English suffrage organisations were set up in Ireland particularly between 1912 and 1914. The diversity of these groups reflected not only different views towards the suffrage question but also reflected the complex political situation in Ireland.

Like other branches of Irish politics this area was characterised by splits and disagreements. It must be asked whether or not this diversity held the movement back or did it make it stronger in that it catered for many different groups and thus embraced more women? Did the fact that the movement lost women particularly from 1913 on to the Nationalist movement emphasise its adaptability or its weakness? A look at the characteristics of these groups may help shed light on this matter.

It is clear that their main common concern was that certain women should have the vote. They did not agree with the present suffrage situation where two thirds of men had the vote and no women were eligible for the Parliamentary franchise. This they felt was out of keeping with successive governments' commitments to a widening democracy. The unenfranchised woman was incongruous in a society where women had to pay taxes, owned property, could go to university, were qualifying as doctors and could sit on Local Government, School and Poor Law Boards. Their experience and success in the latter areas resulted in a politicisation and a growing confidence in their ability to participate fully in political life as Susan Day has conveyed in *The Amazing Philanthropists*. A number of the Irish suffragists had Local Government experience which surely must have whetted their appetites for further political involvement. For example at the Poor Law elections in Limerick in 1911 six women were returned for Limerick city wards. It was observed that "all the ladies are convinced and strenuous suffragists".[24] In Ireland, as elsewhere, the suffragists were up against the usual anti-suffrage arguments which ultimately condemned women to the domestic sphere. The women also had the problem in that they were looking for the vote from a foreign government. They all saw the necessity of getting the Irish MPs on their side since it was imperative that if there was a Home Rule Bill women would be enfranchised under it. /

Socio-economically they were on the whole middle-class, fairly well educated and many were Protestant, thus a fairly privileged sector of Irish society. However, this predominance of the minority religion has often been exaggerated, and has led to the neglect and dismissal of the movement by historians as being of little importance and on the fringe of mainstream Irish Catholic society. On a closer look many who had been classified as 'Protestant' came from a wide section of Irish society. Others, particularly in the IWFL, who had been christened as Roman Catholic had abandoned their religion by the time they became committed members of the movement (no doubt because it and they had conflicting views on the role of women). As shall be seen in Chapter 6 there was an independent Catholic women's suffrage organisation in Ireland.[25]

Of course there is no doubt that the suffragists were middle-class, as the movement evolved out of two groups: the genteel drawing-room ladies' society and the intellectual young graduates leaving university. Many of the latter were not typically middle class in that their beliefs were more revolutionary and experimental than conformist. As elsewhere, the middle-class nature of the movement in Ireland was only to be expected. It was only those with the leisure time and the education who would have opportunity to be concerned with such an abstract thing as suffrage. The women in the Dublin biscuit factories had more mundane and immediate things to be concerned with. Looking back on the movement from 1930 the socialist Helena Moloney recalled: "The women's movement, now unhappily long spent, which aroused such a deep feeling of social consciousness and revolt among Irish women of a more favoured class, passed over the head of Irish working woman and left her untouched."[26] Olive Banks in her analysis of the makeup of British feminists examined their occupations. Nearly half her sample were not in the real sense employed, however they still built up a professional reputation for themselves by writing and publishing on a variety of topics. The others were involved in the professional occupations open to women at that time. Many were teachers, some were professional writers and a small number had become doctors.[27] These professions and their distribution appear to have been similar among the ranks of the early twentieth-century Irish suffragists which had its share of teachers, writers and doctors.

The limited middle-class aims of the movement can clearly be appreciated when it is observed what exactly was being fought for. On the issue of adult suffrage all the Irish suffrage groups were extremely vague. The IWSLGA had as its first aim to "promote extension of Parliamentary franchise to all qualified women", meaning qualified in property terms.[28] The Munster Women's Franchise League wished "to obtain the vote for women as granted to men".[29] The Irish Women's Franchise League declared that it was not "asking for the vote for every woman. It demands that those women who qualify for voting in exactly the same way as men shall be enfranchised. It demands the removal of the sex disqualification."[30] The following extract from the *Irish Citizen* series / 'The Suffragist Catechism' illustrates the timid nature of the women's demands:

> Does that not mean you want every woman to have the vote?
> No?
> Why not?
> Because every man has not got the vote. Men have to qualify for the vote in certain ways. . .
> What we ask is that women who qualify in the same way should have the same right to vote as men who qualify.
> Then you approve of restricting the vote to people of property?
> Not necessarily. Some suffragists do and some don't. What they are all agreed on is whatever entitles a man to vote should entitle a woman also—that she should not be forbidden to vote simply because she is a woman.
> Then if all men had the vote would you be in favour of all women having the vote?
> Certainly. Equal voting rights for the two sexes is our demand.[31] //

In November 1911 Margaret Cousins sent letters to Asquith the Prime Minister, Birrell the Chief Secretary of Ireland, and Redmond, the leader of the Irish Parliamentary party, expressing dissatisfaction with the proposed introduction of a Manhood Suffrage Bill. She said there was no demand for this in Ireland while there was a demand for a Women's Suffrage Bill.[32] The Conservative and Unionist Women's Franchise Association went further. They argued, as a point in its favour, that "women's suffrage will help delay adult suffrage".[33] In a letter to the *Freeman's Journal*, Frank Sheehy / Skeffington declared that "neither the IWFL or any other Irish Suffrage organisation had officially put forward any claim that women should sit in the Irish House of Commons. They claim that women should be included in the electorate for that House from the beginning. It is claimed however that a proportion of the nominated Senate should be women. But this is a minor matter. The vital thing is to give every Local Government elector, man or woman, a share in the election of the popular House."[34] It is in connection with this proposed upper house, the Senate, that the elitism of the least elitist Irish suffrage organisation becomes apparent. In reply to the assertion that no Irish woman would be qualified to sit in the upper House the *Irish Citizen* supplied a list of forty women (the total number of proposed senate seats). The *Citizen*'s list was composed of women from well-connected families (several had titles) and most had university degrees. The proposed Senate was intended to be a corporate body representing different interests in the country yet no skilled woman from industry or agriculture appeared on the list.[35]

Perhaps it is unfair to assume from hindsight that they could have been more radical in their demands. After all the demand for women's suffrage on any grounds seemed ludicrous to many. It may be argued that the suffragists felt justified in taking small steps but there is little to hint that they were willing to take bigger ones later if required. The belief that the suffrage represented property was a prevalent one and an old one and it therefore involved a large intellectual leap to declare that the suffrage should represent individuals. Certainly an air of impatience can be denoted in the *Irish Citizen* towards an adult suffragist who was, apparently, a frequent attender at the suffragist open air meetings:

At question time our old friend the adult suffragist came forward. There is surely not a suffragist speaker who has not met him. Although Mr Carpenter pointed out that we are out to obtain the parliamentary vote as it is, or may be granted to men, he was not satisfied, but after the meeting carried on an argument with two of our women right down to O'Connell's bridge . . .[36].

On the whole the suffrage movement was an urban movement appealing to the women of Dublin, Belfast, Cork and Limerick. Societies were started in the smaller towns as well and there were determined efforts to bring the 'news' to countrywomen but the thrust and direction of the movement came from the cities.

Any examination of the Irish suffrage movement should include the Irishwomen's Suffrage Federation since it linked together a few of the Irish suffrage groups. One of these was the Belfast Women's Suffrage Society, which had originally been a branch of Mrs Haslam's IWSLGA but had later decided to become independent. In 1912 it had a membership of several hundred confined to the Belfast district.[37]

The Irishwomen's Reform League was also in the Federation. It was founded by Louie Bennett and was based in Dublin. It was particularly concerned with women in industry and with encouraging trade unionism as well as being interested in attaining the franchise. Louie Bennett was born in Dublin and came into contact with feminist ideas through her wide reading while she was growing up. Her sister started an anti-marriage league in Alexandra College, one of the first seriously academic colleges for women. Bennett's biographer, R.M. Fox, saw her first step out of 'quiet middle-class life' when she became interested in the suffrage movement. Clearly he did not see the suffrage movement as a middle-class phenomenon unlike a number of feminist historians today.[38] Bennett's feminism was certainly of an all embracing type. She was not only interested in the suffrage, she also wished to improve women's conditions in industry and she was involved in work for the Women's International League, an organisation set up during the war to link women in their desire for peace.

The Irishwomen's Reform League had its offices in South Anne Street in Dublin. As part of its concern for women's lives in general it kept an eye on what was going on in the law courts and one of its members, M.E. Duggan, who had a law degree, made regular reports for the *Irish Citizen* and other suffrage papers on how the forces of justice were treating women. Since she had been a student of law at Dublin University she had come to appreciate the dilemma facing women who could not change their legal position without the franchise. Duggan also campaigned to get women admitted to the legal profession.[39]

Yet another fairly important movement in the Federation was the Munster Women's Franchise League. It was founded by the writers Somerville, Ross and Susan Day and had its headquarters in Cork. It was a rather strange organisation in that it embraced nationalist and unionist women.[40] One of its members Mary McSwiney was to find that her nationalist feelings would force her to leave the movement. It was 'non-militant, non-sectarian, and non-party'. It had branches all over Munster from remote areas in Kerry to prosperous towns in North Cork.[41] There were branches in Waterford, Limerick, Nenagh and Tralee.[42] In the report of the Federation in 1912 it was stated that the Munster Women's Franchise League "have added four new branches to their organisation, thereby, of course strengthening the Federation. Also Miss Day has known so well how to use the advantages gained by affiliation with the Federation, that the MWFL is now the most successful of suffrage societies in Ireland."[43] Despite this claim it was overall a very genteel group with very little clout.

Thus the Irishwomen's Suffrage Federation brought together scattered groups about the country, with the main centres being in Belfast, Dublin, Cork and a few Munster towns. The inspiration for its foundation apparently came from both North and South.

The idea of forming a Federation of Irishwomen's Suffrage Societies was first publicly launched by Miss L.A. Walkington, LLDMA of Strandown, Co. Down. She suggested it to the Committee of the Lisburn Suffrage Society, by whom it was well received. She then consulted with Miss Day, Hon. Sec. Munster Women's Franchise Association, and found that this lady had formulated a similar plan in the early part of the year 1911 and had vainly tried to secure the co-operation of other Irish suffrage societies.[44]

The inaugural meeting was held at the Shelbourne Hotel in Dublin on August 21 1911. Louie Bennett, its honorary secretary, said almost two years after the formation of the organisation, "We are firmly resolved that the Irishwomen's Suffrage Federation, shall remain truly and purely an Irish organisation."[45] Its aims besides linking together scattered suffrage societies, were to carry out propaganda for the movement and to be an association which would exist after enfranchisement. In this it was similar to the English National Union of Women's Suffrage Societies. It did not desire to focus on the vote alone. It was a fairly solid organisation turning out annual reports which gave an account of activities of its member groups from 1911 to 1917. It was responsible for arranging all-Ireland suffrage conferences, getting together petitions, organising deputations to Irish MPs and English politicians. Talks were organised, suffrage libraries were established throughout the country. The Federation was responsible for trying to spread news of the suffrage movement to remoter parts of Ireland and viewed it as a great success when it managed to infiltrate Galway. In 1914 it noted in its annual report that "at the close of our last year we had 14 societies in our Federation, and today we have 26 . . . We have established this year our first suffrage society in Galway, and a great deal of hard spade work had to be done before the Galway Society was successfully launched."[46] As part of its mission of linking suffrage societies it set up a Northern Committee "in response to the need felt for a closer co-operation among Northern societies".[47] Dora Mellone was secretary of the Northern Committee and she reported on its success in 1913 announcing the establishment of twelve new societies in the previous year.[48] The Federation also had a London Committee "who shall advise the council in Ireland on questions relating to English policy".[49] This committee would act as a reminder to Irish MPs at Westminster of their duty to Irish women. As a necessary part of all this bonding they described themselves as 'non-party': that is they did not attach themselves to any political party and "we have all denominations".[50] Another feature of the Federation was its non-militancy and this was to prove contentious when militant suffragists stepped up their campaign. /

The Irishwomen's Suffrage Federation's aim of linking together scattered suffrage societies was successful only to a limited degree. There were political and religious suffrage societies who wished for various reasons to remain separate./ The religious suffrage groups remained apart in order to associate the suffrage aim with religious ideals; however they had no hostility to the rest of the movement in general. The long-standing IWSLGA decided not to join as it felt "under existing circumstances, a union of Irish suffrage societies was impracticable, and that the Association can act more effectively by acting independently".[51] The Irish Women's Franchise League also announced that they would not take part though they were "always prepared to enter into friendly co-operation with other Irish suffrage societies and to speak on common platforms".[52] According to Susan Day of the Munster/ Women's Franchise League the IWFL refused to become a member because the Federation worked on constitutional and non-militant lines.[53] Underlying certain groups' desire to be independent was a tension based upon the belief that their way of approaching the problem was the only way and the right way.

/ However, an organisation which stood out in its aloofness from the other suffrage groups, was the Conservative and Unionist Women's Suffrage Association which established an Irish branch in 1909 in Dublin. Its president was Lady Arnot. Its establishment prompted the *Englishwoman's Review* to state "The Irish Woman's Suffrage and Local Government Association may now be said to be a centre with a left, or Nationalist wing, and a right or Unionist."[54] Members of this Conservative and Unionist organisation were on the whole upper middle-class ladies, with many who were titled and very much part of the ruling elite. Their gentle demands for women's suffrage were not a break from their inherent conservatism, but rather stemmed from a desire to consolidate the interests of their sector of society since they were very much against adult suffrage. However, associating with other Irish women's suffrage groups left them open, ironically, to accusations from their fellow Unionists of being pro-Home Rule.[55] This was extraordinary considering that a number of Irishwomen who belonged to suffrage groups were frequently accused of being pro-British. The *Irish Citizen* sympathised with the plight of the Unionist women ". . . official Unionism, is as blind as official Nationalism to the urgency of the women's demand, or rather it sees just as clearly as the rival machine the shattering effect which the women's movement is bound to have on all the machinery of party and caucus, and accordingly gives it no support."[56] /

Though the Federation had an ecumenical and non-sectarian basis and it had an overwhelming desire for everybody to be friends, it would seem that its diversity prevented it from having any real effect. It succeeded certainly in creating an awareness and solidarity among many women but whether or not this improved the situation in concrete terms is debatable. //

// The Irish Women's Franchise League was a very different organisation. It was not just comprised of, or led by, a group of people looking for the vote they symbolised more than that. They were very much part of the *Fin de Siècle* era and the Irish Renaissance, with an opinion about everything and visions for an ideal society.[57] Their support of women's suffrage was at first just part of, and indeed arose out of, their overall philosophy and approach to life. The individuals involved in the IWFL Frank Skeffington, Hanna Sheehy and her sisters and their husbands Tom Kettle and Cruise O'Brien, the Cousinses, the Palmers, the Oldhams, and Mary Hayden were all part of the intellectual life that was going on in Dublin at the beginning of the twentieth century.

They mixed in the same circle as the actors the Fay brothers, the writer and poet Padraic Colum and his wife, a writer in her own right, Mary Colum, James Joyce, James Stephens, "A.E." and W.B. Yeats. They were involved in the productions at the National Theatre and in the Irish language revival attending the popular language classes. They cycled to each other's homes and had discussion groups. A number of them were vegetarians,[58] anti-inoculation, anti-vivisection, anti-smoking and were involved in the setting up of Irish organisations in support of these issues.[59] They would meet in the vegetarian restaurant in Dublin "which was a rendezvous for the literary set"[60] and "became a place of propaganda".[61] In his book *Under the Receding Wave*, C.P. Curran comments "These were the days when in London the Eustace Mils restaurants mixed moral principles with dietetic statistics on their depressing menu cards and the same atmosphere pervaded the old vegetarian restaurant in College Street [Dublin]."[62] At the restaurant they would discuss life and politics. Some were fascinated by the supernatural and claimed to have psychic experiences. This led them into theosophy, a study of the mysticism of the East and participation in *seances*.[63] Others declared themselves to be atheists. Among the clubs they belonged to were the Contemporaries and the Dublin Parliamentary Debating Society[64] where debates were frequently held including some on women's suffrage. One of the newspapers they were involved in was the *National Democrat*. Another was *Dialogues of the Day*.

Before they officially formed a suffrage movement a number of them had made their opinions on the position of Irish women known. The most obvious case is that of Frank Sheehy Skeffington and the stand he took over women not being treated in the same way as men in University College Dublin.[65] (When he married Hanna Sheehy they both took each other's names.) Others had taken part in debates, met foreign suffragists and had written on the matter. The very fact that many of the women were graduates at this time shows an unwillingness to conform to the norm of femininity. Margaret Cousins recalled that the last piece of advice her headmistress gave her was "that I should not be so independent."[66] It was advice she did not heed as she went on to get her music degree and taught music, determined always to be financially self-reliant. Hanna Sheehy Skeffington had an MA and taught at a girls' school. During the militant period of the movement she was to lose a job after having spent some time in gaol.[67] In the movement itself there were three professors: Professor Mary Hayden, first woman professor of Irish history, Professor Oldham and Professor Tom Kettle. The preponderance of academics, writers and poets marked the movement off from other suffrage organisations. However the intellectual nature of the IWFL did not make them an armchair movement. On the contrary they were the most active and most militant of all the suffrage groups in Ireland.

The IWFL was formed out of a discontent with the already existing suffrage organisations. According to Frank Sheehy Skeffington the IWSLGA "failed entirely to awaken popular enthusiasm or sympathy, and the masses of the population never heard of it". He continued saying the formation of the militant movement in England made the younger women aware of the older organisation's "inertia and ineffectiveness". However they did not immediately form a new organisation because they feared the size of the task before them and they were restrained above all "by personal respect for the veteran leader, Mrs Haslam". What finally roused the Irish women

out of their lethargy, he asserted, was the County Council
Bill of 1907. This made English and Scottish women eligible
to sit on County and Borough Councils but not Irish women,
since it was reckoned that there was no demand in Ireland.
Frank Sheehy Skeffington wrote:

> There were curious rumours at the time, which have never been denied,
> as to the precise agency by which this exclusion was effected. Sir Henry
> Campbell Bannerman declared in the House that he was willing to
> include Irishwomen if there was any demand; and it was said that some
> of those who ought to have been foremost in pressing the claims of
> Irishwomen acted in a contrary direction. The general moral was plain.
> English women had secured this privilege because they had an active
> militant Suffrage agitation; Irishwomen had been denied it because they
> had not.[68]

Hanna Sheehy Skeffington approached the Cousinses and
others about forming "a militant suffrage society suitable to
the different political situation of Ireland, as between a
subject country seeking freedom from England, and England
a free country".[69] Replying to a contemporary's observation
that the new movement would have the support of a
considerable section of the Irish public providing it conducted
itself in an "orderly and seemly fashion", Frank Sheehy
Skeffington replied that the IWSLGA had conducted itself
in such a fashion for about forty years. Just like the
constitutional suffragists in England they were faced with the
same lack of result. "Our new league sets out in a spirit of
whole hearted admiration for the brave women who have had
the courage to abandon 'orderly and seemly' methods for
the only tactics which have ever proved effective in such an
agitation: and we intend to act in their spirit while modifying
their policy in such details as the difference between English
and Irish conditions may seem to require."[70]

However, despite this declaration the IWFL did not feel
the need to practise a policy of militancy in Ireland until
nearly four years after its formation. First, they tried to
persuade Irish members of Parliament to help them. When
this had clearly failed by 1911 they felt that such a "method
had been carried as far as it was possible to carry it without
the stimulus of more active pressure".[71]

When the League was eventually formed there were a number of men involved. While they helped in the running of the IWFL's newspaper, the *Irish Citizen*, and were frequent and articulate speakers on its platforms, on the whole they took a back seat and were associates rather than members of the movement; none of them went to gaol for the cause. Margaret Cousins remembered that "we members of the Irish Women's Franchise League were particularly encouraged by the understanding friendship of many well-known men who stood by us in all kinds of new demands for loyal support."[72] Some of these men are examined in greater detail in Chapter 7. Two who should be mentioned here are James Cousins and Frank Sheehy Skeffington. Both wrote articles in favour of improving Irish women's situation in a number of Irish and English newspapers and journals. James Cousins as a poet and Sheehy Skeffington as a playwright used these skills to publicise their belief in women's suffrage.[73] While on face value it does seem strange to see men involved in the most radical of Irish suffrage movements, it becomes more understandable when one examines the individual personalities involved. Both were pacifists, Cousins was a vegetarian, both had abandoned the religion of their birth.

In her study of British feminists Olive Banks came up with some observations on her male sample which are interesting to note when looking at the Irish situation. She found that the suffrage movement was almost exclusively female unlike the socialist movement which transcended social and gender barriers to a far greater extent.[74] Nevertheless she argued that there were some men in the movement should not be seen as surprising. Banks's men were highly educated and were usually in professions rather than business, a number were involved in journalism and writing in one way or another.[75] The men did not necessarily learn their feminism from their wives, but the women often sought out men like these as husbands. In order to be sure that the men shared their views the women insisted on some symbolic sign like omitting the word 'obey' from the marriage ceremony or combining each other's surnames.[76] The partnerships did not just involve mutual agreement upon ideological grounds but a willingness on the men's part to put up with certain discomforts. They had to cope while absent wives were serving prison sentences, although as Banks points out, domestic servants helped ease the absence.[77] /

Irish male suffragists like Cousins, Sheehy Skeffington, Palmer and Oldham were all very supportive while their wives were in prison. They, too, confirm what Banks had to say about the British male suffragists: "Nor, with rare exceptions, were these men 'womanisers'. Instead they stand out as remarkably affectionate husbands."[78] The fact that men played a role in the extreme section of the Irish suffrage movement must have, to some extent, diluted antagonism from the surrounding society. The women in the IWFL, though militant, could hardly have been accused of being separatist. However, it is true that on occasions these men / were made to appear as figures of fun and ridicule.

The IWFL was formed with the following aims. It wished to obtain the Parliamentary franchise for Irish women on the same terms as Irish men. Its membership was open to women of "all shades of political opinion" who approved of its objects and methods.[79] Its growth in numbers was reflected in / periodic changes of location in its headquarters. In October 1909 it took new offices in the Antient Concert Rooms which included a large hall where weekly meetings were held on Tuesday evenings.[80] By this stage the IWFL had a total of 700 members and numerous associates.[81] By 1913 it had over 800 members and the League had become so large by the end of that year it had to move into larger headquarters in Westmoreland Street. By now they had held meetings throughout Ireland in all but four counties.[82] In her autobiography Margaret Cousins remembered these tours: "In rousing and educating opinion in country towns our experiences were very varied. Usually we set off two by two on tours. There were difficulties in securing places for meetings, difficulties in finding hotel accommodation or a press which would urgently print our notices of a meeting. Very rarely did we find a local man or woman who would preside."[83] In July 1912 the IWFL carried out an 'Open Air Campaign' in the west of Ireland. This involved Mrs Crichton, Miss Jameson, Mrs Cousins and Mrs Baker travelling by day in a side-car and camping by night.[84]

In November 1911 Cousins wrote to the *Freeman's Journal* that reports which stated that women's suffrage propaganda had not yet touched Irish rural constituencies was quite untrue "Such typical extreme points as Dingle and Ventry in Co. Kerry, Clifden in Connemara, and Dunfanaghy in the very North of Donegal have all heard the women's demand explained at representative meetings and have unanimously approved of our claims to the parliamentary vote."[85] Open air meetings were held throughout the summer months, often attracting passers-by out on evening strolls. In the summer of 1910, eighty-eight new members had been enrolled at the open air meetings.[86] These meetings were held in Phoenix Park, Beresford Place, Kingstown and Bray. The speakers usually stood on the back of a fourwheeled lorry. The IWFL tried to have two women speakers and one man. "We did not ask the people to come to us. We had the lorry placed where the people themselves were accustomed to gather, and they never failed to come and listen and ask questions at the end of the hour."[87] Obviously public speaking did not always come naturally to the women and Margaret Cousins rehearsed open-air speaking "in a field behind our house with only an ass for my audience".[88] These meetings were seen as a great success, and their temporary cessation was always regretted when the winter approached.

The IWFL aimed to keep itself before the public eye at all times. Thus it sought to pursue issues which would gain maximum publicity. When visiting English politicians like Asquith and Churchill came to Ireland the women constantly harassed them.[89] As was the case in England the IWFL did everything they could to resist the success of the 1911 census. Besides holding meetings and debates with other political groups such as the Irish Socialist Party,[90] the IWFL sought to attract the public through entertainment. Suffrage plays were performed. Among these were 'Lady Geraldine's Speech' and 'How the Vote was Won'.[91] Short stories and poems were written, and Suffrage recitals were also held.[92] It was reported in June 1912 that "The Votes for Women Quartette won first prize for string quartettes at the Sligo *Feis Ceoil*."[93] These efforts gained them maximum publicity—and were frequently reported in national and provincial newspapers.

Although the IWFL desired to be non-political it not surprisingly encountered difficulty in remaining aloof from the cross currents of Irish politics as will be seen in Chapter 7. Margaret Cousins admitted "While the League stands neutral as regards Home Rule, it cannot pretend friendliness toward any Government or Party which endeavours to kill the great movement for which it stands."[94] However, looking\ with hindsight at the lives of IWFL members as opposed to members of other groups, it would appear to be fairly clear that their sympathies lay with Home Rule and not with Unionism. Indeed as McKillen's article showed after 1916 many of them turned to nationalism.[95] If the suffrage was to/ be offered by anyone in a position to give it the women would take it. Thus when Edward Carson, the leader of the\ Unionist party, declared that women would be enfranchised under the Provisional Government, he threatened to set up in Northern Ireland, his proposal was welcomed enthusiastically by the IWFL as well as other suffrage groups (thus further alienating them from the Nationalists).[96]/

The *Irish Citizen* was the newspaper set up by the IWFL. It was published between 1912 and 1920, weekly for the first half of its life and then monthly or even less frequently from 1916 to its death in 1920. Although its first issue declared that its aim was to reflect the views of "suffragists of all schools and parties" of opinion it was clearly the organ of the IWFL. The founders and chief forces behind the IWFL, Frank and Hanna Sheehy Skeffington and James and Margaret Cousins, were responsible for the appearance of this exclusively Irish suffrage magazine. Thus the newspaper's editorials and prominent columns tended to reflect the militant leanings of the IWFL much to the dislike of its non-IWFL readers and contributors. Despite this it did provide space for other suffrage groups to publicise their activities and express their opinions.

In attempting to present the picture in Ireland, in its determination to gain the vote, and in the move from a slightly concealed militancy to advocation of direct action, the *Irish Citizen* can be seen at its best between its foundation in 1912 and the advent of war in 1914. During this time the suffrage movements grew faster than before and infiltrated

areas of the country that had never previously seen a
suffragist. After that, despite the determination of the *Irish*
Citizen to place the vote first "before all else", other events
began to cloud the horizon and thus, to some extent, changed
the nature of the newspaper. //

The *Citizen* first appeared on May 25 1912. It, like all the
subsequent issues, had the following motto on its front page:

> For men and women Equality
> The Rights of Citizenship;
> For men and women Equality
> The Duties of Citizenship.[97]

Following the example of suffrage magazines elsewhere it
had the word 'citizen' in its title. This, explained James
Cousins in the anniversary issue in 1913, was because

> The new paper was to be the organ of human relationship, of adjustment
> between the needs of the community; in short, of citizenship; and not
> merely of citizenship as an academic idea but of social reconstruction
> in which the feminist and masculine sides of humanity should share
> equally the work of life, and enjoy equally the products of their work.
> Hence came the name of our paper; hence also the motto that will
> never, I trust, disappear from its front page.[98]

By the publication of its fifth issue in June 1912 the *Citizen*
claimed that 3,000 copies were circulated each week—and it
reckoned that over 10,000 people read it.[99] The *Citizen* lasted
until 1920 when its presses were smashed up by the Black
and Tans in the Irish War of Independence. /

While a number of different suffrage groups existed in
Ireland, on many occasions they organised suffrage events
together. A case in point was the 1911 census, the IWFL
and the Belfast Women's Suffrage Society joined forces in
their efforts to resist it.[100] This was following the example
of Mrs Despard's Women's Freedom League in England
who took the well-worn slogan 'No Taxation without
Representation'.

> Throughout Ireland Census resistance in spite of great difficulties of
> the Irish Census Act was warmly adopted, not only by members of the
> League but by many sympathisers. All four provinces were represented,
> many ladies journeying especially to Dublin for the occasion. Some

actively resisted, some "duplicated", finding themselves unlawfully entered by the "head of the house", and large bodies evaded. Our warm thanks to many ladies who offered hospitality . . . It is interesting to note that all classes, from the titled lady to the working girl were represented in this unique form of protest. On Monday many Census resisters and evaders thronged the gallery of the City Hall and followed with interest the debate on Women's Suffrage in the Corporation . . .[101]

The evasion of the census was not just an exercise in undermining the machinery of state but was also of profound psychological and symbolic importance to the women involved.[102]

Suffrage groups came together for all-Ireland meetings which were held when there was a relevant Bill or proposal coming up before Parliament. These 'mass meetings' of Irish women were not only comprised of suffrage groups but were on occasions attended by other women's groups like the nationalist women Inghinidhe na h-Eireann and the Women Worker's Trade Union and even the Ladies Committee of the Irish Drapers' Assistants.[103] Writing about one such meeting, Hanna Sheehy Skeffington gave her impressions of what she perceived to be the solidarity and unity of purpose of the audience as she looked down from the platform

> The spirit of the audience, as judged from the platform, was throughout deeply earnest and, to my mind at least, stirringly militant. It was a woman's audience: one felt, moreover, that every woman present represented many others, and as their chosen delegate. It was an audience of experts: every subtle point, every political allusion was at once appreciated; those women were unanimous as to what they wanted and how what they wanted was best to be achieved. Moreover . . . they were so strong in their sense of absolute right, of unswerving sex-faith and constancy, that they did not take over-seriously the prospect of politicians' wiles and delay.[104]

In 1913 Irish suffragists decided that a week should be devoted "to Suffrage propaganda". The result was "a project which was crowned with success". The Suffrage week was held from May 1 to May 8, during which "a vast quantity of Suffrage literature was sold daily on the streets, while flower and street vendors were to be found in all principal thoroughfares; the collecting boxes too received generous donations . . . . This week devoted to outdoor activity was invaluable from a propagandist point of view, and brought many new members into the organisation, whilst its financial result was highly satisfactory."[105]

With this success in mind a Suffrage Conference was held in Dublin in December of the same year for four days organised by the Irishwomen's Suffrage Federation.[106] Its papers ranged from 'The Present Position of Women's Suffrage in Ireland' to 'Women's Trade Unions and the Vote'.[107] There, Irish women in unison demanded that the Imperial Parliament grant them suffrage, they said that any future Irish government would have to give them a share in power and they condemned forcefeeding and the Cat and Mouse Act.[108]

/ Thus there was the situation in Ireland where there were several different suffrage groups; each formed to meet different needs. Yet they still desired, where possible, to speak with one voice. This desire was reflected in the fact that many women belonged to a few suffrage organisations. For example, Susan Day was a member of the Cork branch of the IWFL as well as being one of the founding members of the Munster Women's Franchise League. Mary Hayden, a member of the Irish Women's Franchise League, was also a founding member of the Irish Catholic Women's Suffrage Society. Louie Bennett was a founding member of the Irishwomen's Suffrage Federation, the Irishwomen's Reform League and the Irish Women's Workers' Union. She was also for a time a member of the Irish Women's Franchise League and even ran speakers' classes for its members, where it was hoped further women for the open air meetings in Phoenix Park would be recruited.[109] Speakers' classes were also run by the Munster Women's Franchise League for anyone who desired to join.[110] /

Of course, what eventually happened in many cases when issues conflicted too much was that the women resigned from those groups which tested their loyalty most. While this might have seemed to be a compromise it did not mean that open dissent was avoided. It was not. In some cases it was very clear where the suffrage women stood. For example they were unanimous in their condemnation of women who tended to perpetuate the existing situation like those who welcomed

Asquith when he came to Dublin. The *Irish Citizen* "carefully examined the published list of the women who were present at the Asquith meeting and who, by their silence or applause, acquiesced in the insult to their sex. It is satisfactory to find, with not more than four exceptions, these are women of the parasite type—women whose individualities are mere reflections, and who have no importance save as the wife or daughter or sister of some man."[111]

The very fact that so many different suffrage groups existed in Ireland meant that controversy between them could hardly be avoided. A suffragist group did not feel it could just stand by while another group pursued the same policies with different methods, especially when they felt that those methods were going to ruin the outcome. The suffrage movement in Ireland polarised into two groups—the IWFL and the rest. This was so because the IWFL so obviously deviated from what had been the norm in women's suffrage circles. There was resentment about the way the IWFL seemed to push itself forward and appeared to be representing Ireland as a whole. This was particularly with regard to the *Irish Citizen*. Dora Mellone of the Irishwomen's Suffrage Federation wrote to Frank Sheehy Skeffington on this issue. "The paper is practically useless as run at present outside Dublin, as the party for whom it caters in reality only exists in this city."[112] Others also felt alienated from *The Citizen*, particularly its attitudes towards militancy and for a time withdrew their subscriptions.[113]

Militancy was one of the most divisive issues among the suffrage groups. It posed a moral dilemma for suffragists all over the world. At some stage in Britain, America, Australia and elsewhere a decision had to be made on what stance to take. The decision usually resulted in a polarisation between the supporters and opponents. Considering the middle-class nature of the movement, militant methods and opposing authority by force was an anathema to many women. Militancy posed the problem of alienating potential supporters among women and among politicians. It would also result in usually law-abiding citizens making court appearances and facing possible gaol sentences. However, at the same time a number of women became militant because they no longer believed constitutional methods could help them. In Ireland the argument was conducted along the same lines and had a similar outcome. /

The IWFL believed that the constitutional methods had failed. Indeed as had already been pointed out this belief was a key factor in their formation. In May 1912 Frank Sheehy Skeffington wrote that "The Irish Women's Franchise League was formed in 1908, in avowed sympathy with the militant movement but with the expressed desire to avoid militancy in Ireland . . . The defection of the Irish members in March of this year . . . shows that this method has been carried as far as it was possible to carry it without the stimulus of more active pressure."[114] In an early issue of the *Irish Citizen* militancy was seen as inevitable: "Every student of history and politics knows what is the result of ignoring a just demand constitutionally put forward. Forces which are denied their natural outlet are apt to liberate themselves through another means, often in such a manner as to seriously decompose the authorities who have dammed up the normal channels."[115] On the eve of going into prison in July 1912 Hanna Sheehy Skeffington summarised the path that had been taken by suffragists up to that time:

The secretary of an Irish suffrage society wrote the other day rather proudly, that her organisation goes back to 1876. The Irish Women's Franchise League dates from 1908, and already it has run the gamut of constitutionalism, and is now knocking at the prison door. Weekly, nay daily, meetings, petitions, country campaigns, deputations, open-air demonstrations, processions, resolutions from local bodies, heckling of Cabinet Ministers sojourning in Ireland, election propaganda, have been tried on public opinion and on members of Parliament . . . This is the point we have now reached: thus closes the chapter of constitutionalism opened in 1876. It was a pretty tale, full of friendship, of election pledges and platform appeals from those who "have always been our best friends", but who were always fatally debarred from action at "critical junctures", and who in the sacred cause of party were regretfully obliged to shelve our cause when there was a likelihood of its winning. The chapter might have been a serial in time but for the "disgraceful tactics" of the militants. As it is it will be interesting material for the psychologist working on a research thesis on Female Patience in the 19th century.[116]

Or indeed the historian!

However the IWSLGA, the subject of Sheehy Skeffington's criticism, were not convinced and continued to disapprove of militant methods. Militancy and its morality were not the only things in contention here. The anti-militants felt that much more was at stake. They felt that the general public and the politicians were already wary and suspicious of the women's suffrage movement and had to be wooed gently. Militancy would confirm for some that these women were indeed lunatics and for others it could put an end to wavering support. Thus those who disagreed with militancy felt that they now had to be much more careful in promoting their cause. In the IWSLGA's annual report for 1912 Mrs Elizabeth Christie reported that "owing to the actions of the extreme branch of the militants we have refrained from prosecuting our cause in public, as the majority of people were made antagonistic to it by these violent and unwise methods."[117] In the report for 1913 she wrote that "On March 11, 1913 we sent out a letter to the principal districts all over Ireland protesting most strongly against the unwise and violent actions of the militants, and entreating all women suffrage societies who had sincerely at heart the advancement of our work to declare their disapproval of such wanton methods."[118] The IWSLGA objected to militant methods because "they tend to degrade and vulgarise one of the noblest movements in the history of the world,—the elevation of women to their rightful place in our social and political organism."[119] Louie Bennett of the Irishwomen's Reform League wrote in 1913 that "We have proclaimed that we wish our deeds to speak for us; we have proclaimed a policy of action, of constructive rather than destructive action. We think the origination of a society such as the Girls' Protection League pleads our cause much more efficiently than many broken windows."[120] However, as might be expected, considering her all-embracing outlook, she described herself as not "a militant nor an anti-militant but as a non-militant". Thus she would not openly condemn women endeavouring to get the vote by whatever methods possible.[121] However, she was "very curious to know by what train of reasoning militant suffragists arrive at the state of becoming peace advocates?"[122] Her disagreements with the IWFL came to a head when for a time she withdrew the IRL contributions to the *Irish Citizen*. When she decided to resubmit she wittily remarked to Frank Sheehy Skeffington that she had heard someone say that the *Citizen* had become "much more interesting since the IRL ceased to contribute to it!"[123] Another suffragist writing to the *Irish Citizen* felt "bound to express to you my very strong feelings against militancy for several reasons—in particular because if the *Irish Citizen*[124] is to become the organ of militancy I individually cannot in any way support it."

Militancy was such a divisive force among the women, so much so that when a Suffrage Conference in Dublin was planned for December 1913 it was decided that despite its relevance to the movement at that period the subject was not to be discussed.[125] Despite these disagreements over what was a major issue for the women, the militants pursued militancy and the non-militants expressed sympathy for them, and visited them while they were in gaol.

Nationalism proved to be an equally divisive issue. Many of the same people mixed in both suffragist and nationalist circles but after a while their greater loyalty would become apparent. For a while people wavered between the two. For example the Sheehy Skeffingtons would see Countess Markievicz (the founder of the Fianna and prominent member of the republican movement) on the stage, work with her in soup kitchens for the Dublin poor, meet her socially and later visit her in prison.[126] Hanna Sheehy Skeffington wrote that Markievicz was only "a mild suffragist" who held that "suffrage would come with a lot else when Ireland was free."[127] While Markievicz as late as 1919 wrote that Sheehy Skeffington much preferred to work from the 'Women's Platform'.[128] Few women were able to avoid a conflict in their loyalties and on some occasions found that they had to make a choice. In February 1911 Miss Deborah Webb sent her usual annual subscription for the Irish Party to the IWFL instead. She wrote that "Closely analogous to the cause of Home Rule there is another cause which I consider yet more radically important and which is in greater need of support. To this cause I have even longer been a subscriber and I shall now add to my subscription what I used to give to the Parliamentary fund."[129] In June 1912 the *Irish Citizen* reported that Patricia Hoey who had served for many years as secretary to the principal branch of the United Irish League in London and had worked on behalf of Home Rule candidates in London elections had been refused entry into the Irish Party convention in Dublin in 1912 because she was a known suffragist. It concluded "That she could be so treated should be a warning to all women who put their party interests before those of their sex."[130]

However some women in Ireland were making tracks in the opposite direction. These obviously politicised women saw themselves as having a role in Ireland's future but were not immediately concerned with women's suffrage. They, along with many Irish men, were looking for Home Rule for Ireland. A woman writing under the pseudonym 'Maire' revealed to the *Catholic Bulletin* in October 1912 her feelings on why suffrage was more important to English women than to Irish women. "I attended the Suffrage Meeting in the Phoenix Park on 8th September. It left me envious of the Englishwoman. She had all she wanted with the exception of a mere vote. An English ruler, an English Parliament, an English army and navy, whose uniforms her husbands or sons might wear with pride. She stood there a free woman, and wondered what the Irishwoman was doing, or why she took such scant interest in the suffrage question." 'Maire' went on to point out that the situation was entirely different for Irishwomen. She asked:

> But in the present woman war, where stands the Irishwoman? With our language dying, our traditions fading, our faith paling, the landmarks of our nationality disappearing around us one by one, has the Irishwoman's money and time and energy and place in her heart for a fight for a class. The rights of a class when the issue of a nation's existence is at stake! Granted that an Irishwoman wants a vote, she wants something else more; to nationalise her land, to keep it Ireland and not West Britain. The suffrage movement is turning thoughts of the average Irishwoman Englandwards. That is its greatest danger in the present state of this country.[131]

Another nationalist was Irish language enthusiast and academic Agnes O'Farrelly. She objected to the policy pursued by suffragists at election time when they campaigned against any politician, be he Nationalist or Unionist if he did not support woman's suffrage. She declared that though she believed in woman's suffrage she could not join the IWFL because she believed in Home Rule and could not support a group who opposed its proponents at election time. "Are we or are we not fighting for the vote before all other things? Some of us certainly are not . . .", she added that "I have enough belief however in the instinct of fairplay amongst Irishmen, to give me confidence that one of the first acts of an Irish Parliament will be to enfranchise the women of the country."[132] There were other women who agreed and had full confidence in Irish men's sense of fair play. In the *Catholic Suffragist*, Christie O'Connor wrote "To this down-trodden and long-suffering nation the enfranchisement of women does not seem such an urgent domestic necessity. With many women Home Rule is the first consideration. All the grievances under which they labour are 'made in England'. Their troubles are not so obviously the outcome of male domination as in the sister country . . ."[133]

The suffragists had problems with regard to the nationalist organisations. Firstly because women's suffrage was low on their list of priorities—if it was there at all. Secondly because women seemed to play an auxiliary role in them. Some of the nationalist women had been involved in suffrage groups but had left when they felt their sympathies with nationalism and suffragism conflicted so much as to be incompatible. One such woman was Mary McSwiney. She was a teacher in Cork City. Her outlook on life can be appreciated from a comment she once made that she could not teach Irish History from the English standpoint any more than she could teach the Reformation from a Protestant standpoint.[134] She was a member of the Munster Women's Franchise League and attended suffrage meetings on Saturdays. She found she had to defend herself against accusations from Nationalists that she was joining in with the Unionists to get the vote.[135] However, she herself by 1914 was calling Irish suffragists "Britons first, suffragists second, and Irish women perhaps a bad third."[136]

McSwiney seemed to find the choice between her sex and her country harder than many. It was quite a while before she came to any decision. As Margaret Ward points out in

Unmanageable Revolutionaries, McSwiney, especially in the period before 1913, argued for the necessity of the vote "regardless of the compromise that would entail".[137] She did not share the view of Inghinidhe na hEireann that to accept the franchise from a 'hostile Parliament' would be humiliating and would undermine the success that had been achieved by nationalist groups in developing a spirit of nationhood.[138] But in early 1914 she was beginning to come to the conclusion that "self-government for Ireland [was] the most important question in the country at present and must be paramount until Home Rule is attained."[139]

The IWFL consistently observed what was going on within the Nationalist ranks with regards to women and made appropriate comments. The Irish Volunteers, an organisation founded because "Ireland armed would be able to make a better bargain with the Empire than Ireland unarmed", did not escape their sharp criticism. The IWFL wrote that they had learned that the Volunteers had decided to enrol women "of course in a purely subsidiary capacity, to help the men and do as they are told". They welcomed the fact that some of the women refused to fit in with this role and went away determined to form a volunteer corps of their own which would not be dictated to or controlled by the male volunteers,[140] but later they were to be disillusioned by even this group. However the inaugural meeting of the Volunteers, as Margaret Ward points out, was to set the scene for women playing a subsidiary role within the movement. She writes a number of women had attended the inaugural meeting, their presence confined to a gallery specially set apart for them. "Through this separation, the work of female activists during the past decades was symbolically dismissed and women again relegated to the role of passive observers, excluded from any meaningful participation in political events."[141]

By July 1914 the IWFL felt that Irish women should have nothing whatsoever to do with the Volunteers. Because by this stage they felt that the Volunteers had been taken over by Ireland's biggest anti-suffragist John Redmond, the leader of the Irish Party. They used strong language in their condemnation of the women involved. They saw defenders of the Volunteers like Mary McSwiney, Helena Moloney and

Miss Jacob as "slavish with regard to the men at the head of the movement". They asked "What are the suffragists on / the Irishwomen's Council going to do? Redmond had obviously showed his contempt for them by setting up the Irish Volunteer Aid Association to do precisely the same work the Irishwomen's Council had been doing because he had been unaware of their existence."[142]

Mary McSwiney was shocked at the type of language used in the *Irish Citizen* article written by Frank Sheehy Skeffington. He asserted that women who supported the Volunteers showed "a crawling servility to the men of their party, deserve nothing but contempt and will assuredly earn it—not only from the free-minded members of their own sex but also from the very men to whom they do homage."[143] McSwiney wrote an angry reply "'Slaves' and 'campfollowers' and such choice epithets can only degrade the man who uses them towards the women whose pride it is to help their country in her fight for freedom."[144] The *Citizen's* attack on the Nationalist women made it clear to McSwiney which side she was on and in the late spring of 1914 she formed the Cork branch of Cumann na mBan (Women's Club, a nationalist women's organisation formed in April 1914). When the Munster Women's Franchise League decided to support the British War she decided to leave the organisation.[145] /

/   There have been a number of studies concerned with the Irish nationalist women's groups, these groups are not in themselves of concern in this chapter and book.[146] However, it must be said that in the period under study they are of relevance since they provided an alternative for women wishing to get involved in the future of their country. The nationalist women felt no qualms, to them it was merely a question of which came first, their country's independence or women's suffrage. They felt the latter would naturally follow once the former was achieved. Both allegiances were ways of liberating themselves and getting involved in the body politic. The suffrage women rightly felt however that the nationalist women were not, with one or two notable exceptions, spearheading the nationalist movement and thus were creating a precedent for a new state where women would continue to be the supporters and helpers rather than leaders. /

It is often assumed that the nationalist movement gradually deprived the suffrage movement of a number of its members.[147] Indeed three studies of the Irish suffrage movement have the theme of nationalism versus suffragism. MacCurtain and Cullen Owens argue that nationalism damaged the suffrage movement in Ireland and made it very weak. McKillen, on the other hand, argues that the situation was not quite so polarised, and that in the period after 1916 the section of the suffrage movement represented by the IWFL became more nationalistic and the nationalist women became more feminist in their perspective.[148] There was some movement into the nationalist camp, however, all the suffrage groups mentioned at the beginning of the chapter still existed in 1917 one year after the Easter Rising and were intent on getting the Representation of the Peoples Bill through Parliament. To a certain extent it could be argued that the very existence and urgency of the nationalist issue strengthened the suffrage movement. It made the suffragists determined that whatever type of new Ireland would emerge Irish women would be a part of it.[149]/

This chapter has set the scene for the rest of the book. While on the one hand the number and diversity of suffrage groups in Ireland could be interpreted as a sign of weakness and lack of leadership, on the other hand it could be seen as a sign of the strength and popularity of the idea since it reached so many different people. As we shall see in the next chapter, the idea did not originate or stay in Ireland. Irish women went abroad to inspire others and many foreign women came to speak to groups in Ireland about what they were doing abroad. //

Notes

1. The journals *Englishwoman* and *Englishwoman's Review* are excellent source material for a detailed study of such movements in the latter half of the nineteenth century in Ireland.
2. Mary Cullen, "How Radical was Irish Feminism between 1860 and 1920?" *Radicals, Rebels and Establishments*, Patrick Corish (ed.), (Appletree Press, 1985). Anne V. O'Connor, "The Revolution in girls' secondary

education in Ireland, 1860–1910", *Girls Don't Do Honours: Irish Women in Education in the 19th and 20th Centuries*. Mary Cullen (ed.), (Women's Education Bureau, Dublin, 1987) pp. 44–5. Eibhlin Breathnach "Charting new waters: women's experience in higher education, 1879–1908", *Ibid*, pp. 55–78.

3. Sheehy Skeffington Papers (Hereafter referred to as SSP) in National Library of Ireland (Hereafter referred to as NLI), Dublin. Ms 21, 259 (i).
4. Countess Aberdeen (ed.), *Women in Politics, The International Congress of Women 1899* (T. Fisher Unwin, London, 1900).
5. *Ibid*.
6. Susan Day, *The Amazing Philanthropists* (Sidgwick and Jackson, London, 1916).
7. Susan Day, *Women in a New Ireland* (Munster Women's Franchise League, Cork, 1912) p. 3.
8. *Englishwoman's Review*, April 15, 1903, pp. 122–3.
9. *Irish Citizen*, June 15, 1912, p. 31.
10. Marian Ramelson, *Petticoat Rebellion* (Lawrence and Wishart, London, 1967), pp. 113–18.
11. Dora Mellone, *Englishwoman*, October 1913, p. 1.
12. *Registration of Women Electors under the Local Government Act*, 1904. See also *Englishwoman's Review*, July 15, 1904, p. 189.
13. *Irish Citizen*, (Hereafter referred to as *IC*) May 25, 1912, p. 7.
14. Anne O'Connor, *op. cit.*, p. 32.
15. *Englishwoman's Review*, August 15, 1879, pp. 337–42.
16. *Ibid*, 1887, March, p. 37.
17. *Ibid*, January 15, 1898, pp. 53–5.
18. Margaret Ward, *Unmanageable Revolutionaries* (Brandon, Dingle, 1983).
19. *Englishwoman's Review*, February 15, 1877, p. 70.
20. *Englishwoman's Review*, April 15, 1878, p. 177.
21. *IC*, May 25, 1912.
22. *Ibid*, May 17, 1913.
23. *Ibid*, May 25, 1912.
24. *Votes for Women*, (Hereafter referred to as *VFW*) June 30, 1911, p. 651.
25. See Chapter 6.
26. Helena Moloney, "James Connolly and Women" *Dublin Labour Year Book*, 1930.
27. Olive Banks, *Becoming a Feminist: The Social Origins of "First Wave" Feminism* (Harvester Press, Brighton, 1987), p. 11.
28. *IC*, June 15, 1912.
29. Day, *Women in a New Ireland, op. cit.*
30. Ms 94109 PA, NLI.
31. *IC*, Suf. Cat.
32. *VFW*, November 26, 1911.
33. *Conservative and Unionist Franchise Review*, November 1912, p. 11.
34. *Freeman's Journal*, June 22, 1912.
35. *IC*, June 1912, p. 14.
36. *IC*, July 11, 1914, p. 61.

37. *IC*, May 27, 1912, p. 4.
38. R.M. Fox, *Louie Bennett* (Talbot Press, Dublin, 1957), p. 17.
39. *VFW*, May 20, 1910, p. 552.
40. Maurice Collis, *Somerville and Ross: A Biography* (Faber, London, 1968). John Cronin, *Somerville and Ross* (Bucknell University Press, 1972).
41. *Report of the Irishwomen's Suffrage Federation 1912–1913*, p. 5.
42. Day, *op. cit.*
43. *Report of the Irishwomen's Suffrage Federation 1912–1913*.
44. *The Irishwomen's Suffrage Federation First Annual Report 1911–1912* NLI 399631.
45. *IC*, May 17, 1913, p. 418.
46. *Irishwomen's Suffrage Federation Second Annual Report 1912–1913* NLI 3996 314.
47. *Ibid.*
48. *IC*, May 17, 1913.
49. *ISF First Annual Report*, p. 10.
50. *IC*, May 13, 1913, p. 418.
51. *Annual Report of IWSLGA 1911*.
52. *VFW*, September 29, 1911, p. 821.
53. Cork Constitution, May 16, 1912, p. 8.
54. *Englishwoman's Review*, April 15, 1909, p. 102.
55. This accusation was levied every time the Home Rule Bill came up before Parliament.
56. *IC*, June 22, 1912, p. 36.
57. Ulick O'Connor, *Celtic Twilight* (Gill and Macmillan, Dublin, 1983).
58. Margaret Cousins, *A Woman's Place in the Vegetarian Movement* (Dublin 1910).
59. SSP Ms 27, 256 (iii).
60. C.P. Curran, *Under the Receding Wave* (Gill and Macmillan, Dublin, 1970) p. 89.
61. Cousins, *We Two Together* (Ganesh, Madras, 1950) p. 106.
62. C.P. Curran, *op. cit.*
63. Cousins, *op. cit.*, pp. 106–7.
64. SSP Ms 22, 269.
65. See Chapter 6. In February 1900 Sheehy Skeffington gave a paper on "The Progress of Women" to the Literary and Historical Society of University College. He also wrote an essay for the college newspaper on "A Forgotten Aspect of the University Question".
66. Cousins, *op. cit.*, p. 60.
67. Hanna Sheehy Skeffington, "Reminiscences" in *Votes for Women*, A. D. Sheehy Skeffington and Rosemary Owens (Dublin, 1975).
68. *VFW*, November 11, 1910, p. 83.
69. Cousins, *op. cit.*, p. 162.
70. SSP Ms 22, 270.
71. *IC*, May 25, 1912, p. 3.
72. James Cousins's poem "The Suffragette" and Frank Sheehy Skeffington's play "The Prodigal Daughter" portrayed women suffragists in a positive light.

73. Cousins, *op. cit.*, p. 171.
74. Banks, *op. cit.*, p. 106.
75. *Ibid*, p. 110.
76. *Ibid*, p. 39.
77. *Ibid*, p. 40.
78. *Ibid*, p. 14.
79. *VFW*, November 26, 1908, p. 151.
80. *VFW*, October 15, 1911, p. 45.
81. *Ibid*, May 5, 1911, p. 519.
82. *IC*, July 4, 1914, p. 51.
83. Cousins, *op. cit.*, p. 167.
84. *IC*, July 6, 1912, p. 55.
85. *Freeman's Journal*, November 6, 1911, p. 10.
86. *VFW*, October 21, 1910, p. 46.
87. Cousins, *op. cit.*, pp. 166–7.
88. *Ibid*, p. 166.
89. *IC*, May 17, 1912, also *IC*, July 6, 1912.
90. *VFW*, May 13, 1910, p. 542.
91. *Ibid*, April 22, 1910, p. 486.
92. *Ibid*, April 29, 1910, p. 506.
93. *IC*, June 15, 1912.
94. *IC*, May 25, 1912, p. 3.
95. Beth McKillen, "Irish Feminism and National Separatism 1914–1923", *Eire/Ireland* xvii: 3, Fall 1981, pp. 2–67, xvii: 4, Winter 1982, pp. 72–90.
96. Nicholas Mansergh, *The Irish Question* (Toronto, 1965).
97. *IC*, May 25, 1912.
98. *IC*, May 17, 1912.
99. *IC*, June 22, 1912, p. 35.
100. *VFW*, March 24, 1911, p. 400.
101. *Ibid*, March 31, p. 434, *ibid*, April 14, 1911, p. 466.
102. Cousins, *op. cit.*, pp. 201–2.
103. *IC*, June 8, 1912, p. 21.
104. *Ibid*.
105. *Report of the Executive Committee of the IWFL 1913*, p. 9.
106. SSP Letter from Louie Bennett to Hanna Sheehy Skeffington asking if the IWFL will support the conference. SSP Ms 22,662 (ii).
107. *IC*, November 1913, p. 193.
108. See Chapter 4.
109. *VFW*, May 6, 1910, p. 526.
110. *Ibid*, January 5, 1912, p. 230.
111. *IC*, July 27, 1912.
112. SSP Ms 22,662 (ii).
113. *Ibid*.
114. IC, May 25, 1912, p. 3.
115. *IC*, June 8, 1912, p. 20.
116. *Irish Review*, July 1912.
117. *Report of the Executive Committee of the IWSLGA for 1912*, p. 7.
118. *Ibid*, p. 17.

119. *Ibid*, p. 7.
120. *IC*, May 17, 1913, p. 419.
121. Fox, *op. cit.*, p. 18.
122. SSP Ms 22,265.
123. *Ibid*.
124. *IC*, June 29, 1912, p. 44.
125. *IC*, November 1, 1913, p. 192.
126. *Prison Letters of Countess Markievicz* (Virago, London, 1986) p. 76.
127. *Ibid*, p. 12.
128. *Ibid*, p. 192.
129. *VFW*, February 17, 1911, p. 331.
130. *IC*, June 1, 1912, p. 9.
131. *Catholic Bulletin*, October, 1912, p. 791.
132. *Freeman's Journal*, September 30, 1911, p. 4.
133. *Catholic Suffragist*, August 15, 1916, p. 73.
134. R.M. Fox, *Rebel Irishwomen* (Talbot Press, Dublin, 1935), p. 34.
135. Charlotte Fallon, *Soul of Fire* (Mercier Press, Cork and Dublin, 1986), p. 19.
136. *Ibid*, p. 22.
137. Margaret Ward, *op. cit.*, p. 71.
138. *Ibid*, p. 70.
139. Fallon, *op. cit*, p. 17.
140. *IC*, December 13, 1913, p. 241.
141. Ward, *op. cit*, p. 90.
142. *Ibid*, July 4, 1914, p. 52.
143. *IC*, 11 April, 1914. Fallon, *op. cit.*, p. 18.
144. *Ibid*, July 25, 1914, p. 75.
145. *IC*, August 1, 1914.
146. Lil Conlon, *Cumann na mBan and the Women of Ireland* (Kilkenny People Ltd, 1969). Ward, *op. cit.*
147. Margaret MacCurtain and Donnacha O'Corrain (eds) "The Vote and Revolution" in *Women in Irish Society: The Historical Dimension* (Arlen House, Dublin, 1978), pp. 46–57.
148. McKillen, *op. cit.*
149. See Chapter 7.

· 3 ·

Insular but not Isolated

Irish suffragists did not and could not operate solely within their own context. They were clearly influenced by other women (and indeed men), intellectuals and activists, writers and visitors, pacifists and militants from a variety of countries throughout the world. The written words of women of international repute and influence like Mary Wollstonecraft, Carrie Chapman Catt and Olive Schreiner were read by Irish women, and their philosophies were pondered upon if not always accepted. It is seldom pointed out or appreciated how many well-known women in history had connections with Ireland. Mary Wollstonecraft's mother was from Ireland and she herself spent some time in Co. Cork as a governess. Wollstonecraft's sister ran a school in Dublin at least until 1818.[1] Florence Nightingale, who, if not a feminist, was a rebellious woman, spent time in Dublin with the Sisters of Mercy in the early 1850s.[2] Likewise women left Ireland and helped shape feminism abroad. Among these were Anna Wheeler and George Egerton, Eve Gore Booth and Margaret Cousins.

Wheeler received Mary Wollstonecraft's *Vindication of the Rights of Women* (1792) through a circulating library and consequently decided to leave her husband and change her life.[3] She collaborated with a Corkman, William Thompson, in an influential tome—*An Appeal of One Half The Human Race, Women, Against the Pretensions of The Other Half, Men*, which was published in 1825. She also had a strong influence on Daniel O'Connell the leader of Catholic Emancipation.[4] Thompson had thought that Mary Wollstonecraft's *Vindication* had been "too narrow"[5]. One admirer of Thompson's and Wheeler's book has called it "the first voice of a nineteenth-century man against the subjection of women" and "the most significant [work] relating to women in the three quarters of a century between Mary Wollstonecraft's *Vindication of the Rights of Women* of 1792 and John Stuart Mill's *Subjection of Women* of 1869."[6] This admirer explained the attraction of the book's two authors thus ". . . though he had long reflected on the inequalities of sexual laws, she had actually suffered from them."[7] Wheeler became an associate of the British socialist Robert Owen and had an influence in Owen's attempts to create a feminist socialism. In *Eve and the New Jerusalem*, Barbara Taylor outlines Wheeler's contributions to early socialism.[8] /

Chavelita Dunne or George Egerton left Ireland in the 1880s and through her novels was to have a significant influence on feminists. Patricia Stubbs has described Egerton's stories as "very nineties and very feminist". *Keynotes*, a collection of short stories celebrated the 'new woman' and portrayed her as strong and independent. Back in Dublin Egerton's publisher found that he had occasionally to modify some of her more forthright passages.[9] She was part of the post-Ibsen generation and provided some of the reading material of the early twentieth-century suffragists. Another\ Irish woman in Britain was Eve Gore Booth, the sister of Countess Markievicz. She and her sister had started up a suffrage society in Sligo. Gore Booth has been quoted as saying "All of us, men and women alike, have duties to our neighbours and to our country and to society at large."[10] She took this duty seriously and was to play a significant role in the women's trade union movement in Britain and wrote widely on women's issues.[11] She has been credited with inspiring the young Christabel Pankhurst who took one of the courses Gore Booth was giving to mill girls in Manchester.[12] But when Pankhurst moved towards militancy Gore Booth remained a pacifist.[13] /

/ Margaret Cousins left Ireland in 1913 and became very involved with, and even went to gaol for, the Indian women's rights movement. Her life in the sub-continent is the subject of another volume altogether. Even those who stayed at home, through their actions, sometimes served as an inspiration for feminists abroad. The Ladies' Land League of the early 1880s, which took over the running of the Land War when the male Land Leaguers were imprisoned, was frequently and reverently referred to by foreign women. They showed how women, too, could lead a national organisation.[14]

Thus there was a tradition of contact before the beginning of the twentieth century, and Irish women were not isolated in their country either physically or intellectually. Some of this was due partly to the fact that Ireland was an island whose people had constantly to look outwards for stimulation and often move outwards out of necessity. As with other philosophies, Irish Catholicism and Irish Nationalism, what developed was uniquely Irish, very different from the continental brands, so too with Irish suffragism. The women had the advantage of selecting what suited them and rejecting what they found to be unsuitable to Irish circumstances. This tradition of exchanging ideas enabled the dialogue to flow more freely when a structured and organised movement was founded in Ireland. However like most dialogues it contained certain tensions. Misunderstandings were frequent, friendships and motives were distrusted. In an examination of the relationship between Irish suffragists and women elsewhere it might be possible to glean the characteristics which made the Irish women unique, and to see to what extent they shared the attributes of international suffrage organisations. How far were the Irish women influenced by and part of that worldwide movement, which was rampant in the early part of the twentieth century, and to what extent was their character shaped by Irish circumstances? Such a study will help assess the context in which the Irish movement was regarded by suffragists abroad and thus indicate whether or not the movement was a significant one in world terms.

The women in the first structured suffrage movement in Ireland, the IWSLGA, were aware of precedents abroad and sought to bring a variety of outside speakers to its meetings. There was a consciousness of the heritage left by people like Mary Wollstonecraft and Anna Wheeler. John Stuart Mill's attempt to enfranchise women in 1866 with the presentation of a petition in Parliament served to inspire the formation of the IWSLGA in 1876. Suffragists in Ireland were encouraged by the enfranchisement of women in some American states. They were well read and realised the importance of keeping in touch with what was going on abroad. Mrs Dockrell represented the IWSLGA at the International Congress of Women in London in 1899, and her comprehensive report to the Congress about the progress of women in local government in Ireland was subsequently published with the Congress's proceedings.[15] /

It is clear also that suffragists, particularly in Britain, were aware that there was a significant movement in Ireland for women's suffrage. Millicent Fawcett, the leader of the English National Union of Women's Suffrage Societies had contact with Irish suffragists in the 1880s and 1890s and was a regular visitor to Ireland. However she was distinctly anti-Home Rule, and was a sympathiser of the boycotted English landlords in Ireland in the 1890s and sought to alleviate their sufferings by fund-raising, a fact that the IWFL seemed to have forgotten when she visited them some twenty years later, but which did not bother the genteel lady suffragists of the 1890s. During these early visits to Ireland her advice was sought on a proposed Local Government Bill which threatened to exclude women since "Not five women in the South here know what county councils are." One of her Irish contacts was Belfast suffragist, and founder of the Belfast Ladies Institute in 1875 (and later of the Irish Women's Suffrage Society), Isabella Tod.[16]

In contemporary surveys of suffrage movements in the late nineteenth and early twentieth centuries, the Irish suffrage movement gets particular mention as being unique and distinctive. This is evident in the books by Blackburn, Zimmerman and Fairfield.[17] An entry into the minute book of the IWSLGA in 1903 on the death of Helen Blackburn noted that she ". . . was the warmest and most strenuous friend our Irish society has ever had. Her generous 'Record of the Women's Suffrage Movement in the British Isles' will remain as an abiding monument to her unselfish zeal and industry."[18] Periodicals such as *Englishwoman* and *Englishwoman's Review* gave detailed reporting not only on suffrage movements but also on moves for secondary and

higher education of women in Ireland as well as their progress
in Local Government matters, and the improvement of
industrial conditions. While it is true that Ireland was often
seen by these journals as yet another county or province of
Britain it is clear that they realised the independent nature
of the Irish movement. Weekly suffrage magazines and
newspapers also gave lip-service to Irish women's efforts.
The *Irish Citizen* told its readers in July 1912 "All readers
of the *Irish Citizen* ought to buy this week's *Common Cause*
in recognition of the publicity given in it to Irish women's
efforts for enfranchisement."[19]

Other English journals such as *Votes for Women, The Vote,
Men's League for Women's Suffrage, The Anti Suffrage Review,
Church League for Women's Suffrage* and others all had 'Irish
Sections' where they reported the latest meetings, gave
membership updates, and discussed actions of Irish suffragists. This attention to, and interest in, Irish affairs was
observed by Frank Sheehy Skeffington. In a letter written in
1914 he revealed:

> We receive a considerable number of applications from England for
> copies of the *Irish Citizen*, and we are frequently asked whether it can
> be had through any of the English Suffrage Societies (just as some Irish
> Suffrage Societies stock *Votes for Women, The Vote* and *Common Cause*).
> At present Henderson's (Charing Cross Road) are the only people who
> sell it in England; but it would obviously be more convenient for
> scattered readers to be able to obtain it through their own suffrage
> societies . . .[20]

Likewise Irish women themselves kept in touch with what
was going on outside the country by reading foreign suffragist
literature and newspapers. English suffrage papers were
periodically sold on Dublin street corners. However, as will
subsequently be seen this was not always viewed as beneficial.
In March 1910 *Votes for Women*, the suffrage newspaper
owned by the Pethick Lawrences, referring to its sales in
Ireland, reported that it "continues to sell throughout the
country" and gave a list of its individual sellers.[21] It claimed
at one meeting alone to have sold 350 copies in Dublin.[22]
The Irish Women's Suffrage Society regularly stocked and
sold *Votes for Women*.[23] Margaret Cousins remembered in her

autobiography that this weekly "gave us in Ireland details of the first deputation of women, headed by Mrs Pankhurst, to Parliament, and their arrest and imprisonment as common criminals. There was later the exciting and inspiring account of the first meeting organised by the Women's Social and Political Union which packed the Albert Hall, London."[24] The *Irish Citizen* as a matter of course presumed its readers read *Votes for Women* and *The Suffragette*.[25] It also acknowledged that much of the international information in its pages came from *Jus Suffragii* which was the newspaper of the International Women's Suffrage Association.[26] The IWSLGA too spoke of *Jus Suffragii* as "our international organ" for information.[27] *The Citizen* also on occasion received the South African newspaper *The Woman's Outlook*[28] and conveyed its contents to *Citizen* readers. Thus the suffragists in Ireland were admitted to the world of international suffragism through its media. Olive Banks has made a similar observation in her study of British feminists noting that a "factor in recruitment to feminism which is hard to tie down but is nevertheless of great significance is the spread of information. Feminist journals have clearly played a part throughout the whole of the period, not only as a source of propaganda, but as a way of bringing people together."[29]

As well as reading English weekly suffragist newspapers Irish women were strongly influenced by feminist literature. Louie Bennett, leader of the Irishwomen's Suffrage Federation and trade unionist, wrote that her sisterhood with women was realised through reading Richardson, Fielding, Miss Burney, Jane Austen, the Brontës, Eliot and Ibsen. She felt that they were responsible for arousing women to the need for independence. Writing about the literature of the 'new woman' she commented "so in her literature, she shrieked for freedom. Not realising at first that it was that terrible gaolor Custom, rather than man, that held her in bondage, she shrieked against man." The South African feminist and writer Olive Schreiner was greatly admired by Bennett, who wrote of *African Farm* "It is a cry of rebellion against many things in heaven and earth, but most of all against the injustice of women's position in the world."[30] Bennett did not feel that the independence of Irish movements would be compromised by an appreciation of a common grievance among women throughout the world. She wrote that while her organisation was truly an Irish organisation "independent of any similar English organisation" she hoped that "every Irish suffrage society will work to keep alive the consciousness that the women's movement is a world wide movement; that we suffragists are working for all women and that we recognise the bond of sisterhood uniting women of every nationality."[31]

The author, clergyman and friend of the suffragists, George Birmingham, told Frank Sheehy Skeffington to "tell your wife from me that I [am] reading a work by a perfect whirlwind of a feminist, a Mrs or Miss (She would probably disdain both titles) Charlotte Gilman Perkins . . . there is no doubt that the reading was good for me . . . ."[32] Despite muddling up the author's name, his enthusiasm for the book is obvious and must have influenced his supportive attitude towards the suffragists in Ireland. As an undergraduate the young Skeffington's reading foreshadowed his future politics. While reading Meredith's *Diana of the Crossways* he followed "every word of it with his pencil, underscoring each line with impulsive assiduity and exclamatory markings".[33] He admired Meredith more for "his social criticism and attitude towards women than his briary wit". According to one source Skeffington introduced his wife to the writings of John Stuart Mill[34] and we are assured by her daughter-in-law that she had Ford Maddox Ford's picture of the English suffragist couple the Pethick Lawrences hanging in her room.[35] She was not only inspired by foreign suffragists but by intellectuals and philosophers also. Of Thoreau, she wrote that he said "the time may arise when the prison may be the only place of honour left to an honest man. Many a brave Irishman has proved the truth of the axion in the past. It is now for Irish women to realize citizenship by becoming 'criminalised'."[36]

The availablity of foreign suffragist literature is also evident from the book lists of the suffrage libraries and the book reviews in the *Irish Citizen*. Lists of the latest books in the Feminist circulating libraries were regularly published. The Irishwomen's Reform League announced its 'interesting additions' in June 1914. These included A.C. Fox Davies *The Book of Public Speaking* and Willis J. Abbot's *Notable*

Women in History. The Irish Women's Suffrage Society had a Pass-it-on-Library and had thirty or so members "who appreciate books on the women's question we are able to circulate through the kindness of a lady sympathiser across the water."[37] They advertised their library as a place where "members read sections from ancient and modern literature illustrative of the different types of women."[38] The Irishwomen's Reform League's library was seen to be a "valuable asset to the suffrage cause in Ireland in many by-ways. It must, for instance, help to keep the movement on a fine intellectual plane, and in doing much to rouse interest those who are quicker to respond to an intellectual than to an emotional, philanthropic or moral influence."[39] The library in South Anne Street in Dublin had acquired copies of *Daughters of Ishmael* by Reginal Kaufman; *The Case for Women's Suffrage* edited by Brougham Villers, and Cadbury's *Women's Work and Women's Wages*.[40] However, the suffragist libraries did not focus on intellectual and theoretical issues alone—the IRL library also had received (unnamed) books dealing with management and proper clothing of infants.[41] C.P. Gilman's book *What Diantha Did* was recommended by the South Anne Street library to all "who are interested in the domestic side of the feminist movement."[42]

The *Citizen* book-reviews were concerned with the latest additions in suffrage literature as well as relevant previously published books. From these reviews it can be seen that Irish women were exposed to the same literature that their American, British and continental counterparts were reading. Thus there was a common intellectual understanding among women who were often 5,000 miles apart. On the *Citizen*'s 'Bookshelf' on June 13, 1914 was Frances Swiney's *Women Among the Nations* which considered "the Primitive Woman, the Woman of the Old Civilisations, the Woman of the New".[43] A review of *Shelley, Godwin and their Circle* by H.N. Brailsford was said to be specially notable for its fine chapter on Mary Wollstonecraft, who a century earlier had with regard to women "anticipated all their main positions, and formulated the idea which the modern movement is struggling to complete".[44] Another review recommended the books of militant English suffragist Elizabeth Robins which included *Where are you going?*, *The Convert and Suffragette Sally*. The reviewer spoke of the "amount these do, have done and are still doing, in opening people's minds to the dreadful need of Votes for Women . . .".[45] Christabel Pankhurst's *The Great Scourge and How to End It*, in which she accused the majority of men as being carriers of venereal disease and advised women to be cautious about getting married, was given a very enthusiastic review.

> Miss Pankhurst's book has been attacked as extravagant, fanatical and hysterical. The subject is one on which fanaticism might well be excused, and of which the horrors might easily generate hysteria; but there is no justification for these charges against Miss Pankhurst. Her approach to the subject of prostitution is an eminently sane, practical and common sense one . . . Let no one urge that its circulation is not needed in Ireland. The comparative freedom from the Great Scourge of our agricultural districts is gained at the expense of our cities where it is concentrated. Remember, Dublin has a greater percentage of deaths from syphilis than London.[46]

As well as keeping an eye on the latest suffrage literature from abroad the *Citizen* brought anti-suffragist literature to the attention of its readers. *An Expurgated Case Against the Rights of Women's Suffrage* written by Sir Almroth Wright, the prominent anti-suffragist who was born in Ireland and educated in Trinity was duly reviewed and provoked some correspondence including a vehement reaction from George Bernard Shaw.[47] The *Citizen* published feminist tracts, articles, pamphlets and comparative studies of other countries. It also had a special 'British and Foreign Notes section'. When looking at countries with enfranchised women the *Irish Citizen* was always quick to point to the flaw in the Antis' arguments.[48] Interest in the American suffrage movement wove its way through a number of issues of the *Irish Citizen*. Articles appeared on 'How the Vote was won in Illinois', 'Women Displace Southern Pacific'[49] and 'Woman Suffrage in America; an Irish Woman's Impression'.[50] The author of the last article wrote that "The suffrage campaign in America is carried on with an amount of intelligence and serious thought which is, regrettably, not so obvious in the English movement; . . . A man speaker the other day declared that

American women did not need to be militant because their men are not so thickheaded as Englishmen . . ."[51]

As well as specific suffrage news, anecdotal reports appeared illustrating how women were better off abroad. One such was 'The Tune of the Stars and Stripes' which recounted the grievance of Irish women concerning their low status in the eyes of the law and reflecting a growing movement which demanded the right of Irish women to become lawyers

> It is now known that, as far as openings for professional women are concerned, America is one of the most advanced. The other day in New York Grace O'Neill, "a frail looking woman of 26 years acted as a special judge in a divorce suit, and acquitted herself admirably". Should an Irish woman go to America she would be eligible for like responsibilities—remaining at home the same woman will be deemed unworthy of entering the legal profession. Small wonder our sisters are emigrating in ever increasing numbers.[52]

Another article on a similar theme was 'The Legal Position of Women in the British Isles'. It expressed the opinion that Irish women fared much worse even than the women across the water

> There are important local variations to these laws in Scotland and Ireland. Generally it may be stated that those in Scotland are more favourable, those in Ireland are more prejudicial . . . In Ireland the legal position of women is bad. The Married Women's Property Act of 1908 does not apply to Ireland. Divorce is, in practice, possible only for the rich, so that the inequality of requiring proof of cruelty or desertion by the man and not by the woman is more theoretical than practical; nevertheless it exists. A private Act of Parliament, very costly to obtain, is necessary for a complete divorce. Magistrates have not the power to grant separation orders as in England.[53]

Comparatively women in many countries abroad did seem to be a lot better off. One article looked at the experiences of women in Finland which was among the few countries who gave women equal voting rights before the First World War. It argued that since they had received it Finnish politics was in a much better state.[54]

Irish women were further stimulated when foreign suffragists took an active interest in them. Letters came from abroad reassuring them that their actions had beneficial

consequences far afield. In January 1914 a letter arrived from
Mrs Alice Park 'the well known Californian suffragist'. She
wrote that actions of suffragists in different countries helped
the cause in general. ". . . Every outbreak in England,
Scotland and Ireland gives all women everywhere great
publicity in newspapers great and small, without any effort
on part of women outside the British Isles. Publicity is an
absolute necessity in pushing a forward movement."[55] The
National American Women's Suffrage Association frequently
sent messages of encouragement to the *Irish Citizen*. The
South African feminist and author Olive Schreiner, who was
referred to as "that fine feminist",[56] also kept in touch with
Irish suffragists. Among other international correspondents
were American suffragists Jane Addams, Alice Paul, a New
Jersey Quaker and suffragist, and her lieutenant Lucy Burns,
the only prominent American suffragist leader of Irish
Catholic ancestry.[57] Letters also appeared periodically from
the Australian suffragist Vida Goldstein.[58]

It was not just in the columns of the *Irish Citizen* that
foreign contacts are evident. In other areas, in people's
correspondence and memoirs, autobiographies and biographies, the link between the Irish movements and those outside
the country is visible. Sir Horace Plunkett the pioneer of the
cooperative movement in Ireland and founder of the Irish
Country Women's Association had spent a number of years
in Wyoming where women were enfranchised in 1869.[59] He
wrote articles on women's suffrage which not only attracted
the attention of Irish suffragists but also of the English
NUWSS leader Mrs Fawcett whom he subsequently met and
liked but thought "the rest a queer lot".[60] One of his
biographers, Margaret Digby, recounts him amusing "the
House with an impromptu speech on Woman Suffrage, drawn
from his Wyoming experience back in 1892."[61] Later he was
to meet Lady Constance Lytton who "was recovering from
her gaol experiences as a suffragette". She told him "a most
thrilling tale of prison life".[62] When her real identity was
discovered her treatment in prison altered considerably—a
fact which was used as propaganda for the suffrage cause.[63]

Among Hanna Sheehy Skeffington's papers are letters from
an admirer in the Isle of Man,[64] a French feminist,[65] the

Labour leader John Burns,[66] not to mention the amount of correspondence from the various English suffrage leaders. Her husband Frank wrote to the American suffragist Jane Addams among others.[67]

While the written word may have indeed the power to convert, the actual charisma of the speakers had far more impact and many speakers came to talk to the Irish suffragists. They came from Norway, Australia, Britain and America as well as other countries. Meetings were addressed in Dublin, Cork, Limerick and Belfast and some of the smaller towns. The visitors spoke of the progress women had made in their own countries and generally engendered a feeling of world sisterhood among their listeners. They also spoke to non-suffragist groups like university students and accepted invitations from their debating societies. Women who had wide experience on the suffrage front came and related their experiences. One of these was Mrs Mary Gawthorpe. She was an English suffragist, a member of the Independent Labour Party and representative of the Women's Labour League. She was also an organiser of the WSPU and had undergone imprisonment in Holloway. She was regarded as a very "effective speaker"[69] and was invited to speak to the Solicitors' Apprentices Debating Society at the Four Courts in Dublin in November 1908. She appeared on the platform with Margaret Cousins.[69]

/ One of the early visitors who had a large influence on the Cousinses and the Skeffingtons and gave a theosophical slant to certain parts of the Irish suffrage movement was Annie Besant. She was the organiser of the 1888 match girls' strike and a member of the Social Democratic Federation. As a child James Cousins had been told that Besant was "an agent of the devil".[70] Nevertheless he went to hear her in London[71] and was instrumental in bringing her to Dublin. In 1909 he wrote to Frank Sheehy Skeffington "I fancy a good number of the Contemporaries would like to hear Mrs Besant and to bring friends."[72] The Irish Theosophical Society was set up as a result of her visit.[73] Indeed Annie Besant had such a strong influence on the Cousinses that they answered her call to join her in journalist and education work in India.[74] /

Another visitor with a spiritual slant was the Rev. C. Hin-

scliff, founder of the Church League for Women's Suffrage
(London). He came to speak to the Irish Women's Suffrage
Society (Belfast), addressed a number of meetings in October
1912 and started a branch of the Church League for Women's
Suffrage in Dublin in 1913.[75] Charlotte Despard the sister
of Lord French, the last Lord Lieutenant of Ireland, and
the leader of the English organisation, the Women's Freedom
League (a breakaway group from the WSPU) came on a
number of occasions and addressed several open air meetings.[76] She spoke to the Irish Women's Franchise League
and was described by Margaret Cousins as one of the "rare
Catholics who were Theosophists".[77] At one meeting she told
her audience that in the "great intellectual and moral qualities
which men and women had in common, there was no sex".
She confessed that she had never really cared for a man who
"was not part a woman". A Despard fund was organised by
the *Irish Citizen* to enable Mrs Despard to travel around
Ireland in September 1912.[78] However when her organisation
began to have designs on running the Irish suffrage movement
such help was not as forthcoming.

The more charismatic and famous the speakers, the larger
the size of the crowds and the greater the publicity. Mrs
Emmeline Pankhurst, the leader of the English militant
suffrage movement, the WSPU, made a few visits to Ireland
and during the early years of the militant Irish movement,
the IWFL, she was a very popular figure. Veteran suffragist
Mrs Lister reflected in 1977 on the reasons she joined the
Irish Suffrage movement. "I was young and enthusiastic.
Mother told me about Pankhurst."[79] Mary Colum, another
Irish feminist, nationalist and writer remembered in her
autobiography the Pankhursts coming to Ireland "the Pankhursts fought magnificently, but when they made speeches
they talked like lawyers and politicians."[80]

In October 1910 Mrs Pankhurst came on a week's visit
and addressed meetings in Cork,[81] Dublin, Dundalk, Belfast
and Derry.[82] In anticipation of her visit the *Freeman's Journal*
wrote "It is expected that Mrs Pankhurst in her first visit to
Ireland will achieve success as brilliant as was hers recently
during her trip to the United States. She has undergone
imprisonment on various occasions, and is, in very truth, the

heart and brain of the militant movement."[83] In Dublin she
addressed a meeting at the Palace Skating Rink at Rathmines
"It was probably the largest gathering assembled in Dublin
in connection with the woman suffrage cause. The extensive
floor of the rink was almost wholly occupied, the majority
present being, of course, ladies."[84] Her visit was looked upon
with interest by the Press in general in Ireland and noted by
the police in particular.[85] According to the *Evening Telegraph*
(Dublin) "Mrs Pankhurst's strong and magnetic personality
will, no doubt, win many new recruits for the movement in
Ireland while her brilliant ability will do much to dispel
prejudice and ignorance."[86] In its coverage of the visit the
Irish Independent concluded "She has further been endowed
with that most beautiful thing in a woman—a low sweet
voice."[87] She was accompanied on her tour by Margaret
Cousins who remembered that in Cork "The Town Hall had
a capacity audience, all seats paid for, and I felt very happy
at the ovation she received from my country-people on her
first appearance in Ireland."[88] On a return visit in April 1911
Mrs Pankhurst addressed meetings in Dublin where she was
presented with a Kilmainham brooch in Celtic workmanship
with the name IWFL, and she urged Irish women to join
the next deputation to the House of Commons.[89] Equally
enthusiastic was Deborah Webb whose poetic tribute included
the verse:

> To us an inspiration thou hast been,
>   Thy eloquence is purifying fire;
> Thy lovely face transfigured we have seen
>   To somewhat of thy zeal we would aspire.[90]

As will be seen, there was to be a limit to the amount of
English zeal acceptable to the Irish suffragists.

Two of Mrs Pankhurst's daughters also visited Ireland.
Christabel's reputation preceded her. Such was the excitement
when she came in March 1910 that "long before the time
large crowds besieged the doors and although the hall holds
2,000 persons many had to be excluded and some of the
more ardent were heard knocking on the door during the
progress of the meeting."[91] It was little wonder so many
turned up since the IWFL had spent twenty pounds on

publicity posters.[92] Christabel Pankhurst addressed the IWFL
again in October 1911, she conveyed to the League "the
intention of WSPU to support, by every means in their
power, the claim of their Irish sisters".[93] However that
support would subsequently be seen as too intrusive.
Christabel Pankhurst was a rather flamboyant and fanatical
personality. She intrigued enthusiastic followers in Ireland.

Of her visit it was glowingly said "She came, we heard
and saw; she conquered", words, perhaps, that must have
been regretted when accusations that the Irish suffrage
movement was part of the British one had to be answered.[94]
She frequently wrote of Irish women's fight for suffrage in
Votes for Women and was particularly concerned that Irish
Nationalist MPs were capable of preventing both Irish and
English women being enfranchised. In an article written in
October 1911 she argued that all the objections that had been
voiced against women getting the suffrage had once been
used against giving Irishmen independence. In both cases the
objections had the same replies.[95] However, despite such
assertations of solidarity and support there was a feeling
among a number of Irish suffragists that Christabel did not
give one whit about Irish independence and if it had to suffer
in order for women's suffrage to succeed—so be it.

Sylvia Pankhurst who corresponded with Hanna Sheehy
Skeffington[96] came to Ireland in August 1914.[97] She had
supported the Dublin strikes of 1913 and campaigned for the
release of the socialist James Larkin.[98] As a socialist she was
extremely concerned and wrote about the condition of the
Dublin working classes.[99] She was to return after the war in
1919 to talk to what remained of the IWFL and had very
definite ideas for the new Independent Ireland which reflected
her socialist philosophy. According to her biographer she
startled her Irish audience by urging them:

> not to tinker with parliamentary reformism, but to make propaganda
> by direct action, the seizing of farms and factories by the workers, for
> instance, and the setting up of Workers Soviets. Irish Nationalism . . .
> though it might have the *appearance* of being revolutionary (like the
> pre-war suffrage movement), was in fact riddled with reaction; it must
> rid itself of the blinkers of pseudodemocracy and get into line with the
> forces of significant radicalism.[100]

Other regular British visitors included the Pethick Lawrences.[101] They had been defended by the Irish Nationalist MP T.M. Healy against the charge of 'conspiracy'.[102] Mrs Pethick Lawrence visited Ireland in 1913 and 1914. Her concern for Irish women embraced issues wider than the suffrage one. She and her husband were a middle-class couple who first became socialists and later suffragists.[103] She had taken six little girls from Dublin during the 1913 Lock Out to her home. She, surprisingly, had managed to overcome the fears of the Catholic clergy about pagan England by getting a local Catholic priest to look after their spiritual welfare. This was a feat since many children were prevented from going to English homes because of a widely held belief, fuelled by the Archbishop of Dublin, that a period spent in England would put the children on the path for Hell.[104] In Pethick Lawrence's autobiography *My Part in Changing the World* she remembered "When in January, I went to Dublin to speak to a suffrage meeting, all the little green frocked and green capped bunch were sitting on the platform between their proud parents."[105] It would appear that no damage had been done. Mrs Fawcett continued to repeat the visits she had made to Ireland in the 1880s and 1890s.[106]

Mrs Colby, the chairman of the National American Women's Suffrage Association, came from the United States and "her clever accounts of suffrage work in America gave much pleasure".[107] She was a particular success on her visit to Cork. Six hundred people attended an 'at home' in the City Hall where she told them about the movement in America.[108] In Belfast she explained "how women use the vote in the US when they have it."[109]

Another American visitor was Mrs Helen Frazer. The Irishwomen's Suffrage Federation reported that she "spent a month in Ireland . . . drew large new members to the Federation".[110] In October 1914 the *Irish Citizen* drew attention to the 'enthusiastic reception' that had been given to Mrs Alice Park, a woman who frequently corresponded with Irish suffragists.[111] These Americans always gave special hope to the Irish women coming from a country where some women had been enfranchised, where there were many contacts with Ireland and funds were ample. Women in rich and powerful American families attempted to exert their influence on Irish politicians looking for money.[112] Sympathetic male Americans also came to speak to Irish suffragists. The Rev. William Sperry of Fall River, Mass. spoke to the Irishwomen's Reform League about the suffrage movement in Massachusetts.[113]

A woman who spent quite some time in Ireland was Miss Helga Gill from Norway.[114] Norway had given women a limited franchise in 1907 and full voting rights in 1913.[115] Gill came in the summer of 1911 and came again for six weeks in 1912 and gave talks at several meetings. She was 'on loan' from Mrs Fawcett's NUWSS.[116]

From Australia (whose Senate asked the British government to grant women the vote as it had so many beneficial effects there)[117] came Mrs Vida Goldstein. She was a prominent leader of the Australian suffragist movement and admirer of the Ladies Land Leaguer of the 1880s Anna Parnell. She had attempted to get elected to the Australian senate and failed. Despite her aspirations for women she advocated a white Australia[118] and seemed in general to be quite conservative. She addressed a number of meetings in the South of Ireland in the Autumn of 1911.[119] This was an extension of her visit to England where she had been invited by the WSPU. In the Albert Hall, it was claimed, she had addressed more than 10,000 people. She met George Bernard Shaw while in England—no doubt reinforcing the Irish man's feminism. When she was back in Australia she occasionally sent messages of goodwill to meetings of Irish suffragists and letters to the *Irish Citizen*.[120] And a glance at the *Irish Citizen* would indicate that her thoughts and writings were of quite an influence on the Irish women.[121]

Listening to and seeing these women gave encouragement to suffragists in Ireland. However they could go one step further: go abroad and see other women in action for themselves. Those who could afford it or who had the financial backing of their organisations did so and felt invigorated by their experience. This movement out of their own sphere indicated a willingness to expose themselves to wider experiences and to support their sisters abroad. Nearest to home they went to London. Irish suffragists got the ferry boat from Kingstown and were usually greeted by representatives from one or other of the main English suffrage organisations the NUWSS and the WSPU who were often instrumental in inviting them.[122] While there they met English suffragists, attended their meetings and demonstrations and took part in protests of various kinds. A group of women from the IWSLGA led by Mrs Dockrell joined an English suffrage deputation to the English prime minister in 1906.[123] Also in that year Margaret Cousins attended a meeting of the National Council of Women in London and on her return to Ireland she was inspired to join the IWSLGA. However she was quickly to become disillusioned with their timidity[124] and became a founder member of the IWFL.

The Haslams, the founders of the first Irish suffrage movement in 1876, the IWSLGA, frequently went to London. In 1908 Mr Haslam read a paper on 'The Rightful Claims of Women'.[125] In 1913 they were still to be seen participating in a Hyde Park suffrage demonstration.[126] The Haslams were highly regarded by the *Englishwoman's Review* "These two veterans of whom one has passed and the other is approaching the age of fourscore, are a lesson and encouragement to younger women."[127]

Other Irish suffragists also addressed British suffrage meetings. Frank Sheehy Skeffington spoke to a WSPU 'at home'.[128] James Cousins addressed them in July 1910, "I was to give a message from Ireland". He bought a "pair of socks, and a cravat, both of the greenest green that the shops of London could arise to" in honour of the occasion.[129] In 1913 he gave a talk to the Liverpool branch of the WSPU on 'White Slavery its Cause and Cure'.[130] English suffragists would have been familiar with some of his ideas as they frequently appeared in the columns of their suffrage newspapers.

Certain tensions existed between the English and Irish women which will be elaborated upon further, below. Suffice it to say here that Irish women saw nothing wrong with using English knowledge and techniques to further their cause at home. This philosophy extended to Irish suffragists doing their training in England. The Irishwomen's Suffrage Federation conceded that "The NUWSS also gave valuable help by receiving several of our members for one month training in organisation work in town and country."[131] Margaret Cousins went to work for the militant WSPU for three weeks in the summer of 1909.[132] "It was a helpful apprenticeship for our campaign later in Ireland. The daily programme began by chalking the pavements in the morning with announcements of meetings for the day. This was at first a back-aching job . . . The mid-day hours were spent selling the newspaper *Votes for Women*."[133] As shall be seen in the next chapter a number of Irish women got involved in militancy in England and even got sentenced to terms in Holloway. This was all seen as good practice for the home ground.[134]

Margaret Cousins was one of the Irish delegates invited to attend the Parliament of Women in Caxton Hall by Mrs Pankhurst in 1910. From Caxton Hall women made their way in groups of twelve to the House of Commons to protest to Asquith about the omission of women's suffrage from the Liberal Party program in the coming general election. The Irish women first went to the Chelsea home of Augustine Birrell, the Chief Secretary of Ireland, and broke all its windows.[135] Since there was not a policeman in sight to arrest them they proceeded to Downing Street. Cousins was amongst the many women arrested. Her crime was throwing bits of a flower-pot at Lloyd George's residence.[136] She was subsequently sentenced to a month in Holloway gaol.

Irish women were visible at many English suffrage demonstrations, they marched in parades and appeared on platforms in London carrying Irish flags and sometimes accompanied by Irish pipers.[137] In July 1910 members of an Irish contingent were given the following instructions for a demonstration the following day. They were to assemble at Cleopatra's Needle, then they were to "march preceded by twelve Irish pipers and the national flag of Ireland, to their own platform (No. 6) in Hyde Park".[138] Later there was to be a dispute over the payment of these pipers.[139] The instructions included a little warning which was an indication of the conflicts that were already beginning to divide the British and the Irish women. They were reminded that "At a time like this every other question but that of Woman Suffrage must be dropped, and a special appeal is made to every patriotic Irish woman to fall in and do her share towards accomplishing this, remembering that 'unity is strength'."[140]

To some extent there was still a semblance of unity in July 1912 when an Irish platform was featured at the Hyde Park suffrage demonstration. The speakers included Miss Hoey, Miss Agnes Kelly, Miss Smethwick, and Miss Lennox, and the platform was again decorated with Irish flags.[141] Again in 1913 Irish women participated in another Hyde Park demonstration.[142]

With the introduction of the Cat and Mouse Act in 1913 Irish and English women joined forces to get it repealed. As well as holding demonstrations of solidarity in Ireland, Irish women joined similar protests in England. In response to a request from the NUWSS they sent Miss Mellone and Miss Chenevix who "acted as our delegates at the Caxton Hall Conference on the Cat and Mouse Act".[143]

Women travelling from Ireland were often joined by Irish women in London[144] who were inspired to join the London Irish branch of the IWFL and the ISF when they saw their countrywomen coming to London.[145] Both the IWFL and ISF set up branches of their organisation in London.[146] Of course Irish women did not just go to London to see their English sisters. More importantly they also went to lobby Irish MPs. With regard to Mr Asquith's abortive Reform Bill the ISF annual report of 1912 said "We also arranged that Miss Rosa Barrett and Miss Blanche Poe should spend a week in London lobbying Irish members in connection with the Bill. These ladies were assisted in the work by Mrs Spring Rice and the Hon. Mary Massey."[147] Irish MPs were hardly endeared to the women when they met them again across the other side of the Irish Sea. Nevertheless the women (though not technically their constituents) felt that they should not be allowed to forget the wishes of their countrywomen.

Irish women returned from these visits across the water filled with ideas for action at home. Their trips even inspired some to write poetry. "Miss Webb read a stirring poem inspired by the last militant deputation to Westminster."[148] The visits to England played a major role in the life of the

Irish suffrage movement. In one way these trips externalised
the problem for Irish women. After all they were looking for
the franchise from a foreign government. They went to
London to attract the attention of that government and their
own representatives who had seats there. There was only a
limited amount they could do in Ireland since it did not have
a legislative body with the power to grant them the franchise.
Their horizons must have been broadened by moving out of
the disapproving Irish situation, taking part in the pageantry
of the demonstrations and meeting other women with similar
grievances. While they were often seen as oddities at home,
in London they composed only a small group in the
mass demonstrations. This proved to be a great source of
exhilaration and inspiration for the Irish women. While not
adopting English strategy completely, the Irish women were
able to select what they thought suitable to the Irish situation.
Finally by coming into contact with British women the Irish
women came to appreciate what made them different and
unique.

The suffrage movement in the United States was also
observed by Irish suffragists. Just as the States had beckoned
many Irish campaigners before him it was to lure Frank
Sheehy Skeffington in 1915. The purpose of his visit was to
get support for his anti-conscription in Ireland campaign.[149]
Here again the great foe was John Redmond the leader of
the Irish Party. As shall be seen in Chapter 7 Redmond was
strongly opposed to women's suffrage and thus became the
target of the suffragists of whom many, though militant in
the suffrage sense, were pacifist in the war sense. When
Redmond began his campaign to get Irish men to fight in
what was essentially seen as a British war he aroused the
further wrath of many Irish suffragists and pacifists. As far
as they saw it he had been the chief instrument in blocking
women getting the vote; now he was trying to get his
countrymen to fight someone else's war.

Frank Sheehy Skeffington avidly watched what was going
on in the American suffrage scene while he was there. He
met and addressed a number of suffragists. Writing home he
reported on the excitement in New York when it was
suggested that women stay off their jobs for one day to show

their strength in the labour market. He was enthusiastic too when the states of New York, Pennsylvania and Massachusetts were to vote on the Women's Suffrage Amendment to the Constitution. Undeterred when neither of these events came off he wrote to his wife that he had been to a suffragist parade "the finest I have ever seen . . . About 30,000 marched up Fifth Avenue . . . Some 5,000 men were in the march . . .".[150] After Sheehy Skeffington's murder in 1916 by Captain Colthurst,[151] his wife went on a tour of the States to publicise his death and try to get the United States to put pressure on Britain to bring the murderer to trial. While she was there she had observations to make on American suffragism. She had an audience with President Wilson and on the whole admired his policy towards women's suffrage in the States[152] but more than likely agreed with a National American Women's Suffrage Association document which declared that President Wilson should begin setting the world right for democracy by giving women the vote.[153]

> Since my return to Ireland I have often been asked my view as to President Wilson's personality . . . I think the President's attitude towards progress may best be illustrated by his action upon a matter of internal American policy, namely: The Women's Suffrage Federal Amendment. It tends to show that while President Wilson is not the type of lone pioneer who would push ahead against any odds, he is guided by what one may call a policy of enlightened expediency, and there is no statesman in the world today who knows better the exact time to come in on the right side and to press a reform home to a successful issue.[154]

Some Irish women attended the Congress of the International Women's Suffrage Alliance, held at Budapest in June 1913. The Irishwomen's Suffrage Federation was represented at the Congress by Mrs Metge, Hon. Treasurer of the Northern Committee.[155] Lady Dockrell again represented the IWSLGA.[156] Attempts by twenty-one Irish women to attend the Peace Conference at The Hague in 1915 run by the Women's International League for Peace and Freedom were blocked by the British Government as were the efforts of a number of British women of whom only two attended. All but one of the Irish members, Louie Bennett, were refused permits to travel and even then travel was made impossible because of the closing of the North Sea until the conference was over.[157] This happened despite the efforts on the part of Irish women and Hanna Sheehy Skeffington spent a week in London trying to make some headway but to no avail.[158] The IWFL subsequently held a protest meeting in Dublin.

// However this did not prevent attempts by Irish women to be present at future congresses and more importantly trying to achieve separate representation from the English women. Frank Sheehy Skeffington wrote to the founder and president of the Women's Peace Party, Jane Addams, on this matter in October 1915. The Party's aims included a 'Concert of Nations', an international police force and an early cessation of hostilities.[159] He urged her that it was of the utmost importance that the Irish women had separate representation from the English women.[160] The Women's International League for Peace and Freedom had already met at a conference in Spring 1915. It believed that women were naturally peaceful and should organise to stop the war.[161] Sheehy Skeffington believed that Irish women should be allowed to make a separate case since not only was their situation a lot different from the English one but they believed they belonged to a separate nation. //

This is an illustration of how Irish women felt unity with other women but yet apart. In August 1914 Hanna Sheehy Skeffington wrote in an article on 'The Duty of Suffragists' with regards to the war. "There is one 'bright spot'—and it is a real one, not a will-o'-the-wisp in this, namely, the fine solidarity of organised womanhood. With one voice at the International Alliance and through the entire suffragist press it spoke bravely and firmly against the insensate devilry of war."[162] The advent of the Great War certainly emphasised the solidarity of women of different nationalities who wanted nothing to do with the men's war. This is evident in the writings of a number of Irish suffragists not least Frank Sheehy Skeffington's article on 'War and Feminism'.[163]

// The patriotism the war brought out in the English WSPU was reflected among some suffragists in Ireland, particularly those who had unionist sympathies. However many Irish women, particularly those in the IWFL, felt that the war had nothing to do with them.[164] It was relevant in so far as they had to unite with other women for peace. They believed women should have nothing to do with the war—a feeling prevalent in other European countries (and indeed America) not unlike the sentiments of many socialists.[165] While the war brought out solidarity to some extent it also emphasised the problems that had always existed between Irish suffragists and those outside.

Even though there was flow of movement and thought between the Irish movement and world suffrage organisations throughout the early twentieth century—there were a few problems. Despite all the Nationalists' claims of the suffrage movement in Ireland being a British movement, the Irish women, particularly the IWFL, were determined they should go their own way and not listen to the dictates from abroad. They were aggrieved when the media insinuated otherwise. ". . . The attempt is being continued to make it appear that the women's movement is a foreign importation into Ireland. It will not do. The suffrage movement in Ireland is one of native growth, managed and controlled within Ireland, and wholly independent of inspiration from outside. Not for long, in view of palpable facts, can even the dullest dupes of the Irish press believe otherwise."[166] In this way their suffragism was not truly international. When it came to obliterating national differences with their sister women abroad they could not do so, particularly when it came to cases of suspected imperialism and sabotage of their movement. And, not surprisingly, the most suspected imperialist was their close neighbour, Britain.

In the nineteenth century there had been attempts by the English suffragists to set up branches in Ireland. However they often came to the conclusion that Irish women could best look after their own needs. In looking at the early history of the suffragists in Ireland Dora Mellone wrote, "Many have sought to help Ireland and have earned only the distrust of the Irish". She continued that suffrage work "in Ireland remained almost stationary until Irish women themselves took the matter in hand and made it the living issue which it is today . . . Ireland of all countries is blessed or cursed with a history. That history is one record of ill wrought to

Ireland by people from without. One invader after another
has come to Ireland seeking his advantage alone . . .".[167] Miss
Christie O'Connor of the Irish Catholic Women's Suffrage
Society observed, "Irishwomen are invited to join hands with
their English militant sisters and help them in their struggle
for freedom. But they are apt to reply that their English
sisters gave them no help or sympathy during the famine, or
in bad times when they and their children were ejected from
their homes."[168]

The early twentieth century witnessed the establishment
of the branches of a number of British suffrage societies in
Ireland. Branches of the Conservative and Unionist Suffrage
Association, the NUWSS, the Church League for Women's
Suffrage, the Anti-Suffrage League and the Men's League
for Women's Suffrage were all gradually set up. For some
suffragists particularly those not in the IWFL the English
influence did not present any problems. These were usually
middle-class, Protestant and basically conservative despite
their gestures towards feminism. As was seen above some of
their members received training in England. Finance was
also available and taken from the English NUWSS. In the
annual report of the Irishwomen's Suffrage Federation it was
acknowledged that "Last year the NUWSS gave a donation
of £100 to the Federation for a special propaganda campaign
. . .". However it did add that it hoped "in future to provide
the 'sinews of war' entirely from our own resources . . .".[169]

In 1907 in the pre-IWFL days Frank Sheehy Skeffington
wrote in his newspaper the *National Democrat* in praise of
the WSPU that he hoped that they "will proceed from
violence to violence until their end is attained. And I have
no doubt that they will. These women are of the stuff of
which martyrs are made."[170] However with the growth of
the imperialistic ambitions of some of the English suffrage
organisations like the Pankhursts' WSPU and Despard's
Women's Freedom League the Irish women really grew
perturbed, especially those in the IWFL. It is clear from the
formation of a number of Irish suffrage groups at this time
that the Irish women wished to remain separate. According
to James Cousins "we had no desire to work under English
women leaders: we could lead ourselves."[171] Hanna Sheehy

Skeffington in a paper addressed to the United Irish League, referring to the English suffragists, reminded her audience that ". . . though they are with us in our sex's war for freedom, yet in our national struggle they are with the men of England and against us."[172]

This dilemma basically was the crux of the problem in the relationship between the English and Irish women. To emphasise their separateness and maturity an Irish suffrage newspaper was founded to cater to Irish women's needs rather than having them dependent on 'Irish sections' in English newspapers for information of progress in their own country. The paradox in the English/Irish relationship is nowhere clearer than in the fact that the Cousinses and Sheehy Skeffingtons received two hundred pounds to set up the *Irish Citizen* from their friends, the English suffragists, the Pethick Lawrences.[173]

The birth of the *Irish Citizen* was appreciated from all points of view in Ireland. The honorary secretary of the Limerick branch of the IWSLGA wrote ". . . dealing as your paper does, primarily with the movement in Ireland, it appears to us more intimate than newspapers across the channel."[174] According to *Irish Freedom* ". . . Hitherto the suffrage movement had to import its literature from England, now it has an organ in Ireland and for Ireland. That is a step in the right direction."[175] Of course having an Irish suffrage newspaper was ultimately a retort to those who accused Irish suffragists of being unpatriotic and part of an English movement, proclaiming that this was not so.[176] Having a newspaper of their own was a way of distinguishing themselves from the English movement, it gave a stamp to their Irishness, and it acted as a type of ambassador for Irish feminism.

Thus, understandably, there was great indignation when the WSPU announced their intentions of setting roots firmly on Irish soil. There was a feeling of *déjà vu* about the prospect. It was as if Ireland, having experienced Anglo-Saxon male imperialism was now to suffer the female version. However, with missionary-like zeal the women from the WSPU did not see it quite like that. *The Citizen* in September 1912 reported a meeting of the WSPU in Ireland. They came,

it noted, because Asquith was brought into Ireland by
Redmond and the English militants followed, three of them
ended up in prison and the WSPU came to support their
women.[177] This most militant, and many would say least
democratic, of the English organisations first set up a branch
in Belfast and later one in Dublin. The British women saw
themselves doing everything above board and notified the
Irish women of their intentions. Yet the Irish women, not
surprisingly, saw more than a subtle difference between
English women going on the Irish lecture circuit and
attempting to run the movement in Ireland.

A rather tense correspondence was carried out between
Hanna Sheehy Skeffington and Christabel Pankhurst on the
subject. Pankhurst pointed out to Sheehy Skeffington how
successful their organiser Dorothy Evans had been in the
North of Ireland. She continued that so far as she was
concerned "there ought not to be a distinction between the
English and Irish Movement any more than there is a
distinction between the English Movement and the Scottish
Movement . . . It is not as though English interests were not
at stake in Ireland. They are. Indeed, it may almost be said
that the Nationalist Members hold the fate of the suffrage
cause for the whole kingdom in their hands". While she did
believe that there could be special Irish societies she felt it
was necessary to have the WSPU in Ireland. "We feel if only
in the interests of English women that we must be represented
in Ireland, not only in Ulster but in Nationalist Ireland too.
Since Mr John Redmond is to so large an extent the arbiter
of the fate of English women, English women must plant
their foot on his native heath." She added rather irrelevantly,
considering the size of the populations, that she had no
objections to Irish organisations setting up branches in
England. To add insult to injury, Pankhurst felt that yet
another reason for setting up a branch in Dublin would be
the attraction of membership to women who had not yet
joined a suffrage movement. She concluded her letter by
saying that in a few days a Miss Margaret Edwards would
be at her post in Dublin and told Sheehy Skeffington that
"I know that there has been some feeling that only Irish
women can appeal to the Irish. The same thing used to be

said in Scotland but experience proved that it is not nationality but personality that counts. After all the Suffrage Movement has united women of different races. We are all one in the Woman's Suffrage faith."[178]

Sheehy Skeffington wrote back saying that the feeling of the IWFL was very much against the step but they felt they could do little to prevent it. She hoped to "continue our friendly relations with the WSPU to whose inspiration we are much indebted for the wonderful impetus it has given to the movement everywhere". However she hotly disputed the analogy drawn between Ireland and Scotland. "The position of Ireland is very different from that of Scotland—you know that as well as any Irishwoman—therefore your analogy with Scotland does not hold. The fact that the IWFL has always been frankly militant in word and deed differentiates it from the National with which you suggest comparison—it seems to me that under the circumstances it would have been wiser to have tried to cooperate with the local militant society, as you always have hitherto done most helpfully than to scatter militant forces and dissipate militant energies by the introduction of the English militant organisation."[179]

The feeling was prevalent among Irish women that there was quite a difference between the English and Irish situation as far as the suffragists were concerned. Mary McSwiney felt that the British suffragists were using the Irish women for political gain. "What is good for England is not good for Ireland in suffrage tactics, anymore than in other matters; and as Irishwomen we are concerned with our own country first."[180] When the WSPU arrived officially in Dublin they were criticised from every angle. The *Irish Times* reported WSPU speakers being heckled in Phoenix Park. Mrs Brigid Dudley Edwards wrote

> The WPSU have begun badly in Dublin. They have stood aloof from the protest against the gross miscarriage of justice of which Mrs Sheehy Skeffington, the leader of the IWFL has been the victim. Yet when Mary Leigh and Gladys Evans, members of the WSPU hungerstruck in Mountjoy Mrs Sheehy Skeffington risked her life in a sympathetic hungerstrike with them.[181]

A Miss Carre wrote to the *Irish Citizen* saying that she felt there was no point in creating dissent between different suffrage groups.[182] By May 1914 the *Irish Citizen* felt that the WSPU had done "little or no good in Ireland and some positive harm".[183]

The dividing of forces became evident in the selling of newspapers. Paradoxically they had once symbolised unity. They now were a focus of dissent. "The Irish Women's Franchise League confine their attention to this corner, and the Women's Social and Political Union vend their wares at Poyntz's corner. Occasionally the WSPU invade the territory of their Irish sisters but these seldom (if ever) make reprisals."[184] While it is true that Irish women were going to England to participate in demonstrations tensions were growing.[185]

The offices of the WSPU were raided by the police in April 1914 and women were arrested on the charge of possessing explosives.[186] The IWFL breathed sighs of relief when the WSPU pulled out of Ireland when the war began, as they had changed the whole thrust of their movement. Their new emphasis of throwing themselves behind the war and becoming involved in the recruitment drive did little to mend their relations with the pacifist IWFL, rather it emphasised yet another difference between them. This illustrates the main differences between the militant suffrage movements in Ireland and England. While on the surface they may have appeared almost the same, the fundamental philosophies behind the two organisations were very different. For a number of years before the war the WSPU had grown into a dictatorial organisation in the hands of Mrs Pankhurst and her daughter Christabel which culminated with the expulsion of the Pethick Lawrences from their organisation. Sylvia Pankhurst's socialist beliefs took her off in a different direction.[187] The vigour with which the WSPU participated in the war effort was merely a redirection of the energy that had gone into the militant suffrage campaign. Whilst back in Ireland the IWFL's opposition to participation in the war can not be solely explained on nationalist grounds. It was rather an extension of their whole philosophy of life which embraced a dislike of eating meat, of smoking, taking alcohol and a belief in well-being and peace.

During the war little was done to improve relations with either the British suffragists or their government.[188] In an article written by Hanna Sheehy Skeffington in 1919 about her visit to the United States, which was undertaken to publicise the death of her husband murdered three years previously, she spoke of the threat she posed for the British authorities and how they attempted to deal with her.

The British Agents in the United States are naturally very perturbed at the Irish propaganda on behalf of our small nation. They dislike particularly propaganda of such Irish exiles as myself who had come directly from Ireland, and could speak with first hand knowledge. As one of them observed: "My objection to Mrs Sheehy Skeffington is that she has a lot of damaging facts". Accordingly a trap was laid for me. I was invited by a Women's Society in Toronto to cross the frontier and lecture there on Woman's Suffrage. I realised that Suffrage was being possibly used as bait to get me on hostile ground, where I might be interned, and politely refused the invitation.[189]

The antagonism between the Irish suffragists and Mrs Pankhurst and her followers was increased when she was selected as one of Britain's 'regular army of lecturers' turned into the United States "not only to put her case for the war before American audiences, but to vilify, whenever possible, these nations that did not agree with her imperialist ambitions". Mrs Pankhurst was sent to make an appeal to the women of the United States. Sheehy Skeffington commented that Americans were puzzled at the "curious specimens" of British 'democracy' who were sent to the States as Britain's spokesmen.

It seemed as Imperialists of the "Morning Post" brand were furnished with credentials. For instance while Mrs Pankhurst's campaign, Anti-Russian and Anti-Irish, was facilitated by the British Government, Mrs Pethick Lawrence, the distinguished Suffragist and Pacifist leader, was refused pass-ports to America where she was invited by American Suffragists to help their campaign.[190]

If the relationship between the Irish and English women was sometimes uneasy it was not just because of their proximity. The friendly relationship with the American suffragists was for the main part one of mutual admiration with the American suffragists taking a big interest in what was going on in Ireland both with regards to Home Rule and to women's equality. This was part of a long tradition of American interest in Ireland. However, this relationship also became strained during the war. While in America in 1915 Frank Sheehy Skeffington wrote "Just what is weak about the big suffrage movement here—[is] its timidity."[191] An article which appeared in the *Irish Citizen* during the war implied that American suffragists had put suffrage "on the shelf for the duration of the war".[192] From the perspective of 1919 Hanna Sheehy Skeffington repeated the points made in that article

> When America entered the war the same situation was created with regard to the Woman Suffrage Movement as occurred in Great Britain in 1914. Many of the so called Constitutional Suffragists turned their backs on suffrage and preached to their followers the urgent need of winning the war before all else. Their leaders such as Dr Anna Howard-Shaw and Mrs Chapman Catt put suffrage on the shelf as did some of their British sisters, and told their followers that to ask for a vote just then, when their country was in a war to make the world safe for democracy was to be unpatriotic, if not pro-German . . . A comfortable and decent burial was accordingly arranged for the suffrage corpse, and the interment would have taken place duly but for the militant section known as "The Nationalist Women's Party", headed by Alice Paul, a Quaker, and Lucy Byrne, an Irishwoman.[193]

Such reflections which she had made all too clear in the columns of the *Irish Citizen* during the war angered many American women who felt that they also certainly had not put the war first. Indignant letters were written to the *Irish Citizen* demanding a retraction and a correct portrayal of the situation. However this was but a small blot on the relationship between the movements in Ireland and America.

From the aforesaid it can be seen that the Irish suffrage movement, therefore, was significant in world terms. It fed on the writings and actions of foreign women, while at the same time its thoughts and progress were reported abroad. It was admitted to the intellectual world of feminist literature and was influenced by, as well as influencing, feminists in other countries. Irish women saw themselves within a comparative context and constantly assessed their situation with regards to the status of women elsewhere. Foreign suffragists visited Ireland and Irish suffragists went abroad. However there was a constant tug between the desire to be part of an international movement and at the same time to remain independent. This tug was to dominate the relationship between the Irish movement and the international movement. To a large extent it was exasperated by the complex relationship between Ireland and England. It was very important to the Irish suffragists that they should not be branded as part of an English movement, as this would have labelled them as unpatriotic. This factor dominated the suffragists' relationship with outside movements. To be subsumed into an international movement would have considerably lessened their impact in Ireland while at the same time the belief that they were part of an international movement served to strengthen their motivation. That motivation helped them persist in their militant campaign and survive their gaol sentences.

Notes

1. Clare Tomalin, *The Life and Death of Mary Wollstonecraft* (Penguin, Harmondsworth, 1977; Pantheon, New York, 1983).
2. Showalter, "Florence Nightingale and Suggestions for Thought", *Signs*, Spring 1981, p. 405.
3. William Thompson, *An Appeal of One Half of the Human Race, Women, Against the Pretensions of the Other Half Men* (first published 1825 republished by Virago, London, 1983).
4. Margaret MacCurtain, "The Historical Image", *Irish Women: Image and Achievement*, Eilean Ni Chuilleanain (ed.) (Arlen House, 1985), p. 44.
5. William Thompson, *op. cit.* Introduction by Richard Pankhurst, p. viii.
6. *Ibid*, p. xvi.
7. *Ibid*, p. viii.
8. Barbara Taylor, *Eve and the New Jerusalem* (Pantheon, New York and London, 1982).
9. Patricia Stubbs, *Women and Fiction* (Harvester Press, Brighton, 1979).
10. *Prison Letters of Countess Markievicz* (Virago, London, 1986). Introduction, p. xvii.
11. She had quite an influence on Christabel Pankhurst and persuaded her to take a Law Degree. Mitchell, *The Fighting Pankhursts* (Jonathan Cape, London, 1967), p. 28. See also Fox, *Rebel Irishwomen* (Talbot Press, Dublin, 1935).

12. *Prison Letters, op. cit.*, p. xviii.
13. *Ibid*, p. xxx.
14. Joseph Lee, *The Modernisation of Irish Society 1848–1918* (Gill and Macmillan, Dublin, 1973), p. 86.
15. Countess Aberdeen (ed.), *Women in Politics, The International Congress of Women 1899* (Fisher and Unwin, London, 1900).
16. Haslam Papers, British Library.
17. Strachey, *Millicent Garrett Fawcett* (John Murray, London, 1931), p. 148.
18. *Englishwoman's Review*, April 15, 1903.
19. *IC*, July 6, 1912, p. 50.
20. SSP, p. 21, 19-11-14.
21. *IC*, July 6, 1912, p. 50.
22. *VFW*, September 27, 1912.
23. *Ibid*, March 10, 1911, p. 378.
24. Cousins, *op. cit.*, p. 163.
25. *The Suffragette*, January 10, 1914.
26. *Jus Suffragii* (The Right of Voting) organ of the International Women's Suffrage Association, later International Alliance of Women, later International Women's News.
27. Report of Executive Committee of IWSLGA, pp. 11–12.
28. *IC*, July 4, 1914.
29. Banks, p. 140.
30. R.M. Fox, *Louie Bennett*, pp. 33–5.
31. *Irishwomen's Suffrage Federation First Annual Report 1911–12*, p. 6.
32. SSP Ms 21,617 (VII).
33. Leah Levenson, p. 185, C.P. Curran, *Under the Receding Wave*, p. 11.
34. R.M. Fox, *Rebel Irishwomen*.
35. Andre Sheehy Skeffington, Harrison Tapes.
36. SSP Ms 21,639.
37. *IC*, May 17 1913, p. 419.
38. *Ibid*, November 2, 1912, p. 191.
39. *IC*, May 17, 1913, p. 419.
40. *Ibid*, November 2, 1912, p. 191.
41. *Ibid*, June 13, 1914, p. 27.
42. *Ibid*, vol. 1, No. 1, p. 8.
43. *Ibid*, June 13, 1914, p. 27.
44. *Ibid*, January 24, 1914, p. 283.-
45. *Ibid*, July 18, 1912.
46. *Ibid*, January 24, 1912, p. 284.
47. See Chapter 4.
48. *IC*, May 25, 1912, p. 5.
49. *IC*, January 10, 1914, p. 266.
50. *Ibid*, August 15, 1914.
51. *Ibid*.
52. *IC*, August 15, 1914.
53. *The Vote*, June 6, 1913, p. 92.
54. *IC*, November 2, 1912, p. 188.

55. *IC*, January 10, 1914, p. 269.
56. *Ibid*, November 8, 1913, p. 200.
57. Aileen S. Kraditor, *The Ideas of the Woman Suffrage Movement/ 1890–1920* (W.W. Norton, New York, 1981), p. 28.
58. *IC*, June 15, 1912.
59. Evans, *op. cit.*, p. 14.
60. Margaret Digby, *Sir Horace Plunkett: An Anglo American Irishman* (Basil Blackwell, Oxford, 1949), p. 68.
61. *Ibid*, p. 71.
62. *Ibid*.
63. Banks, *op. cit.*, p. 141.
64. SSP 17/8/14 Ms 22,666 (iv).
65. SSP 22/1/14 Ms 24,099.
66. *Ibid*.
67. SSP Ms 21,620 (vii).
68. Banks, *op. cit.*, p. 141.
69. Cousins, *op. cit.*, p. 165.
70. *Ibid*, p. 74.
71. *Ibid*, p. 125.
72. SSP Ms 21,620 (vii).
73. Cousins, *op. cit.*, p. 125–7.
74. *VFW*, March 24, 1911, p. 413.
75. *IC*, May 17, 1913, p. 418.
76. *IC*, May 17, 1913, p. 418, *IC*, June 29, 1912, p. 47, Cousins, p. 130.
77. Cousins, *op. cit.*, p. 170.
78. *IC*, May 1912.
79. Mrs Lister, Harrison Tapes, Fawcett Library, London.
80. Mary Colum, *Life and Dream* (Macmillan, New York, 1947).
81. *VFW*, October 7, 1910, p. 5.
82. *VFW*, September 10, 1910, p. 799, *Ibid*, September 6, p. 811.
83. *Freeman's Journal* quoted in *VFW*, September 30, 1910, p. 847.
84. *VFW*, October 14, 1910.
85. Police Reports, Public Records Office, Kew.
86. *Evening Telegraph*, June 19, 1910.
87. *VFW*, October 14, 1910, p. 26.
88. Cousins, *op. cit.*, pp. 172–3.
89. *VFW*, October 14, 1910, p. 30, *VFW*, March 24, 1911, p. 413 on Mrs Pankhurst's visit to Belfast.
90. *VFW*, October 28, 1910, p. 55.
91. *VFW*, March 18, 1910.
92. Cousins, *op. cit.*, p. 171.
93. *VFW*, October 20, 1911, p. 42.
94. Cousins, *op. cit.*, p. 172.
95. *VFW*, October 20, 1911, p. 41.
96. SSP Ms 22,666 (v).
97. SSP Ms 22,666 (iv).
98. Ramelson, *op. cit.*, p. 148.
99. *IC*, August 15, 1914.

100. Mitchell, *op. cit*, p. 84.
101. *IC*, May 17, 1913.
102. T.M. Healy, *The Defence at Bow Street*, Box D-K 396 11B Fawcett Library.
103. Banks, *op. cit.*, p. 120.
104. F.S.L. Lyons, *Ireland Since the Famine* (Weidenfeld and Nicolson, London, 1971), pp. 279–86.
105. Emily Pethick Lawrence, *My Part in Changing the World* (Victor Gollancz, London, 1938), p. 302.
106. *Irish Times*, January 18, 1910, p. 6, *Ibid*, February 4, 1910, p. 5.
107. *Irishwomen's Suffrage Federation Second Annual Report 1912–1913*, p. 5.
108. *IC*, November 8, 1913.
109. *Ibid*, November 1, 1913, p. 190, quoted from Belfast *Evening Telegraph*.
110. *Irishwomen's Suffrage Federation Second Annual Report 1912–1913*, p. 5.
111. *IC*, October, 1914.
112. Hasia Diner, *Eirin's Daughters in America, Irish Immigrant Women in the Nineteenth Century* (Johns Hopkins University Press, Baltimore and London, 1983).
113. *IC*, July 6, 1912, p. 56.
114. *IC*, July 6, 1912, p. 50. See also *IC*, May 17, 1913 report from Munster Women's Franchise Association on her visit the previous year.
115. Evans, *op. cit.*, p. 216.
116. *Irishwomen's Suffrage Federation First Annual Report 1911–1912*, p. 10.
117. Ramelson, *op. cit.*, p. 139.
118. *Ibid*, p. 213.
119. *IC*, June 8, 1912, p. 17.
120. Leslie Henderson, *The Goldstein Story* (Stockland Press, Melbourne 1973), p. 90.
121. *IC*, June 15, 1912, p. 291.
122. *IC*, June 21, 1912, p. 10.
123. *Englishwoman's Review*, July 16, 1906, p. 169.
124. Cousins, *op. cit.*, p. 79.
125. *VFW*, June 6, 1908.
126. *IC*, May 17, 1913, p. 410.
127. *Englishwoman's Review*, July 16, 1906, p. 168.
128. *VFW*, July 24, 1908.
129. Cousins, *op. cit.*, p. 199.
130. Alan Denson, *James H. Cousins and Margaret E. Cousins. A Bio-Bibliographical Survey* (Kendal: Alan Denson, 1967), p. 137.
131. *Irishwomen's Suffrage Federation First Annual Report 1911–1912*, p. 9.
132. Denson, *op. cit.*, p. 88.
133. Cousins, *op. cit.*, p. 169.
134. See Chapter 4.

135. Cousins, *op. cit.*, p. 117.
136. *Ibid.*, pp. 174–6.
137. SSP Ms 22,662 (i).
138. *VFW*, July 22, 1910, p. 715.
139. SSP Ms 22,662 (i).
140. *VFW*, July 22, 1910, p. 715.
141. *VFW*, July 12, 1912, p. 674.
142. *Irishwomen's Suffrage Federation Report 1913*, p. 5.
143. *Irishwomen's Suffrage Federation Second Annual Report 1912–1913*, p. 10.
144. SSP Ms 22,256 (ii).
145. *VFW*, July 1, 1910, p. 685, *VFW*, March 10, 1911, p. 378.
146. *VFW*, March 31, 1911, p. 434 *Ibid*, May 12, 1911, p. 534.
147. SSP Ms 22,259 (iii).
148. *VFW*, April 21, 1911, p. 485.
149. F.S.L. Lyons, *op. cit.*
150. Leah Levenson, *With Wooden Sword* (Gill and Macmillan, Dublin, 1983), pp. 185–6.
151. *Ibid*, pp. 222–6.
152. Aileen S. Kraditor, *op. cit.*, pp. 209–10, Wilson's attitude towards women's suffrage.
153. Evans, p. 226.
154. Hanna Sheehy Skeffington, *Sinn Fein in America* (Davis Publishing, Dublin, 1919), p. 23.
155. *Irishwomen's Suffrage Federation Second Annual Report 1912–1913*, p. 10.
156. *IWSLGA Annual Report 1913*, p. 6.
157. R.M. Fox, *Louie Bennett*, p. 43.
158. Levenson, pp. 171–2, *IC* March 20, 1915, *IC* May 8, 1915.
159. Evans, p. 226.
160. SSP, October 7, 1915.
161. Evans, *The Feminists*, p. 196.
162. *IC*, August 15, 1914.
163. Frank Sheehy Skeffington, "The War and Feminism" republished in Levenson, *op. cit*, pp. 241–9.
164. See the *Irish Citizen* throughout the war.
165. Boxer and Quartet, *Socialist Women* (Elsevier, New York, 1978).
166. *IC*, September 14, 1912.
167. *Englishwoman*, October 1913, pp. 1–7.
168. *Catholic Suffragist*, August 15, 1916, p. 73.
169. *Irishwomen's Suffrage Federation Second Annual Report 1912–1913*, p. 11.
170. *National Democrat*, February 1907, pp. 10–12, Levenson, p. 67.
171. Cousins, p. 164.
172. Levenson, p. 84.
173. *Ibid*, p. 123.
174. *IC*, September 14, 1912, p. 130.

175. *IC*, July 6, 1912, p. 56.
176. See Chapter 7.
177. *IC*, September 14, 1912, p. 129.
178. SSP Ms 22,664.
179. SSP Ms 24,134.
180. Fallon, p. 19.
181. *Irish Times*, September 23, 1912.
182. *IC*, December 6, 1913, p. 230.
183. *Ibid*, May 1914.
184. SSP Ms 21,641.
185. *IC*, June 13, 1914, p. 26.
186. Cullen Owens, *Smashing Times* (Attic Press, Dublin, 1984), p. 71.
187. Mitchell, *The Fighting Pankhursts*, *op. cit.*
188. *IC*, August 15, 1914.
189. Hanna Sheehy Skeffington, *Sinn Fein in America*, *op. cit.*, p. 11.
190. *Ibid*, p. 14.
191. Levenson, p. 187.
192. *IC*, March 18, 1917.
193. Hanna Sheehy Skeffington, *British Militarism as I Have Known It* (Donnelly Press, New York, 1917), p. 23.

· 4 ·

Incarceration: Political or Criminal?

The Irish suffrage movement did not remain the passive, docile movement it had been in the late nineteenth century. A significant number of suffragists under the leadership of the IWFL decided in the years before the war to adopt militant methods. As the second chapter has shown, militancy created dissent within the movement. It also made the women's demand seem more urgent and made it impossible for Irish society to ignore them. Now there was a new criminal element in Ireland—middle-class women. A number of suffragists appeared before the magistrates and most refused to pay any fines. Thirty-five women went to gaol and a number of them hungerstruck. These women would normally never have seen the inside of a prison except perhaps in a philanthropic capacity. This was all too much for the pillars of Irish establishment and drew comment and censure from both the press and the church.

Militant suffragism in Ireland was not a mirror image of English militancy. Militancy was not used as a matter of course to gain publicity but rather employed as an expression of disappointment. It was almost always directly related to the fate of the amendments to the Home Rule Bill and other suffrage measures at Westminster. When a measure was defeated the Irish women vented their anger by breaking windows in buildings of the British authorities in Ireland, usually at Dublin Castle, and by damaging the property, or confronting the persons, of their Irish representatives at Westminster who were so often the cause of the defeat of these measures. It also took the form of chalking on pavements, putting oil and ink in letter boxes and raising false fire alarms.

In January 1913 the *Cork Constitution* noted that "small bottles containing black fluid were discovered in letter boxes in the residential district of Dublin yesterday. They were enclosed in an envelope bearing the words 'Votes for Women'. Several letters were damaged."[1] The militants clearly felt they had no other option and were morally compelled to perform acts they would under other circumstances abhor. The *Irish Citizen* quoted Marjorie Hasler in April 1912 as saying "We don't like smashing glass any more than men like smashing skulls, yet in both cases there is, I believe, a strong feeling that something must be broken before a wrong is changed into a right."[2] Fellow suffragist Maud Lloyd had similar sentiments "The government has goaded me, as a self-respecting woman, to make my protest against its insolent and tyrannical attitude to my sex in the one possible way at present available to me—the destruction of government property. I have aimed a blow at the God of this world. Were I a man and not a suffragette, I should probably under equal provocation, have aimed a blow at human life."[3] Writing in the *Catholic Suffragist* in 1916, Christie O'Connor examined the militant movement in Ireland before the war. She wrote "militancy, once kindled, did not blaze throughout the land like a prairie fire." This was because "without the rural population at their back to support and reinforce them, the efforts of the militants in small cities must needs meet with but partial success." She added "Regarding the propaganda itself, Irish suffragists have not received the same incentives to violence. It must be remembered that the Dublin militants were placed in the first division, and were not treated with the brutality which prevailed in the English gaols.[4]

To some extent O'Connor's assessment was accurate, however it was written from the point of view of a non-militant Catholic suffragist. Certainly militancy did not "blaze throughout the land" and was confined to the main urban centres like Dublin and Belfast. The Irish suffragists also appeared to have been treated less roughly than the English and this served to prevent the violence becoming more frequent. Nevertheless militancy was a significant factor in the Irish suffrage movement between 1912 and 1914. This is equally true with regards to those suffragists who were non- or anti-militant. A large proportion of their time was now spent in disassociating themselves from the militants and condemning their actions.

Militant activity on behalf of the Irish suffragists may well have caused consternation and debate. However when the suffragists had been sentenced the controversy did not end. For the women did not see themselves as common criminals but as political prisoners fighting for a cause. The gaoled suffragists waged a battle of wits against the authorities in Dublin Castle, with the governors in Mountjoy, Tullamore and Belfast gaols, with their prison doctors and with the Chief Secretary of Ireland, Augustine Birrell, and the Lord Lieutenant of Ireland, Lord Aberdeen. Some MPs spoke on the prisoners' behalf. Ordinarily conservative Irish newspapers affirmed their claim to political status and recorded the misgivings of concerned citizens and certain public figures with regard to their treatment. English suffrage and non-suffrage papers also reported on their condition. To some they were crazy demented women, to others they were martyrs. The suffrage groups were split in their support of the prisoners just as they had been divided over militancy. The gaoled women were constantly before the public eye, particularly in the period between 1912 and 1914. There were attempts by some Irish MPs to keep the issue before Parliament and there was some confusion over what exactly was meant by 'political status' and whether or not Irish suffragists were being treated differently from the English.

The women who went to gaol were middle-class, well educated and, on the whole, members of the IWFL. According to Dr Elizabeth Fitzpatrick daughter of Mrs Purser, all the women involved ". . . had servants, all were ladies, all came from the middle-class. It was possible for them to do it [get involved with woman's suffrage] than poorer women who needed alleviation of working conditions."[5] A few had relatives who had been in gaol for the nationalist cause and therefore respectability and imprisonment were not necessarily seen by them as incompatible. Mrs Purser was the granddaughter of the Young Irelander William Smith O'Brien who had been condemned to be hanged and was later transported for his part in the 1848 rising. Her favourite place for distributing suffragist literature was at the foot of his statue in Dublin.[6] Both Hanna Sheehy Skeffington's father and uncle had been imprisoned for their beliefs. Indeed her father had been in prison six times in connection with Home Rule and had undergone hungerstrikes. One of Sheehy Skeffington's earliest experiences was going to see him in Kilmainham Gaol.[7]

Some of the women had undergone imprisonment in Holloway and other English prisons and indeed had hunger-struck. Mrs Tanner spent two months in Holloway in 1908. She told a large welcome committee of the WSPU on her release that when she went into prison "woman suffrage was an article of faith with her; now she had come out it was a religion; she went in a reformer; she came out a revolutionary."[8] Another Irish suffragist in an English gaol was Agnes A. Kelly who explained her actions in an article in the *Irish Citizen* 'Why we adopted the hunger strike'.[9]

Some Irish women were forcefed and suffered later on from the experience.[10] Irish women took part in the notorious Black Friday deputation in London in 1910. Mrs Palmer, Margaret Murphy, Margaret Cousins, Jane Murphy, Mrs Earl, Mrs Houston, Miss Webb and Marjorie Hasler were among these.[11] Indeed Hasler's death in 1913 was attributed to her prison experience by Hanna Sheehy Skeffington. Hasler had been in gaol in both London and Dublin, and Skeffington, who had served a month with her in Dublin, wrote "In November 1910 she formed one of the deputations to the Prime Minister on the day afterwards known as 'Black Friday' . . . it was then she sustained injuries to her head and back that resulted in a weakened spine and lowered vitality generally." Sheehy Skeffington believed that this "lowered vitality" was responsible for her inability to resist the measles which killed her.[12]

Even in 1912 when women were already in Irish gaols Margaret Cousins promised Mrs Pankhurst at least six women ready to face imprisonment in England but she regretted she needed the rest back in Ireland to be present at the Irish Party's National Convention. "We shall certainly send you some representatives—at least six; but in view of the fact that a great deal of local militant work will have to be done at the time of the National Convention, several of our members who cannot face imprisonment twice will have to be reserved for this latter occasion. But we are arranging that everyone of our Irish contingent that we send over will be prepared to go to prison as we have sent before."[13] Thus a number of Irish women served their apprenticeship in England for their ordeals in Irish prisons.

Back in Ireland the women were being sentenced to prison from the end of 1911 to the beginning of the Great War in the summer of 1914. Their judges varied in sympathy. Some gave out sentences that almost amounted to political status while others gave sentences with hard labour. On the whole the women were sentenced to terms with special privileges but not the recognition of full political status. In the first case of militant women being sentenced the judge, Mr Swifte, in answer to their demand to being placed in the first division,[14] said he would "have complied with it if he had the power to do so. . .". He added that two of the defendants had addressed the court and they showed they were ladies "of considerable ability". However "their methods were misguided". Mr Swifte said at the close of the hearing that "if the matter were in his jurisdiction he would sentence prisoners to first class division treatment, but that the Prisons Board had the regulation of the treatment of prisoners in their power."[15] In fact it was claimed in a letter to the *Irish Times* that under a little known Act Mr Swifte was entitled to sentence women to this treatment.[16] Another judge Mr Drury was more adamant when he sentenced the women before him in January 1912. In giving his decision he said

he had nothing to do with political motives or any motives. He had to deal with facts and to see that the law was observed. He had many cases of window smashing but never had the misfortune of having suffragists before him. He had very strong views as to people taking the law into their own hands, and although these ladies said they were outside the law, yet the law had to protect them . . . it was intolerable that the ladies who broke glass in this wanton manner should come and ask favours. He had nothing to do with their treatment in prison, and he sentenced each of the prisoners to one month's imprisonment with hard labour.[17]

The court cases were not always tragic and solemn but often took on a carnival atmosphere with the suffragists capitalising on the publicity and attention. At the hearings they were guaranteed the full attention of the press and thus had the opportunity of presenting their cause. Such was the case when Hanna Sheehy Skeffington, the Murphy sisters and Mrs Palmer were in court for breaking glass.

Previous to the hearing floral tributes were left on the bench for the magistrate, carnations and sweetpeas, and on the registrar's desk for Mr Stack, the able clerk of the court. Copies of the *Irish Citizen*, the organ of the suffragettes were circulated amongst the audience, which assumed very much the aspect of a theatrical *matinée*. Mrs Sheehy Skeffington carried a very large bouquet mainly made up of wild flowers.[18]

The women were sentenced to Belfast gaol or Mountjoy gaol in Dublin. Later it was decided to send the women to Tullamore gaol, 60 miles from Dublin, also. This decision upset the suffragists. The IWFL claimed that they were put there "to be away from their friends".[19] The authorities argued that this prison could best provide the conditions for these women who were rather exceptional prisoners. There "relaxations could be carried out without the general interference with the general discipline of a large prison."[20] It was noted that each woman got a large room in the male prison with an iron bedstead and a fire.[21] A report in the *Irish Independent* stated that "The prisoners were treated fairly at Tullamore. They were occupying large rooms which were more spacious and better furnished than ordinary cells. The diet too . . . was fairly good."[22] Certainly they seemed to be an improvement on the cells in Mountjoy where the women were put into small cold cells with plank beds and unwashed blankets. The women also found it an improvement on Holloway where they were addressed by their names and not by numbers.[23] In 'Mountjoy Jottings' Mrs Palmer wrote that prison officials were pleasanter there than in Holloway and the garden was more attractive but the rest of her description was rather bleak.[24] Another Irish woman prisoner,

Countess Markievicz, a few years later imprisoned for
nationalist reasons, had interesting, rather different comparisons to make between Aylesbury, Holloway and Mountjoy.
While in Aylesbury she wrote "It's queer and lonely here,
there was so much life in Mountjoy. There were sea-gulls
and pigeons, which I had quite tame, there were 'Stop Press'
cries, and little boys splashing in the canal and singing Irish
songs, shrill and discordant, but with such vigour . . . . Here
it is so still and I find it so hard to understand what anyone
says to me, and they find the same trouble with me."[25]

Hopes that the women would be isolated from public
attention were soon dashed. When Margaret Cousins arrived
at Tullamore she found the awaiting crowd to be "very
favourable".[26] The *Daily Express* reported in February 1913
"The Tullamore Urban Council have passed a resolution
demanding political treatment for Irish suffragist prisoners."[27]
As it turned out the provincial people of Tullamore soon
became suffrage conscious. Suffrage prisoners were visited
by all the notables of Tullamore society. Their visitors
included the wives of the school inspector and the chairman
of the Urban Council. They were also visited by Mr Rogers,
Tullamore solicitor.[28] The Methodist minister in Tullamore
requested the governor if he could have prisoners, Cousins
and Connery, to breakfast on the morning of their release.[29]
Tullamore Methodist minister James Kirkwood wrote to the
Lord Lieutenant of Ireland requesting that the suffragists
should be treated as first-class prisoners. "I know I am
expressing the opinion all over the country."[30]

When the women arrived off the Dublin train they were
faced with the grim sight of their new home. It was described
by Margaret Cousins thus. "The buildings are massive,
ponderous, handsome. Their feudal appearance and atmosphere form a symbolic setting for the women's cause."[31]

Once the women had settled into prison life whether in
Belfast, Dublin or Tullamore their litany of complaints began
and the governors could hardly ignore their discontent, judging
by the number of pleas and protests they received from the
women. They were unused to such educated and articulate
prisoners. The women wished to send and receive letters
daily and also receive visitors daily. At one point they received

letters and visitors once fortnightly.[32] They complained that the only reading material made available to them was the Bible. The *Irish Citizen* in an article entitled 'Suffragist Prison Reading' asked what was the purpose of limiting the imprisoned women to reading the Bible and a prayer book? It argued that if it is to teach them to avoid militancy it will backfire:

> We can hardly think that a month's close reading of the militant methods of such passages as "Thou shalt dash them in pieces like a potter's vessel", and "The Kingdom of heaven suffereth violence, and the violent take it by force", are calculated to encourage a disposition to "wait and see". The prisoners being out of range of the pastorals printed in the daily press, will hardly have read Cardinal Bourne's statement that violence is contrary to God's law.[33]

Likewise the husband of imprisoned English suffragist Mary Gawthorpe wrote ". . . For reading—the Bible—that book of revelations. What a mockery! And a book called 'A Healthy Home' which she says with a smile, is of no use to her there."[34]

The prisoners disliked being in their cells twenty hours out of twenty-four. Describing her cell in Mountjoy, Hanna Sheehy Skeffington wrote that the effects of this enforced solitude were "harsh and spirit subduing; it finds out the weak joints in one's armour, and brings into play all one's philosophy and resourcefulness." However there were compensations "Yet I have many happy memories of Mountjoy—of pleasant companionship through hours of exercise and associated labour with my fellow suffragists, of kindness from friends who paid us daily pilgrimages, of studious hours far from the madding, mobbing crowd."[35] The women desired to mix with each other and not the other prisoners. Edith Lloyd, sister of prisoner Maud Lloyd, sent a letter to the Chief Secretary stating that she was concerned about her gaoled sister's health and her heavy sentence—six months in the first division for breaking windows. She was particularly worried about her cell confinement. "As she spends her life practically in the open air as a landscape artist, the lack of air and exercise is bound to cause illness . . . ."[36] Margaret Murphy complained that the whitewashed cells were hurting her eyes. They were subsequently repainted.

> With reference to Miss Margaret Murphy's complaint of the possible
> effect of the whitewashed walls of her cell upon her eyes, the governor
> agreed to have the walls recoloured, and to have a new gas burner
> fitted in lieu of the existing one, and her request for a special kind of
> disinfectant to be used in her cell was referred to the Medical Office.[37]

There were several requests from the women to have their own female doctor. This was now becoming more feasible with the increasing number of female medical graduates. Two of the suffragist doctors were Kathleen Maguire and Kathleen Lynn. The suffragists disliked the way the prison doctors treated them. Madge Muir in a letter to the governor of Belfast gaol appealed to him "to relieve me from the medical attention of the doctor here". She objected to being attended by a male doctor and claimed he pressed his stethoscope so hard he gave her two bruises.[38] In the summer of 1912 Margaret Murphy reminded the Lord Lieutenant of Ireland that she had already requested to be treated by her own doctor Kathleen Maguire ". . . as I am undergoing treatment, owing to having been forcibly fed whilst in Holloway, . . . Dr Maguire understands my constitution."[39] Meanwhile her medical officer in prison wrote of her ". . . I beg to report that I regard her as being a woman of neurotic temperament who suffers from indigestion, an ailment frequently complained of by women of this type."[40]

Neurotic was an adjective frequently used to describe the women's 'strange' behaviour. Indeed *Votes for Women* in September 1912 stated that "the government and the Dublin authorities contemplate the removal of Mrs Leigh to a lunatic asylum."[41] According to the governor of Tullamore "it was impossible to prophesy what their action might be as two of them, Miss Margaret and Miss Jane Murphy, had neurotic tendencies."[42] It is therefore not surprising that the prisoners demanded to be treated by doctors of their own choice. The Murphys eventually succeeded in not only getting suffragist doctor, Kathleen Maguire, to treat them but also in getting their own dentist. "Miss Jane Murphy will attend her own dentist at her own expense."[43]

Other concession were also made, vegetable substitutes

were provided for the vegetarian women "on the 31st of January Mrs Cousins was allowed by the medical officer one pint of vegetable soup in *lieu* of meat, being a vegetarian. . .".[44] According to one suffragist, many claimed to be vegetarians "having learned by experience that the food thus obtained was better".[45] This experience was contradicted in Holloway where the husband of imprisoned suffragist and vegetarian Mrs Cobden Sanderson complained that she only got dry bread, tea or cocoa and potatoes.[46]

The women wished to conduct their professions from their cells. This included the running of the *Irish Citizen*. Hanna Sheehy Skeffington hoped "that during my imprisonment my place as a seller of the *Citizen* will be filled."[47] On July 6 1912 the *Irish Citizen* reported that the 'political prisoners' were now being granted some privileges "Mrs Palmer is allowed her typewriter and Mrs Sheehy Skeffington is writing review articles."[48] The women also desired to write letters to the press for publication from their cells.[49]

What lay behind all these complaints was the demand to be treated differently from common criminals. They had not committed their crimes for personal gain but for a cause which they believed would eventually improve the nation. The women repeatedly insisted that they were different and were in prison for political reasons. In a letter to the chairman of the Prison Board Margaret Cousins asserted "I am not a criminal but a political prisoner—my motives were neither criminal nor personal—being wholly associated with the agitation to obtain Votes for Women. I shall fight in every way in my power against being branded a criminal."[50]

Cousins and other suffragists claimed that there were precedents for their demands. "I felt very privileged in being in the historic line of the political prisoners of Ireland who fought for proper status, I could not sell the pass they had won."[51] Many past incidents were often cited to reinforce their arguments—often mistakenly. Both English and Irish suffragists pointed to cases in Ireland's past which indicated that those who saw their ends as political were given preferential treatment. Frederick Pethick Lawrence in a pamphlet entitled 'Treatment of Suffragettes in Prison' asserted that the treatment denied to the suffragettes had been given to such men as Dr Jameson who "raided the Transvaal in time of peace and Mr Ginnell, M.P., imprisoned for encouraging cattle-driving . . .".[52] The latter was a nationalist MP who was to become a suffragist supporter.[53] The IWFL in a letter to Mr Hazleton MP asked him to apply to the Chief Secretary "that our women political prisoners should be given exactly the same treatment as that given to Mr Ginnell and to Mr Farrell within recent years who were allowed visitors and letters daily and on whom silence was not enforced."[54] In her memoirs Mary Gawthorpe wrote "Mr Keir Hardie, Mr Cobden-Sanderson, Mr Pethick Lawrence, concentrating in and outside the House of Commons, demanded the treatment accorded political prisoners, that is of the first class, for the suffragette prisoners. This would give them similar privileges to those accorded rebel Irishmen who had put up their own stiff fight for treatment as political offenders."[55] A flyer published by the Women's Press in London posed the question "Have prisoners in this country ever received first-class treatment because they were political offenders?" It answered

> Yes. The Chartist leader Fergus O'Connor, indited for seditious conspiracy and language was allowed his own clothes and food, and no restrictions were placed upon the visitors, books, letters he received. In short he received full political treatment. In 1868 the Irish prisoners sentenced for "seditious libel" were given first class treatment.[56]

This last reference to the Fenians failed to give recognition to the fact that for much of the time of the Fenians imprisonment they were given worse treatment than 'ordinary prisoners'. Indeed they were treated so badly there was a widespread press campaign to improve their conditions. There were stories of Michael Davitt having to eat on all fours like a dog with his hands tied behind his back.[57] It was not until the accession of Gladstone that their conditions noticeably improved.

The suffragists were baffled as to how some Irish nationalists who had been political prisoners, or had claimed that status, failed to support the women. The *Irish Citizen* commented that Mr Patrick O'Brien who gave a speech on receiving the freedom of the City of Kilkenny said that part of his success was due to having been a political prisoner before he got to represent Kilkenny. Why, asked the *Irish Citizen*, has he no sympathy with women political prisoners?[58] There were even some nationalists who pointed to the double standards of these attitudes. William Redmond MP speaking at a Home Rule meeting in Ireland commented how ironic it was that the Irish nationalists were now treating the suffragists with the same flippancy which they had been subjected to by successive British governments.[59]

In 1908 *Votes for Women* noted that there were also precedents for imprisoned Irish women being treated differently from, and less well than, Irish men. Their source was a book by T.P. O'Connor which referred to the Ladies Land League:

The case is that of the Irish Land League of the eighties. Mr O'Connor shows that while the [male] prisoners were sentenced under the Coercion Act, and were allowed to have communications with each other for six hours out of every day, and to conduct their business, and even plan their campaign, the women were sentenced under the old statute of Edward III and were treated as common criminals.

The conclusion drawn by *Votes for Women* was that the policy of the government in 1881 and 1908 was directed "towards breaking down the spirit of women".[60] Countess Markievicz had a similar gripe to make in her prison letters in 1919 "By the way, according to 'information received', the men are allowed large sheets of paper for letters and two sheets! Trust the English to always make a point of worse treatment for women."[61]

Between 1912 and 1914 the treatment of suffrage prisoners varied enormously. Irish suffrage prisoners were definitely treated better than ordinary women prisoners. This could be explained by the fact that their guardians were unsure how to handle them. They were middle-class and educated and clearly had not committed serious crimes against society. They were articulate, argumentative, wrote over their guardians, heads to their superiors and received prestigious visitors. They were given a number of privileges and many concessions were made. However there was no clear-cut policy. Treatment of the women was not coordinated between the different prisons nor indeed in the same prisons at different times. Thus there was a volume of correspondence written by the women in an effort to make their status clear. Because of the inconsistency in their treatment complaints were often made about unfairness. Daily visits which were received by women in 1912 were at one point reduced to fortnightly visits.[62]

Clearly, therefore, the women's position and status within the prisons was vague and uncertain. This was so because the concept of 'political status' meant different things to different people and for some it did not exist. Therefore it is difficult to pin down exactly what the women's position was during the period under study. As has been shown above there were times when the women were granted a number of privileges which would not have been available to the average prisoner. A report in April 1913 on the Tullamore prisoners Mrs Mabel Purser and Mrs Barbara Hoskins stated that while they were in prison they were allowed to wear their own clothes, have their own toothbrush, associate with other prisoners, use a library book in addition to the usual religious instruction books. The prisoners did not consider these to be sufficient and they both hungerstruck.[63] A letter to the IWFL on 3 September 1912 stated that the "prison authorities, with the sanction of his excellency, have offered these prisoners privileges which are not allowed to ordinary convicts. *Inter alia* they may wear their own clothes, remain in association apart from other convicts, and obtain food other than the ordinary prison fare."[64]

However, and this is most important, the prison authorities and government failed to give it the label of 'political status'. The women were not just interested in obtaining privileges, they were more interested in it being publicly recognised that they had those privileges. Mrs Palmer voiced the dilemma when she wrote "The only complaint we have, we get letters and visitors as privileges and not officially."[65] Privileges may have made the prisoners' lives more comfortable but if they were hidden they were not worth having since the prisoners argued that they were not interested in comfort for its own sake. Margaret Cousins expressed her outrage at the statement by Max Green, the chairman of the Prison Board, that "We have to cod the public" with the retort "the press and the world knew the next day that the three suffragettes in Tullamore were on hungerstrike."[66]

In June 1912 one MP, Atherley Jones, argued in the House of Commons that the suffragists should be granted the status of political prisoner

These women are in the ordinary conventional use of the term, political offenders, and a political offence—whether it be so or not—is not tested by the means largely employed to secure a particular end, but is tested by the end which is in view. When people aim at a change in the Constitution, be it beneficent or otherwise, and pursue any unlawful means, whether they consist of assassination or some trivial and ludicrous offence of breaking windows, it is equally a political offence, and you cannot at all evade the issue by saying that they are not punished for a political offence but for breaking windows. I repeat that whether the offence is a political offence or not—and I speak as a lawyer, and with a sense of responsibility when I say so—it is tested by the end in view and not by the means that are adopted.[67]

The Chief Secretary, Mr Birrell, however had a totally different point of view. Replying in Parliament to a question put by a pro-suffragist Irish MP, Mr Ginnell, he said that it was impossible to grant political status to anyone since that category did not exist. Referring to the Tullamore hungerstrike in February 1913 he stated "These prisoners have refused food for several days on the grounds that they have not been accorded the full privileges of 'political prisoners'—a category unknown alike to the law and to the prison regulations. I have already informed the honourable member to the extent to which the regulations have been relaxed in their favour. No forcible feeding has been resorted to in the case of the prisoners . . . ."[68] Nevertheless petitions and requests were repeatedly made to the prison governor and the Lord Lieutenant of Ireland requesting the political status of suffrage prisoners.[69]

Warnings were issued stating that unless 'political status' was introduced by a certain date they would hungerstrike. *The Cork Constitution* in January 1913 reported that "A memorial has been presented to the Lord Lieutenant of Ireland praying that the three suffragists who were sentenced on Tuesday, and are now in Tullamore gaol, should be treated as political prisoners and stating that if the request were not granted the prisoners would start a hungerstrike."[70] The following day the same threat was reported in *Votes for Women*, it quoted Mrs Pethick Lawrence calling on a meeting in Dublin "to protest against the sentence of hard labour inflicted on the three Dublin suffragettes, and announce that they would begin the hungerstrike on Saturday".[71] At one stage the Irish prisoners believed themselves to have political status and were prepared to hungerstrike in support of the English suffragists in Mountjoy. The *Irish Citizen* announced on August 1912 "the hungerstrike will have begun in Mountjoy prison, unless before that day the political status of the English prisoners as well as the Irish is definitely recognised by the authorities, it therefore behoves all those who desire to save Ireland from the barbarities which have characterised the treatment of political prisoners across the water to act vigorously and promptly."[72]

On occasions it appeared that the status had been conceded. *Votes for Women* reported in 1912 that "it is understood that the authorities are prepared to give her [Mrs Baines] full political privileges but these she could not accept unless they were given also to Mrs Leigh and Miss Evans, but as they fell far short of political recognition the compromise was rejected by the prisoners."[73] In the following February *Votes for Women* stated that "we are informed that the Irish suffrage prisoners have been induced to abandon the hungerstrike a few days ago owing to the promise that political treatment (for which they were striking) would be accorded to them. This promise had not been kept, only certain limited privileges have been granted; and they are, therefore, we understand agitating for full political rights."[74] In June 1913 Mrs Marguerite Palmer, Mrs Dora Ryan and Mrs Annie Walsh, transferred from Mountjoy hungerstruck: "The sole ground on which these prisoners have commenced the hungerstrike is because they have not been allowed to receive a visitor daily and to write and receive a letter daily as a matter of course."[75] Robert Ryan and R.J. Palmer, the husbands of Mrs Ryan and Mrs Palmer, wrote to the Lord Lieutenant expressing anxiety over whether "it has been decided to grant these prisoners the full facilities for communications with their friends which have been previously accorded to political offenders in Ireland—including suffragists whose original sentence involved hard labour. We refer to the right to receive a daily visit and to receive and send letters daily . . . ."[76]

While the women were on hungerstrike their condition was carefully monitored. Doctors reported daily on their progress to the governor who in return reported to the Lord Lieutenant. Their weight was examined, their blood and urine tested and their vomit was scrutinised. They were tempted with "every dainties including fruit grapes".[77] Here the cynical attitude of the male officials in the prison again becomes apparent. J. Stewart was the medical officer for many of the women prisoners. According to Margaret Cousins he looked like Mephistopheles.[78] He declared "Madge Muir's mental condition is I think not normal she is given to lying . . . She is most abusive (to me at least without any cause) she is at times sulky and reticent and before committal it is alleged that she was partly attired in male clothes. This hungerstrike is nothing short of suicide".[79] In a letter written by the governor of Tullamore on June 22 1913 he wrote ". . . The statement that Mrs Ryan lost a full stone in weight is grossly exaggerated. She lost 4 lbs, Mrs Walsh 6 . . ., Mrs Palmer $1\frac{1}{2}$ . . . Before the hungerstrike Mrs Palmer was getting quite fat . . . ."[80]

The women were not on a hunger and thirst strike and therefore could maintain their strength for a much longer period. Mrs Purser's daughter remembered that her mother's hungerstrike "didn't damage her health at all". She was on hungerstrike for two weeks.[81] Hanna Sheehy Skeffington wrote "At first one misses the break of meal time in prison, and does not if one is wise, let one's thoughts dwell upon dainties. In novels one skips the allusions to food hurriedly . . . We were fasting 92 hours before release. Had the strike lasted much longer more unpleasant symptoms would have, doubtless, intervened . . . ."[82] Margaret Cousins remembered that she had no bad effects from the strike apart from some dizziness ". . . I lost weight and found breathing difficult in climbing the stairs to my room. Indeed I found all my powers of reading and understanding enhanced. I felt refined and purified, and I had a keen realization of the Unity of Life and my own oneness with it."[83] However after six days on hunger strike Mrs Hoskins was said to be near death with threatened heart failure. The governor was frightened and let her out on conditional release.[84]

Hanna Sheehy Skeffington wrote in August 1912 "The hungerstrike is a method of passive revolt that was initiated in Russian prisons where 'politicals' adopt it when all else fails. In Russia they do not add the further refinement of cruelty—forcible feeding; it has been reserved to civilised England to adopt that method of 'persuasion'."[85] On the whole forcefeeding was not an issue in the Irish prisons. Only two suffragists were forcefed—and these two were the English suffragists Leigh and Evans. Perhaps this case was an exception since they were English, belonged to the militant WSPU and their crime involved an attack on the English prime minister, Asquith and the leader of the Irish Party, John Redmond.[86] They were being treated in the same way as their colleagues across the Irish Sea. They were also different in that Leigh stated that she was hungerstriking for 'Votes for Women' while the Irish hungerstrikers said they were doing so for political status.[87]

Their hungerstriking and subsequent forcefeeding had quite an impact in Ireland. Irish suffragists went on a hungerstrike in support of them and a wide spectrum of the Irish public was outraged by their forcefeeding.[88] Letters to the press debated the morality of forcefeeding.[89] Numerous petitions from a variety of sources arrived at the Lord Lieutenant's and Chief Secretary's office in Dublin Castle protesting at the forcefeeding.[90] Protests were expressed by such groups as far apart as the British Socialist Party to workers in the London department store of Selfridges. In a letter to Dublin Castle Margaret Cousins wrote "We would respectfully draw your attention to an article in the *Lancet* by most prominent doctors, entirely condemning this system as a means of maintaining life and health in a resisting subject."[91] Augustine Birrell received a telegram on 21 September 1912 "For God's sake stop the brutal feeding of suffragettes in Dublin or the name of Englishman will become hated in the world."[92] It would seem from the following letter that the forcefeeding was drawing unwanted attention and unnecessary support for the suffragists. "The barbarity of the treatment of Mrs Leigh and Miss Evans in our Irish prison is creating . . . bitter feelings in thousands of us who have never up to now paid much attention to the suffragette statement that there is no justice where women are concerned . . . Are these women to be done to death?"[93]

However not everyone felt that the women were totally innocent in this matter. In a letter published in the *Irish Times* the public were confronted with the views of one of their noted countrymen. George Bernard Shaw called forcefeeding 'legalised torture' and 'wanton savagery'. He was totally opposed to this procedure being used upon suffragists or anyone else. However his statements on the English prisoners were ambivalent and open to misinterpretation.

> . . . if the prisoners in Mountjoy are determined to commit suicide by starvation, they must be allowed to do so, and that the government could not be held responsible for their deaths if it could convince the public that the prisoners had plenty of food within their reach. This is the cold logic of the matter, and it has been evident to intelligent observers for some time that the moment militant suffragists overstepped the line which separates what I may call pardonable ructions from offences against public safety which no community can be persuaded to tolerate, they would drive the government back to this cold logic.[94]

A year later Shaw said that "many of the poor reporters had got into such a state of mind that they could not resist saying 'Even Bernard Shaw wants you to starve Mrs Lee.'"[95] T.C. Tobais, a barrister-at-law, wrote to the *Irish Times* to express his views on the subject and to comment on Shaw's letter.

> . . . Speaking generally the law does not approve of doing a man a kindness against his will . . . What is sauce for the goose is sauce for the gander, and if there is any justification for the action of the authorities, there is no getting away from the fact, pointed out by Mr Shaw, that any criminal who had sufficient strength of mind could escape the consequences of his crime by precisely the same methods as Mrs Leigh and Miss Evans have found effectual in gaining their liberty.[96]

It is debatable why forcefeeding was not introduced in the case of the Irish suffragists. Their English counterparts felt that it was because the Irish public would not stand for it: "if forcible feeding has been resorted to it will be regarded in Ireland as a national disgrace. The violence and brutality of the process is revolting to the Irish mind, and moreover, Irish opinion strongly supports the claim for political treatment . . . public opinion is more enlightened in Ireland than in England."[97]

// When it was suggested in the House of Commons by Sir John Rolleston that forcible feeding of suffragists in English prisons might lead to the forcible feeding of Sir Edward Carson, the Ulster Unionist, in an Irish gaol, Mr Healy MP exclaimed: "It will have to be done by Englishmen then for we will not do it."[98] Presumably the English government discovered that orders to feed the Irish suffragists would be resisted and thus decided to make a virtue out of necessity by giving them political privileges without more ado. //

However, since political privileges were not always seen by the women as political status the hungerstriking went on. If the government was not going to forcefeed it had to find another way of coping with the situation. That way was the introduction of the Temporary Discharge of Ill Health Act more commonly known as Cat and Mouse Act in May 1913. The only member of the Irish Party to vote against this was Tim Healy.[99] Its aim was to prevent any unnecessary deaths and to allow the women recover their health after hungerstriking. Once the women had recovered they were to return to prison to serve the remainder of their sentence. They were let out 'on licence'. The reason for the introduction of this act lay in the inability of the authorities to cope with the widespread hungerstriking in England. The Act provoked widespread protest in Ireland as it had done in England. Articles and letters critical of the act appeared in the press and meetings were held to demonstrate opposition to it. *Votes for Women* reported in June 1913 that in Ireland the feeling against the act was so strong that "the Lord Mayor of Dublin has granted the use of the Mansion House for a public meeting of protest against the application of the Cat and Mouse Act to Ireland."[100] On the platform a number of well-known individuals expressed their condemnation. Miss Harrison, the first woman to sit on an Irish council, said that to condone persecution for political views would lay the axe at the root of the tree of popular liberty. Professor T. M. Kettle, an ex MP, who had by this stage been involved in disagreements with the women over militancy and the nationalist cause, said they all believed in treating politics as politics and not as a crime. "He understood that Mrs Palmer was to see-saw between prison and her own house because she broke the fanlight of the UIL offices. He was a member of the executive of the UIL—one of those who bought the new fanlight—and he wanted to say that Mrs Palmer was free to break the fanlight as often as she thought it would forward her cause."[101]

Medical opinion was also sought by those who opposed the Act and was given readily. An unsigned and undated, handwritten statement in the Sheehy Skeffington papers in Dublin (which I conclude was written by the suffragist Doctor Kathleen Lynn because of its similarity to other statements she made) described the effects of the Act on suffragists. She wrote:

> I have been asked to write a short statement of my experience of the Cat and Mouse Act. I attended one victim of the act—Miss Gladys Evans, an Englishwoman, so far it has never been enforced against an Irishwoman. As well as I can remember Miss Evans was released and re-arrested 6 or 7 times in 2 months. Each time she was released she was in the last stage of exhaustion from hunger and thirst strike, in a state of profound collapse, . . . she was so weak as to be unable to walk without support, she was intensely cold, her skin was harsh and dry, her tongue, stiff, dry and leathery and dark brown in colour—Her body was covered with a very irritating rash, . . . she could speak only with difficulty. In this condition she returned each time to her friends and was with the utmost care tended gradually back to some measure of health, only to be rearrested and go through the whole appalling process once more. That is how the British Government, the world's example of chivalry treats its political prisoners. Let Irishmen and women see to it that there shall be no repetition of such barbarism now.[102]

Dr Lynn also wrote about her Irish patients ". . . in the case of Mrs Palmer, Mrs Ryan and Mrs Walsh, now under her care, she found precisely the same symptoms as in the case of Mrs Evans—the rash, the anaemia, the prostration, aggravated in Mrs Ryan's case by a considerable weakness of the heart."[103] She spoke to the Church League for Women's Suffrage in January 1914 "on the torture of forcible feeding and related what she herself had seen". Others including Padraic Colum, the playwright, George Birmingham, the writer, Countess Markievicz and Mr Hubert O'Connor, an Independent Nationalist, added to the condemnations.[104] Petitions were drawn up and signed by thousands. Irish MPs were approached. Churchmen joined in with the opposition.

Women who were let out on licence were in constant fear of reimprisonment. English women on the run from the powers of the Act fled to the homes of their Irish counterparts. According to the daughter of Mrs Purser, English women hid in their house. "Mrs Dager Fox and Mrs Grace Roe used to come and stay with us as guests."[105] It would seem that the threat of the Act inspired more fear than the actual Act itself. Almost a year after its introduction Helen Chenevix, a member of the Irishwomen's Reform League, and therefore non-militant, wrote the following to the Lord Lieutenant: "The Committee of the Irishwomen's Reform League have directed me to draw your attention to the fact that the Cat and Mouse Act which has not been enforced in the case of the Dublin suffragist prisoners is now being put into operation in Belfast, and to plead with you in the name of humanity to discontinue the enforcement of the Act . . . ."[106] On the whole the provisions of the Act were not enforced, largely due to the difficulty of rearresting the prisoners and partly due to the strength of Irish public opinion.

Irish women were in and out of gaol until the outbreak of the Great War. Then like the tacit agreement the English suffragists made with the government that they would suspend all militancy until the aftermath of the war the Irish suffragists, too, cut down on their militancy and therefore on their prison sentences.[107] This two-year period of sporadic imprisonment indicated that the women were serious about their demand. The fact that they were prepared to go to gaol, and in some cases go without food, showed the Irish public that this movement was not a mere whim pursued by idle ladies with nothing better to do. It is difficult to argue that anything more than publicity for their cause was gained. On the whole it was a case of convincing the converted. Those who were already unsympathetic did not change their minds when the women went to gaol. Indeed they were now more convinced of the women's madness. There is no evidence that in England or in Ireland militant action twisted the government's arm toward positive legislation. In the longterm, it could be claimed that the suffragists established certain guidelines on political status and set a precedent for the imprisoned revolutionaries of the 1916 Rising who also adopted the hungerstrike. In the shortterm, they accelerated the growing awareness of Irish society to the movement for women's suffrage in its midst.

Notes

1. *Cork Constitution*, January 31, p. 5.
2. *IC*, April 19, 1912, p. 1.
3. *Ibid.*
4. Christie O'Connor, *Catholic Suffragist*, August 15, 1916, p. 73.
5. Dr Elizabeth Fitzpatrick, Harrison Tapes, Fawcett Library London.
6. *Irish Independent*, February 4, 1913.
7. *VFW*, July 22, 1910, p. 716, *IC*, June 22, 1912, R.M. Fox, *Rebel Irish Women*, p. 73.
8. *VFW*, December 10, 1908.
9. *IC*, May 25, 1912, p. 6.
10. General Prison Board Papers, State Paper Office, Dublin, Ireland, hereafter referred to as GPB. Margaret Murphy was forcefed in Holloway.
11. *VFW*, April 1, 1913.
12. *Ibid*, April 11, 1913.
13. *Ibid*, May 31, 1912.
14. Prisoners in the First Division could wear their own clothes, have access to writing materials and occupy superior cells. See Andrew Rosen, *Rise Up Women!* (Routledge and Kegan Paul, London and Boston, 1974), pp. 75–6.
15. *Cork Constitution*, June 21, 1912, p. 5.
16. *Irish Times*, June 25, 1912, p. 9.
17. *Cork Constitution*, January 29, 1913, p. 8. *Freeman's Journal*, January 29, 1912.
18. *Freeman's Journal*, June 21, 1912, p. 7.
19. *Executive Report of the Irish Women's Franchise League*, 1913, p. 4.
20. *Freeman's Journal*, May 14, 1912, p. 7.
21. GPB Papers, Tullamore, March 6, 1913.
22. *Irish Independent*, February 10, 1913.
23. Cousins, p. 189.
24. *IC*, September 7, 1912, p. 123.

25. *Prison Letters of Countess Markievicz* (Virago, London, 1986), p. 149.
26. Cousins, *op. cit.* p. 190.
27. *Daily Express*, February 1913. See also *General Report of the IWFL Executive Committee 1913*, p. 43.
28. GPB papers, 19 February, 1913.
29. *Ibid*, February 23, 1913.
30. *Ibid*, May 31, 1913.
31. *Irish Independent*, February 28, 1913.
32. GPB papers, February 1913.
33. *IC*, February 8, 1913.
34. Mary Gawthorpe, *Uphill to Holloway* (Traversity Press, Maine, 1962), p. 225.
35. *VFW*, August 23, 1912, p. 760.
36. GPB papers, letter from Maud Lloyd to the Chief Secretary, Augustine Birrell, July 16, 1912.
37. GPB papers, Mountjoy Prison, extract from minutes, July 25, 1912.
38. GPB papers, extract from medical officer's journal, July 4, 1912.
39. GPB papers, 17 August, 1912.
40. GPB papers, Mountjoy, 5 July, 1912.
41. *VFW*, September 6, 1912, p. 784.
42. GPB papers, J. Mulhall, vice chairman, June 27, 1912.
43. *Ibid*, July 1912.
44. *Ibid*, J. Boland, governor, March 1, 1913.
45. SSP Ms 22,271.
46. Gawthorpe, *op. cit.* p. 244.
47. *IC*, June 29, 1912, p. 47.
48. *Ibid*, July 6, 1912.
49. GPB papers, February 1913.
50. GPB papers, January 28, 1913.
51. Cousins, *op. cit.* p. 191.
52. "Treatment of Suffragettes in Prison", Pamphlet, Suffrage Box, Fawcett Library, London.
53. Paul Bew, *Conflict and Conciliation in Ireland, 1890–1910: Parnellites and Radical Agrarians* (Clarendon Press, Oxford, 1986), pp. 67–8.
54. *Irish Times*, June 25, 1912, p. 5.
55. Gawthorpe, *op. cit.* p. 245.
56. Flyer, Suffrage Box, Fawcett Library, London.
57. R. V. Comerford, *The Fenians in Context: Irish Politics and Society 1848–82* (Wolfhound Press, Dublin, 1985).
58. *IC*, Sept 7, 1912.
59. *Freeman's Journal*, October 12, 1912, p. 6.
60. *VFW*, September 10, 1908, p. 433.
61. *Prison Letters*, p. 205.
62. *IC*, February 15, 1913, p. 8.
63. GPB papers, April 1913.
64. *Ibid*, letter to the hon. sec. of the IWFL, September 3, 1912.
65. *Ibid*, Mrs Palmer 1913.
66. Cousins, *op. cit.* p. 210.

67. *VFW*, August 23, 1912, p. 760.
68. Extract from Parliamentary Debates, February 11, 1913, in GPB papers.
69. *IC*, May 22, 1912.
70. *Cork Constitution*, January 30, 1913.
71. *VFW*, January 31, 1913, p. 25.
72. *Ibid*, August 16, 1912. See also *IC*, August 1912.
73. *VFW*, August 23, 1912, p. 757.
74. *Ibid*, February 14, 1913, p. 281.
75. *Irish Independent*, June 21, 1913.
76. GPB papers, letter to Lord Lieutenant, June 7, 1913.
77. *Ibid*, report by Dr Edgar Flinn, Belfast Prison, August 6, 1914.
78. Cousins, *op. cit.* p. 192.
79. GPB papers, report by J. Stewart, medical officer.
80. *Ibid*, J. Boland, governor of Tullamore, June 22, 1913.
81. Dr Elizabeth Fitzpatrick, Harrison Tapes, *op. cit.*
82. *VFW*, August 23, 1912, p. 760.
83. Cousins, *op. cit.*, p. 191.
84. *Ibid*, p. 192.
85. VFW, August 23, 1912, p. 760.
86. *VFW*, July 26, 1912.
87. GPB papers, September 27, 1913.
88. *IC*, February 21, 1913, p. 314.
89. GPB papers, protest from the Willesden branch of the British Socialist Party.
90. *Ibid*, Petition from the workers of Selfridges and Co., September 1912. Gladys Evans worked in this store.
91. GPB papers, August 31, 1912.
92. *Ibid*, September 21, 1912.
93. *Ibid*, September 9, 1912.
94. *Irish Times*, September 17, 1912, p. 7.
95. Rodelle, Weintraub, *Fabian Feminist: Bernard Shaw and Women* (Pennsylvania State University Press, 1984), p. 237.
96. *Irish Times*, October 5, 1912, p. 645.
97. *VFW*, August 23, 1912, p. 757.
98. *Ibid*, July 5, 1912, p. 645.
99. Rosemary Cullen Owens, *Smashing Times* (Attic Press, Dublin, 1984), p. 65.
100. *Ibid*, June 1913.
101. *VFW*, July 4, 1913, p. 596.
102. *Ibid*, July 4, 1913, p. 596.
103. SSP Ms 22,664.
104. *Church League for Women's Suffrage*, January 1914, p. 180.
105. Dr Elizabeth Fitzpatrick, *op. cit.*
106. GPB papers, letter from Helen Chenevix to Lord Lieutenant of Ireland, March 6, 1914.
107. Pugh, *Women's Suffrage in Britain 1867–1928* (The Historical Association, 1980), p. 30.

· 5 ·

"The Real Sentiment of the People"

As the previous chapters have shown, the suffrage movement in the pre-war years was vibrant and healthy. Its presence in Ireland did not go unnoticed where it received mixed reaction. The high profile of commentary indicates the extent of impact of the movement. Comments came from four sources: the intellectuals, the press, the general public and the churches. Debate ranged from general support to opposition of the movement. There was discussion on militancy, on the suffragists' relationship with nationalism, religion and socialism and their link with the English suffrage movement. Financial support was sometimes offered, advice was given, letters to the press were written and appearances were made on platforms. Condemnations were made and meetings were broken up. Reaction of the intellectuals, the press and the general public will be investigated in this chapter. Reaction by the church, because of its special importance and influence in Irish society, will be examined on its own in the next.

The prominent intellectuals in early twentieth-century Ireland were generally in favour of the movement. Some expressed the desire to do more if they were not so preoccupied with their own pursuits. The legitimacy of the women's demands appealed to their sense of justice. Their literary skills enabled them to assist the women to some extent. Although Ireland had no H.G. Wells producing an *Ann Veronica* for the movement it did have some aspiring writers who wrote articles on behalf of the cause.[1] The women realised the advantages of having writers on their side. Helena Moloney wrote of the Nationalist women's magazine *Bean na hEireann* that the "best writers in Ireland [gave] their earliest and finest works to our columns".[2] The Irishwomen's Suffrage Federation reported that the president of the Munster Women's Franchise League, Edith Sommerville, herself a writer, submitted paragraphs to many newspapers on subjects of importance to women. The MWFL also appealed to well-known writers to write to the press on their behalf.[3] Their honorary secretary Susan Day published the book *The Amazing Philanthropists*, previously mentioned in Chapter 2, which features a suffragist on a County Cork Poor Law Board. This book served as a platform for women both in local and national politics.[4] When the feminist *Irish Citizen* was inaugurated it seldom had an issue without a word from some writer or other. One of these was James Stephens, the author of *A Crock of Gold* and *The Charwoman's Daughter*. His poem *The Red Haired Man's Wife* found an appreciative audience amongst the suffragists

> I am separate still
> I am I and not you
> And my mind and my will,
> As in secret they grew
> Still are secret, unreached and untouched
> And not subject to you.[5]

Stephens was a regular contributor to the *Irish Citizen*, attender at IWFL meetings and a friend of the Sheehy Skeffingtons.[6] He wrote articles on the male and female qualities of the mind and many of his short stories have the stormy relationship between the sexes as their central theme.[7]

Literary critics have in recent years devoted study to feminist orientations in James Joyce's works and have in some cases found within them great understanding and sympathy towards women. *Women in Joyce* contains a number of articles which examine Joyce's fiction and ask whether it reflected the reality of women's lives in Dublin at the turn of the century.[8] The article on 'Dubliners: Women in Irish Society' by Florence L. Walzi comes to the conclusion that "Joyce's picture of the relationship between men and women is not a pleasant one; but because these characters are harshly vivid and because Joyce ensures that we know their differences and suffering we feel sympathy for them."[9] It is clear from a number of studies of, and by, individuals of this period that Joyce had close connections with the suffragists in real life.[10] He had been to university with some of them and had been their companion in the early 1900s in the years before he left Ireland.[11] He was among those who attended the 'at homes' on Sunday afternoons in the Sheehy household—which he was later to portray in *Stephen Hero*.[12] C.P. Curran remembered that Joyce and Frank Skeffington were 'good friends'[13] though significantly enough Joyce never used the longer version of Skeffington's name and frequently called him 'The Creeping Jaysus'. In *Impressions of a Dublin Playgoer* Mr Holloway wrote that he dropped:

> in for a chat at Cousins where I stayed for a couple of hours. You are always sure to find interesting people there . . . Miss Cousins played a couple of beautiful pieces beautifully, and Mr Joyce a mysterious kind of youth with weird penetrating eyes (which he frequently shades with his hands) and a half bashful, faraway, wistful expression on his face sang some dainty ballads most artistically and pleasingly, some to his own accompaniment.[14]

Joyce was a frequent visitor at the Cousins house though he disliked their vegetarianism.[15] Bonnie Kime Scott has shown how his sympathetic portrayal of Emma Clery in *Stephen Hero* has much basis in reality. Emma Clery attended university in Dublin in much the same circumstances as Joyce's fellow female students—women like Mary Colum, Hanna Sheehy Skeffington and Margaret Cousins.[16] When he left Ireland he frequently sent back messages of support to his suffragist friends and he returned on a visit in 1909.[17] James Cousins recalled in his autobiography that

> Among our variegated friendships was that of James Joyce. When he scraped the clabber of Dublin off his boots . . . he made a ceremonial exit towards Trieste by having a printed copy of what he called *A Catharsis* distributed to his acquaintances. The copy that was dropped into our letter-box on his farewell night showed that he had not forgotten our hospitality to him and our mental and musical exchanges that had presumably cancelled occult and dietic eccentricities. But the point is that Joyce's back of my hand to Dublin did not include me in its vituperation.[18]

Another friend of Cousins was a well-known Dubliner,

George Bernard Shaw, who was a concerned contemporary of the Irish suffragists. Shaw's feminist sympathies, an extension of his adult suffrage beliefs and support for the English suffrage movement, have long been appreciated by Edwardian historians and Shavians alike. He along with eight other writers signed a petition in favour of women's suffrage which was published in the *Times* in March 1909.[19] He argued that "a woman is really only a man in petticoats, or, if you like, that a man is a woman without petticoats."[20] He wrote a number of articles on women's suffrage and related issues and was interviewed a few times on the subject. His articles ranged from the White Slave Traffic to 'Why Women are peculiarly fitted for the vote'.[21] Among his most well-known feminist polemics are *Press Cuttings* and *Mrs Warren's Profession*.[22] *Press Cuttings* is concerned with the suffrage movement three years in the future. The movement provides the background for many of his plays. He felt very strongly about the position of women in society and admitted to having thrown over "the customary polite assumption that women are angels".[23] His activity in promoting the women's cause involved not just literary pursuits but also practical considerations. When he was asked to run for office as a Liberal candidate in 1889 part of his election platform was that women should have the suffrage on the same terms as men.[24] While a London councillor he campaigned to get toilets provided for women in Camden Town which he rather aptly termed as 'The Unmentionable Case for Women's Suffrage'.[25] However he found he had to restrain himself on the subject of women's suffrage. He told the WSPU that after having spoken once he did not intend to speak again. Otherwise he would be spending "all his public life on the 'Suffrage Platform'."[26] Nevertheless he did not stop. The pamphlet 'An Unexpurgated Case Against Women's Suffrage' written by the noted anti-suffragist Sir Almroth Wright could not be left without comment by an incredulous Shaw.[27] Against his fellow Dubliner's arguments, which first appeared in a letter in the *Times*, Shaw claimed that suffragists found themselves in the same position as the journalists in Rudyard Kipling's story. "They it will be remembered saw the sea serpent. At first they thought they had the chance of their lives; then, overwhelmed by the hugeness of the chance, they dropped their pens and were silent. Their luck was overdone: the real sea serpent was incredible."

He proceeded to reject everything Wright had asserted. Not only that but he claimed to be highly insulted by Wright's implications.

> As a matter of fact, Sir Almroth Wright does insult everyman's wife and everyman's mother, including his own; and the 'unexpurgated case' in his title means simply the frankly insulting case. If a man tells a woman that she is relatively to himself an inferior beast, he insults her . . . Sir Almroth attempts no proof: he simply points to the common experience of the world that we are all fools. Woman will not be satisfied with that: she will ask 'Am I a bigger fool than you?' If he answers 'No', his case falls to the ground. If 'Yes', a flatter insult cannot be conceived.[28]

Shaw's sympathy towards and connections with women's suffrage have periodically been examined. Indeed a book entitled *Fabian Feminist* was published in 1984. This book has a number of articles by Shavians about his utterings on the subject and his support of it through his plays and other writings. Yet despite the fact that he was a Dubliner there is not one article, or indeed paragraph, on his connections with the Irish movement—connections which are certainly worth noting.[29] Similarly in an article in *The Shaw Bulletin* by Michael O'Neill on 'Some Shavian links with Dublin' there is no recognition of Shaw's connections with Irish suffragists except the reference to Shaw's *faux pas* when lecturing to an Irish audience who took exception to Shaw's statement that Irish girls had bad teeth.[30]

Shaw was a friend and correspondent of the Sheehy Skeffingtons and the IWFL. As a young journalist James Cousins had reported on Shaw's public lectures.[31] Shaw kept in contact with what was going on in Ireland and his wife subscribed, and gave donations, to the IWFL.[32] When Mrs Pankhurst visited the IWFL in 1910 and addressed a meeting Shaw sent a message of regret that he was unable to attend as he had to return to England.[33] As was seen in Chapter 4, when the issue came to a head in Ireland with the hungerstriking he got involved in correspondence to the *Irish Times* over the morality of forcefeeding. His interest in the suffrage question was widely appreciated. The *Evening Standard* commented in July 1912: "Mr Shaw will be interested to hear that among the books found in the possession of one of the suffragists arrested in Dublin was 'The Devil's Disciple'. Another appropriately enough, since one of the charges is that of attempting to set fire to a theatre—was called 'Flames'."[34]

His name appeared on list of the general committee on the programme of a production of Frank Sheehy Skeffington's suffrage play 'The Prodigal Daughter' which was performed in Dublin in November 1916.[35] Looking back from the perspective of 1918 he wrote to Hanna Sheehy Skeffington

> I have always urged women to press for their representative rights as well as, and even instead of, their voting rights. But I have steadily refused to do the women's own business in the matter. I have seen that miserable domestic pet, the male suffragist, hauled to the platform between stalwart females, and made to sit up on his hind legs and beg. I have heard the clacking of his hollow cackle after the passionate speeches of the women; and I have felt the dignity of my sex wounded to the quick. My personal vanity will not permit me to make such an exhibition of myself. I have never done it and I never will . . .[36]

Yet despite these comments Shaw, through his writings, speeches and actions, had done a considerable amount for the publicity of English and Irish suffrage causes.

Another Irish intellectual, who was a friend of the suffragists was A.E. or George Russell. He was a poet, writer, playwright and painter and like many of the Irish suffragists a theosophist. He first met the Cousinses in the Dublin Vegetarian Restaurant.[37] As editor of the *Irish Homestead* he ensured woman's concerns were provided for. He also contributed a chapter to Sir Horace Plunkett's book, *The United Irishwomen*, entitled 'Ideals of the New Rural Society' in which he supported the idea of women having a far more prominent role in the workforce and being involved in the future of the country. "Men and women have been companions in the world from the dawn of time. I do not know where they are journeying to, but I believe they will never get to the delectable City if they journey apart from each other, and do not share each other's burden."[38] As a close friend of the Cousinses and the Sheehy Skeffingtons he often attended suffrage meetings in Dublin.[39] He too was involved in the production of 'The Prodigal Daughter'. He also was a frequent contributor to the columns of the *Irish Citizen* and had influenced some people towards feminism, among them Louie Bennett.[40]

The writer Padraic Colum and his wife Mary were friends of the Cousinses and frequent attenders at IWFL meetings. Padraic Colum was joint editor of the *Irish Review* and frequently gave space to articles which supported women's suffrage.[41] His wife who was a journalist in her own right was an early practitioner of feminist criticism.[42] Her autobiography provides the historian with a wealth of information about the life of women undergraduates in the early 1900s in Dublin. She describes the restrictions placed upon them yet at the same time the new freedoms and excitement experienced by them that would have been unknown to their mothers.[43]

The poet Yeats also paid lip service to the movement. He came into contact with James Cousins when he endeavoured to enlist his help in the setting up of the Irish National Theatre.[44] Later on he and Maud Gonne attended seances in the Cousins's home.[45] On occasions he sent letters of regret at being unable to attend much publicised suffrage meetings.[46]

Supporters of the suffragists were to be found on the left and right of Irish politics. Both Sheehy Skeffingtons considered themselves to be socialists and the *Irish Citizen* frequently carried articles of social concern. Olive Banks found that the majority of women in her study who were coming into contact with feminism by 1900 also appeared to have had socialist inclinations.[47] While it would be an overstatement to say that the level of interest was as high in Ireland there was indeed quite a bit of contact between the two ideologies and this becomes very apparent on reading Rosemary Cullen Owens's examination of the 'Labour Link' in her book *Smashing Times*.[48] Indeed the IWFL and the Irish Labour Party shared the same premises for a time.[49] The Irish socialist party had a debate on women's suffrage in 1910.[50] Louie Bennett had a leg in both camps being founder of the suffragist Irishwomen's Reform League and the Irish Women's Workers Union. The latter organisation as Cullen Owens points out made its suffrage overtones clear at its inaugural meeting where it was stated "a union such as has now been founded will not alone help you to obtain better wages, but will also be of great means of helping you get the vote."[51] In an article entitled 'How Suffragists are being made in Dublin' *The Vote* declared that "The Irish women and girls fighting for human, and against degrading, conditions of life and labour in Dublin, are becoming suffragists in the course of the struggle."[52] At a meeting of the Munster Women's Franchise League in April 1911 an address was given on 'The Labour Movement and the Suffrage Movement' by a Mr E. Mooney. Taking Professor Karl Pearson's axiom 'There has never been a Labour movement without a Woman's Movement', he drew the analogy between the two and showed how close they were to each other.[53]

However, all did not fit together neatly. A discrepancy existed in class membership between the two groups. The suffragist women were on the whole middle class while the Labour movement drew much of its support from the working classes. The association between the two did not please all suffragist supporters and Labour supporters. Those in the Labour movement were concerned about the suffragists' apathy with regards to adult suffrage. After all if the suffragists were not interested in universal franchise they could hardly be considered as supporters of a working-class revolution.[54] Some suffrage supporters maintained that any association with Labour tainted the respectability of the movement. R.E. Longfield from Mallow wrote to the *Cork Constitution*

> In politics it may be sometimes difficult to say 'non tali auxilo' but if 'Votes for Women' is to be associated with the Labour movement as many people understand it, and with communism and anarchy I am unable to see how any reasonable and law abiding citizen can support it. If it is considered purely on its own merits it has at any rate, a stronger case . . .[55]

A person who believed the two were very much related to each other was the socialist leader James Connolly, a supporter of the suffragists, particularly the IWFL. He was a founder of the Irish Transport and General Workers Union and its members were often to be found in a bodyguard role at suffrage meetings. He often appeared on their platform and was a friend of James Cousins.[56] The IWFL helped Connolly and other socialists during the 1913 Lock Out when they helped set up soup kitchens.[57] In his book *The Reconquest of Ireland* Connolly included a chapter on women and looked at their past, present and future situation in Ireland. He argued that before the English came to Ireland there was a much fairer system of land distribution where the women benefited as well as the men, while the English system of primogeniture favoured the eldest son only. Furthermore, he argued a point which is often put forward by feminist socialists, that the introduction of the capitalist system further meant the repression of women. He observed that the development in Ireland of the women's movement "has synchronised with the appearance of women upon the industrial field, and the acuteness and the fierceness of the women's war has kept even pace with the spread among educated women of a knowledge of the sordid and cruel nature of the lot of their suffering sisters of the wage-earning class." There was, he wrote, a feeling of sympathy in the labour movement towards "the ever spreading wave of martyrdom of the militant women of Great Britain and Ireland". There was also an appreciation "of the genuineness of the women's longings for freedom, as of their courage in fighting for it, produced an almost incalculable effect for good upon the relations between the two movements". Connolly stressed their common interests when he wrote "In Ireland the woman's cause is felt by all Labour men and women as their cause; the Labour cause had no more earnest and wholehearted supporters than the militant women." The working classes and the women were two suppressed groups who could help each other to achieve their aims.[58] While attending a meeting of the IWFL in May 1914 he reiterated what he had written in his book. He told the women that from his standpoint the working class were slaves and the women of the working class were the slaves of slaves. Men, he said could not know what women had suffered; they could only guess.[59] He wrote "When trimmers and compromisers disavow you . . . I, a poor slum-bred politician, raise this my hat in thanksgiving that I lived to see this resurgence of women."[60]

While his suffragism seemed convincing some suffragists felt he could not shake off his desire to dominate. Louie Bennett, who had also helped build up the Irish Women's Workers Union, found him difficult to deal with at times. While she admitted he was "A strong suffragist, he valued only the militant movement." She wrote that he was one of the best suffragist speakers she had ever heard and was a "thorough feminist in every respect: he taught the Transport Union of Dublin to support and respect the women workers' struggle for industrial and political rights."[61] However on occasions she found him "dour and antagonistic" and after one meeting with him in 1914 she came away feeling little reassured "I saw that he was an autocrat at Liberty Hall and that he meant to dominate the Women's union there just as he did every other department."[62] What Louie Bennett saw as autocratic Helena Molony saw as paternal. In an article on 'James Connolly and Women' written in 1930 she remembered "The fatherly care and encouragement he was always ready to give the groups of women and girls in the Irish Women's Workers Union, his anxiety that they should work out their own plans, and run their own organisation, his readiness to listen to their most trivial problems, have left a permanent impression on the minds of those women."[63]

The other major socialist in Dublin circles at this time, James Larkin, also lent support to the women. His sister Delia was a strong advocate of women's rights.[64] And indeed the Irish Labour Party like the British Labour party was intent on women's equality. It supported resolutions that women's suffrage should be included in the Home Rule Bill[65] and members of the Transport Union signed a petition against the Cat and Mouse Act. The British Labour Party was the only party at Westminster that was not hostile to the Women's Suffrage Bills.[66] Thus while there was on the whole strong support from the Irish Labour Party for the advancement of women there is no reason to suppose that it was any different from the relationship between socialism and feminism in other European countries where the socialist goal was ultimately more important.[67] There was in the Irish Labour Party a conservative Catholic and nationalist element which could not rid itself of the traditional views on the role of womanhood. //

Unlike the Irish Labour movement the Irish press was much more heterogeneous in its views. The suffragists were always on the lookout for sympathetic journalists and editors, and quick to condemn those who did not give them a fair hearing. They were very conscious of the power of the press: in promoting, criticising or ignoring their cause, it had a role to play in the fate of their movement. According to an observer of the British suffrage movement, treatment of the women's movement by the press in general was a factor in drawing women into the movement "and the publicity which attended the militant campaign, especially in the early years brought the suffrage issue not only into the open but into the limelight."[68] However the *Irish Citizen* would not have agreed that this was always the case. It complained about the "one eyed press". It referred in January 1914 to the *Evening Herald*'s review of the activities of the militant suffragists in 1913 and complained that almost the whole article was devoted to the English suffragettes. At the end the *Herald* sub-editors had tacked on a paragraph relating to Ireland: ". . . indeed it was obviously bought from some English journalistic syndicate . . .".[69] The *Irish Times*, it complained, "while under pretence of friendliness to the woman's suffrage cause never misses an opportunity of damaging it. . .".[70] The *Times* was also accused of having "one tone for persons whose words were followed by the breaking of glass in London, and another tone for the persons who threatened in certain eventualities to resist the law by armed force." This was a reference to the Unionists' determination to oppose Home Rule by any means. The *Citizen* continued that the Dublin *Evening Telegraph* "has one set of adjectives for the militant woman suffragists, and another for the Manchester Martyrs".[71] The *Citizen* also asserted that the *Cork Constitution* which saw itself as a 'strong upholder of law and order' was not interested in "the law of truth and journalistic decency".[72]

And indeed the *Cork Constitution* reported on the suffragists with a mixture of mockery and humour. It spoke of the "shrieking sisterhood" and the "hatless brigade". The latter was in reference to women's plans to boycott all male hatters. *Cork Constitution* ventured:

> If we might make a suggestion, it is that the Suffragettes should organise a general boycott of mankind. Never to go into his company, to withdraw from his sight, and forbid him their presence. This can only be done by the militant suffragist withdrawing to a desert island. The Government would probably be glad enough to place one or more of Britain's rocky islets at present chiefly occupied by such chattering birds and animals as cockatoos and monkeys, in order that the Suffragettes may have a parliament of their own . . .[73]

In the meantime it felt that the amount of support for these women was small and the amount of suffragists was less. "The Irish public knows right well that the number of women who want votes is small, and the number who don't want votes is legion. Ladies and women can find plenty of useful work to do in their homes—without trespassing on the domain of men."[74] *The Freeman's Journal* mixed up the names of the different Irish suffrage movements.[75] *The Evening Telegraph* believed to the consternation of the Irish suffragists that disorder in Dublin was caused by London organisers.[76] Louie Bennett complained of the press in general when a suffrage week was held in Dublin in December 1913 "No one could deny that the most prominent topic of the week was women's suffrage . . . Yet the press entirely disregarded many of the events of the week, and gave the meagrest possible notices of the most important of them. Are we to believe that the press is seriously endeavouring to cater to the Dublin public?"[77]

This was a frequent complaint of the women. The press not reporting at all was worse than bad reporting. The *Irish Citizen* declared with regards to Miss Patricia Hoey's refused entry to the Irish Party's national convention in 1912 "That no mention of her exclusion should be admitted to the Irish Press is a sufficient justification, were any needed, for the existence of the *Irish Citizen*."[78] In the *Amazing Philanthropists* there was talk of the local newspaper the *Blazer* refusing to advertise suffrage meetings and carefully omitting to report proceedings "unless something unpleasant occurs, when, of course it blossoms forth in gory headlines". It was Susan Day's opinion that newspapers like the fictional *Blazer* believed that the only person able to undertake public duties was someone who had "no breadth of intellect, no culture and no toleration, but who is narrow and reactionary to a degree".[79]

However, the *Irish Citizen* did see some favourable points in the Irish media. It praised enlightened newspapers who commented favourably editorially and who reported on the meetings, demonstrations and declarations of the suffragists. A number of local newspapers played a role in introducing the suffrage movement to their community by reporting on local meetings, carrying advertisements and occasionally carrying favourable editorial comment. One such newspaper was the *Enniscorthy Echo*. In one of its editorials it was stated that pioneers of every cause in Ireland had faced a 'cold welcome'. It likened the task of the suffragists to that of Davitt's in arousing the farmers, to Parnell's struggle for Home Rule and to Fr. O'Growney's efforts to save the Irish language. It concluded "But they [the suffragists] are working for an idea—votes for women—and they care not for the trouble or the risk . . . In a few years when they have won their fight we shall be on their side."[80] This sort of coverage was much more pleasing to the *Irish Citizen*. Likewise it was happy to inform its readers of the fair reports which appeared in the *Midland Tribune*.[81] In May 1913 it triumphantly reported that the secretary of the Galway Society of the Irishwomen's Suffrage Federation "has scored a victory so far unique in Ireland: she has persuaded the editors of two local papers, representing opposite sides in party politics, to publish half a column of suffrage matter every week."[82] For those who read English newspapers there was also some good news. In June 1912 the *Citizen* informed its readers that the London *Standard* "publishes daily a 'Women's Platform' in which all phases of feminist activity are represented, together with suffragist news from all parts of the world." It hoped that "before long some Irish paper will arrange similarly to devote a definite portion of its space daily to the serious interests of women, instead of the 'cookery and fashion' twaddle which they appear to think good enough for feminine consumption."[83]

For its part, the Irishwomen's Suffrage Federation had much praise for the press. Clearly the very nature of the pacifist Federation made the press less antagonistic towards them than it was to the militant and more self-assured IWFL. In its annual reports every year the Federation acknowledged that the press had been fair to them. "The work of the Irishwomen's Suffrage Federation on the whole, received fair recognition from the daily press. Our meetings have generally been well reported, and our correspondence accepted with occasional modifications." Among the papers which supported them were *The Newry Reporter, The Westmeath Independent, The Lisburn Standard, The Cork Examiner, The Cork Free Press, The Michelstown Sentinel, The Waterford Standard, The Midland Tribune* and *Kings County Chronicle.* The Federation felt that the extent of press support was fairly large.

> Our provincial Societies have worked the Press most successfully. We believe that in every town where [there is] a Society it has been found possible to enlist the support of the local Press. This is a great gain in an era of newspapers. . . . In several towns where no Suffrage Society as yet exists, editors of local papers are in full sympathy with the cause, and prepared to help it. This is notably the case in Enniscorthy and Ballina.

There were special words of praise for the *Irish Review*, a journal which existed for four years from 1910 to 1914, which it believed was a "firm supporter of the Woman's Suffrage cause" and indeed it did carry a number of pro-suffrage articles on topics ranging from women secondary teachers to the suffrage movement itself, obviously reflecting the sympathy of its editor Padraic Colum.[84] The *Irish Citizen* too praised the *Irish Review* but had some reservations on Frederick Ryan's article 'The Suffrage Tangle'. ". . . It can hardly be said, however, that Mr Ryan succeeds in disentangling the knot; he repudiates the militant solution but does not present any clear alternatives."[85] The ISF feared that the "Dublin Press is too deeply infected by the time-serving and purely party serving spirit to treat the question of Woman's Suffrage with fairness."[86] The writer Susan Day of the Munster Women's Franchise League wrote to *Votes for Women* in April 1911 "The south of Ireland, for which I am competent to speak, is particularly happy in this respect, for two of the leading newspapers have never closed their columns against us. The *Free Press*, the organ of Mr William O'Brien's party published a most sympathetic article just before Mrs Pankhurst's visit to Cork in October, and both it and the *Cork Examiner* (representing Mr Redmond) published full accounts of the meeting in the City Hall."[87]

The general public like the press reacted in varying ways to the suffrage movement. Public reaction served as a barometer of the success or failure of the educational policy common to most Irish suffrage movements and thus was studied carefully by the women. The suffragist press was vigilant in reporting on crowd reaction although, as might be expected, it tended to focus on positive support. According to an *Irish Citizen* report on 29 June 1912 there was real enthusiasm at some of the MWFL meetings notably one in Passage Co. Cork "where the crowds of seven or eight hundred consisted mainly of workmen from the docks."[88] Another report in May 1913 spoke of an open air meeting in the vicinity of Cork where the crowd listening to the speakers "must have numbered nearly a thousand".[89] Other reports included such comments as "a large crowd of workingmen listened attentively to the speeches and asked many questions."[90] "The working classes have shown themselves friendly and have rallied to our support whenever called upon"[91] and "The meeting was noticeable for the increased number of working women."[92] It is obvious from the terminology used in the reports that class barriers still remained despite the suffragists' attempts to break down sexual barriers. In November 1913 the *Citizen* asserted that despite claims by Lloyd George and others to the contrary, Irish public opinion was supportive "whenever the real sentiment of the people gets an opportunity of expressing itself, free from the dictation and excitement of the politicians [it] is distinctly favourable to suffrage, and generally speaking not hostile to militancy, at least in nationalist districts."[93]

Nevertheless despite all this optimism the *Irish Citizen* and other newspapers found themselves reporting some incidents where crowds showed definite hostility towards suffragists. Indeed this hostility was not confined to one particular socio-economic group. Students in Queens' University Belfast broke up a suffrage meeting "by releasing large quantities of chemicals and snuff".[94] Students in Cork went to a suffrage meeting in the City Hall with the intention of breaking it up but were "converted by the eloquence of the speakers".[95] When Mrs Pankhurst spoke in the City Hall, despite the largely favourable audience, there was some noise at the back of the hall. According to the *Cork Free Press* this was "due to the potency of Irish whiskey".[96] Factory women workers in Blackpool, Co. Cork also objected to the suffragists promoting their cause:

> there were exciting scenes at Blackpool, County Cork, on 4th inst., when Cork militant Suffragettes sought to press literature on the girl millhands of a local flax factory. The girls severely handled the suffragettes. Hats and coats were torn off, and one lady was treated for injuries at the infirmary.[97]

At Castlebar, County Mayo, a group of men tried to disrupt a meeting by singing 'Put me on an island where the girls are few'.[98] However James Cousins praised the women's ability to resist mob pressure "they were as rocks on lorries surrounded by jeering crowds of bipeds who counted themselves as men."[99] Nevertheless on occasions the rocks tumbled.

> The only time in our suffrage decade when I had seen hat pins in women's hands as weapons was on that occasion amongst low-class women who stood in front of the lorry and shouted us down. I watched a poor class of youth with a stone in his hand. In a moment he threw it towards me as I tried to gain the attention of the crowd. Then the idea came into the crowd's head that it should push the lorry out of its place. As they proceeded to do so more stones were thrown at us. The police ordered us to come down from the lorry. There was nothing else to do.[100]

Frank Sheehy Skeffington was often perceived around Dublin as a figure of ridicule.[101]

Nineteen-twelve was a particularly bad year for mob hostility more than likely because the militant campaign was reaching its climax. The hostility was usually expressed in minor jostling and heckling. The *Freeman's Journal* reported on April 1 1912 that a group of women wearing sandwich boards which said 'Votes for Women in the Home Rule Bill' and 'Self Government means Government by Men and Women' were surrounded by an unsympathetic crowd who tore their placards from them and ripped them apart. Despite all this the *Freeman's Journal* was still able to claim "No one, it may be said to the credit of all concerned in the little incident, lost his or her temper . . . ."[102] It is evident from the *Cork Constitution* a month later that tempers were being lost. "Each time the members of the Irish Franchise League attempted a street demonstration they were only rescued from the anger of the humbler class women in the Irish metropolis by the prompt action of the police in surrounding them and protecting them from violence."[103]

In *The Amazing Philanthropists* Susan Day conveys the feeling of people in a small town outside Cork towards suffragists. They believed that "shocking immorality among women is now becoming a feature of the movement; they are freaks, degenerates, 'unsexed females', utterly unworthy of confidence and respect of any decent community." In the book when a suffragist was due to speak to the Local Young Men's Society its governing body was assured that she was not "a fit or proper person to address the young men of Ballybawn; the innocent lambs who . . . would never recover, religion would be abjured, morals blasted, the society disrupted."[104]

There was an awareness among the suffragists that mob hostility was not always spontaneous but was often well planned beforehand by a group with a vested interest. *The Vote* spoke of "an organised mob, who are the same each time, and all of one class" who attended "every suffrage meeting in order to howl down the speakers and unless restrained by the police, to physically ill-treat them, it is most emphatically not made up of the general public. In no city in the world have I heard of a mob of blackguards so cowardly as to confine its attacks to women. Orange violence pales before it—in Belfast men at least attack men."[105] This report referred to the Ancient Order of Hibernians, a nationalist organisation whose growing support in urban working class Dublin at this time was being increasingly felt.[106]

When Asquith visited Dublin in 1912 Irish women held a protest meeting in Berresford Place which was addressed by Mrs Cousins and Mrs Connery from the IWFL and Mrs Chambers from the Irish Women's Suffrage Society Belfast. A correspondent to *Votes for Women* described what happened. It was broken up after a half an hour:

> . . . by an organised gang of hooligans, who howled down the speakers and made determined efforts to overturn the lorry which served as a platform . . . On their way to the train the Suffragists were assaulted with showers of stones; some of them had their hats torn off and their clothes torn. Among the women assaulted in this manner were Mrs Wyse Power . . . and Countess Markievicz . . . Mrs Emerson [was] knocked down and kicked savagely . . . For the rest of the evening the gang of hooligans ran amok in the streets, woman-baiting . . . The gang who indulged in this orgy was led by prominent members of the Ancient Order of Hibernians, and there is no doubt that the whole of this hooliganism was inspired from official nationalist quarters.[107]

The following day a similar article appeared in the *Irish Citizen*. It argued that the most sinister feature of the mob campaign in Dublin was the introduction of a trend which was already happening in England which involved the "deliberate enlistment of prostitutes to attack suffragists or women suspected of being suffragist". This, it asserted, alluding to the AOH, was organised by "prominent members of a certain 'Catholic and Nationalist' association, which is filled with zeal against indecent postcards and 'immoral literature'". It continued that a young lady up from the country "not a suffragist or in any way associated with the movement, was seriously assaulted in broad daylight".[108] According to C. P. Curran, Frank Sheehy Skeffington was brought "over and over again at suffrage meetings into violent collision with the bravoes of the Ancient Order of Hibernians".[109] Sheehy Skeffington did not disguise his feelings about the AOH:

> Let me give a word of warning to Mr Joseph Devlin and the Ancient Order of Hibernians: The members of that organisation have been wearing a halo of purity since their famous crusade against indecent

postcards. If, in their war against women who are asserting their rights as citizens, the Hibernians carry out the threats which they have been loudly uttering within the past few days, they may rest assured that their halo will be publicly stripped from them, and an exemplary exposure will be made of the foul mouthed blackguardism which prevails in the bosom of this great "Catholic and National" organisation.[110]

In his play 'The Prodigal Daughter', Sheehy Skeffington portrays a suffragist coming home to her family after a spell in gaol. There are a number of references to the AOH. It was feared that one member of the family was going to be expelled from the Hibernians because of her suffragist associations and that the family in general would be boycotted.[111]

The hostility of the AOH to the suffragists may firstly be viewed in nationalist terms with the AOH seeing the suffragists as essentially part of an English organisation. Secondly in light of their fanatical moral crusade the sight of women demonstrating their beliefs in public encouraged the AOH to break up such displays. Their aggression towards the women was not unique nor unusual, they had already earned the reputation of being "a pest, a cruel tyranny, and an organised system of blackguardism".[112] According to the author of *The Evolution of Irish Nationalist Politics* members of the AOH were often used by Home Rulers like Dillon, Devlin, and Redmond as useful henchmen in dispersing radicals.[113] Therefore at one level their attacks on women could be interpreted as a disapproval of yet another phenomenon among many others which had no place in the future Ireland of these nationalists.[114]

Very different from this overt and violent hostility of the AOH were the comments of the Irish branch of the National League for Opposing Women's Suffrage also known as Women's National Anti Suffrage League. While their anti-suffragist convictions were equally strong they were expressed in a more genteel manner. The Irish notes in the British anti-suffrage magazine the *Anti Suffrage Review*, a journal which has been described by Harrison as a "flabby milk and water performance",[115] convey the select and limited nature of the anti-suffrage movement in Ireland. The group were certainly a class apart from the AOH and appealed to a very different

sector of society. It included such titled members as its
president the Duchess of Abercorn, the vice-presidents
were the Dowager Countess of Drogheda, the Countess of
Pembroke, Viscountess Iveagh, Lady Holmpatrick, and Lady
Beatrix Wilkinson. Its chairman was Mrs Bernard, the wife
of the dean of St Patrick's (the Protestant Cathedral in
Dublin).[116] Their gatherings were cosy and often included
prominent members of Anglo-Irish society.

The opposition of these Irish Antis to suffrage was much
the same as that of the English Antis which is discussed at
length by Brian Harrison in his book *Separate Spheres*.[117]
They belonged to the school who adopted the Ruskinite view
of womanhood. This placed woman in the role of middle-
class helpmeet to man, and mother of his children. There
was no room for working-class women in this philosophy.
The Antis believed that women were mentally and biologically
inferior and would not be able to cope with the stress of
political life. Their place was in the home—the private
sphere—and enfranchisement would cause dissension between
husband and wife. It was also argued that if women wished
to partake in outside interests besides philanthropic work
they should content themselves with local government affairs.

The Irish Antis argued there was not much support for
women's suffrage in Ireland and claimed "the cause is the
hobby of a few odd hundred women of leisure in the larger
towns—notably Dublin, Belfast and Cork."[118] The IWFL
certainly would not have agreed with this. According to the
Antis the lack of support was because the vast majority of
Ireland's population was agricultural. "Ask a woman in rural
Ireland if she is a suffragist and she will laugh in your
face—or else wonder what you are talking about. In our
country districts life is a serious proposition and the country
woman is not fitted either by nature or inclination for the
pursuit of a sex-obsession."[119] Whatever little support there
was they felt it was diminished by the campaign of violence
carried out by some of the suffragists: ". . . Women were
supposed to be more respected in Ireland than in any other
country in Europe. In less than three months the Suffragists
have succeeded in destroying that traditional respect. If no
other achievement stood to their credit, that fact alone would

be enough to brand their cause with shame."[120]

The Antis' arguments did not always lead to a logical conclusion. Though they were absolutely opposed to women's suffrage at a parliamentary level they, like the English Antis, saw nothing wrong with and even praised Irish women's success at local government level. They backed Miss Harrison in Dublin when she was the first Irish woman to stand for election onto a corporation.[121] At the monthly meeting in February they resolved to "assist the Irish Women's Local Government Association in every way possible".[122] Amy Murray, the honorary secretary of the anti-suffrage movement in Ireland, wrote in 1910 that women in the United Kingdom possessed the municipal vote and there was nothing stopping them from using it for "the bettering of human life in general, and of their own sex in particular". She concluded her letter stating that "Imperial affairs are not women's work."[123] This declaration had its basis in the argument that since women did not fight in wars they should have nothing to do with foreign affairs. Of course it became more complicated when it was pointed out that a Home Rule Parliament would only be allocated domestic concerns.

Like the suffragists the Antis too felt that the politicians should be aware of the strength of their feelings and the extent of their support. When they realised in 1910 that the Irish Women's Franchise League had sent a manifesto to electors asking them to press upon candidates to support the extension of parliamentary votes to women Amy Murray then also sent a letter to candidates. "In order that you may not be led to over-rate the importance of this manifesto, as representative of the opinion of the women in your constituency, the Committee of the Dublin Branch of the Women's National Anti-Suffrage League take this opportunity of reminding you that such an extension of the franchise is considered by a very large number of women in Dublin to be contrary to the best interests of the State."[124]

Though the Antis had a number of meetings and claimed to have sent out 200 invitations for one of them the *Irish Citizen* stated that they and their publications were very hard to find. It enquired in September 1912 what were their numbers and whether their sources of funding were Irish or not.[125] One correspondent to the *Irish Citizen* wrote of a railway bookstall which had a poster advertising the *Anti Suffrage Review* but on request was told of its irregularity in actually appearing on the stands.[126] When the *Irish Citizen* finally succeeded in getting hold of the *ASR* they found with satisfaction that a two column article on Dublin contained eight errors of fact.[127] In July 1914 the *Irish Citizen* declared ". . . Their membership is in fact infinitesimal; and but for the subsidies which reach them out of the profit of Guinness Brewery they would not keep going."[128] Suffragists would on occasions attend anti-suffrage meetings to give the Antis a taste of heckling.

Whatever argument there is about the significance and impact of the Irish suffragists it would seem clear that the Antis were of very little importance (despite the fact that the Irish suffragists made little direct headway). Their performance in general would confirm what Brian Harrison said with regard to the English Antis that they were inferior in their propaganda techniques and competed half-heartedly with their opponents.[129] Though the sentiments of the Antis were appreciated in wider Irish society as is evident throughout this book, the Antis themselves held little appeal. They represented the élite and were definitely part of the Anglo-Irish establishment.

The above-described reaction to Irish suffragists, by a wide variety of groups, who differed socially, intellectually and economically, is clearly a confirmation that, whatever the outcome of their actions, they were an important force in early twentieth-century Ireland. It is irrelevant whether or not the reaction was negative or positive—what is important is that there existed a movement in Irish society which forced a large number of people to reinforce or reconsider their ideas of women's role in that society. As the next chapter will show, a powerful and influential group in that society, the clergymen, were equally vocal in their reactions.

Notes

1. H. G. Wells, *Ann Veronica* (Fisher Unwin, London, 1909). When this book was published its portrayal of a young "new woman" who for a

while challenged the mores of her society created a storm in England.
2. R. M. Fox, *Rebel Irishwomen* (Talbot Press, Dublin, 1935), chapter on Helena Moloney, p. 65.
3. *Irishwomen's Suffrage Federation Report* 1911–1912, p. 4.
4. Susan Day, *The Amazing Philanthropists* (Sidgwick and Jackson Ltd, London, 1916).
5. *IC*, September 14, 1912, p. 129.
6. Leah Levenson, *With Wooden Sword* (Gill and Macmillan, Dublin, 1983), p. 105.
7. *Ibid.*
8. Henke and Unkeless (eds), *Women in Joyce* (Harvester Press, Brighton, 1982).
9. Florence L. Walzi, "Dubliners: Women in Irish Society", in *Ibid*, p. 53.
10. C. P. Curran, *Under the Receding Wave* (Gill and Macmillan, Dublin, 1970), Mary Colum, *Life and Dream* (Macmillan and Co., New York, 1947), Joseph Holloway, *Some Impressions of a Dublin Playgoer* (Dublin, 1910).
11. C. P. Curran, *op. cit.*
12. J. B. Lyons, *The Enigma of Tom Kettle—Irish Patriot, Essayist, Poet, British Soldier 1880–1916* (Glendale Press, Dublin, 1983).
13. Curran, *op. cit.*, p. 196.
14. Joseph Holloway, *op. cit.*
15. Cousins, *We Two Together* (Ganesh, Madras, 1950), p. 37.
16. Bonnie Kime Scott, "Emma Clery in *Stephen Hero*", in Henke, *Joyce and Women, op. cit.* See also Bonnie Kime Scott, *Joyce and Feminism* (Harvester Press, Brighton, 1984). Also Bonnie Kime Scott, *James Joyce* (Harvester Press, Brighton, 1987).
17. Cousins, *op. cit.*, p. 216.
18. *Ibid.*
19. Rodelle Weintraub (ed.), *Fabian Feminist* (Pennsylvania State University Press, 1984), p. 85.
20. *Ibid*, p. 156.
21. Reprinted in *Ibid*, pp. 248–50, pp. 255–9.
22. Although *Mrs Warren's Profession* was written in 1894 it could not get a licence for performance until 1925.
23. George Bernard Shaw, "The Unmentionable Case for Women's Suffrage", Fawcett Library Suffrage Box S–Z 396.113 taken from the *Englishwoman*, pp. 112–13, undated.
24. Weintraub, *op. cit.*, p. 10.
25. Shaw, "The Unmentionable Case", *op. cit.*
26. Suffrage Box 89, Fawcett Library.
27. Sir Almroth Wright, *An Unexpurgated Case Against Women's Suffrage* (London, 1912).
28. George Bernard Shaw, *Sir Almroth Wright's Case Against Women's Suffrage Answered by George Bernard Shaw* (Sheridan Prints, Cork, 1912).
29. Weintraub, *op. cit.*

30. Michael O'Neill, "Some Shavian Links with Dublin as Recorded in the *Holloway Diaries*", *The Shaw Review*, Vol. 11, No. 8, March 1959, pp. 2–7.
31. SSP Ms 22,683.
32. Cousins, *op. cit.*, p. 134.
33. *VFW*, Oct. 14, 1910.
34. Quoted in *VFW*, July 26, 1912.
35. Ms 22,683.
36. Ms 24,100 19, October 1918.
37. Cousins, *op. cit.*, p. 65.
38. George Russell, "Ideals of the New Rural Society" in *United Irishwomen, Their Place, Work and Ideal*, Sir Horace Plunkett, ed. (Maunsel, Dublin, 1911), pp. 44–5.
39. Cousins, p. 172.
40. R. M. Fox, *Louie Bennett, Her Life and Times* (Talbot Press, Dublin, 1957).
41. See Chapter 4.
42. Patricia Rimo, "Mollie Colum and her Circle", *Irish Literary Supplement*, Fall 1985, pp. 26–7.
43. Mary Colum, *op. cit.*
44. Cousins, *op. cit.*, p. 160.
45. *Ibid*, p. 121.
46. *VFW*, October 14, 1910.
47. Olive Banks, *Becoming a Feminist* (Harvester Press, Brighton, 1987), pp. 17–18.
48. Rosemary Cullen Owens, *Smashing Times* (Attic Press, Dublin, 1984).
49. Both had offices in the Antient Concert Rooms in Dublin.
50. *VFW*, May 13, 1910, p. 542.
51. Cullen Owens, *op. cit.* p. 77.
52. *The Vote*, May 1, 1914, p. 26.
53. *Ibid*, April 28, 1911.
54. Banks, *op. cit.* p. 111.
55. *Cork Constitution*, May 25, 1912, p. 5.
56. Cousins, *op. cit.* p. 213. See also Cullen Owens, *op. cit.* p. 61.
57. Berresford Ellis, P., *James Connolly: Select Writings* (Penguin, Harmondsworth, 1973), p. 196.
58. James Connolly, *Reconquest of Ireland* (Dublin, 1915), Chapter on women.
59. *VFW*, May 22, 1914, p. 523.
60. Ruth Dudley Edwards, *James Connolly* (Gill and Macmillan, Dublin, 1981), p. 85.
61. Fox, *Bennett, op. cit.*, p. 44.
62. *Ibid*, p. 49.
63. Helena Moloney, "James Connolly and Women", *Dublin Labour Year Book* (Dublin, 1930).
64. *VFW*, May 22, 1914, p. 523.
65. See Chapter 7.
66. Brian Harrison, *Separate Spheres: Opposition to Women's Suffrage 1867–1928* (London, 1978) p. 85.

67. Boxer and Quartet, *Socialist Women* (Elsevier, New York, 1978).
68. Banks, *op. cit.* p. 140.
69. *IC*, January 10, 1914.
70. *IC*, January 10, 1914.
71. *IC*, June 15, 1912, p. 28.
72. *Ibid.*
73. *Cork Constitution*, April, 1912, p. 4.
74. *Ibid*, May 17, 1912, p. 8.
75. *IC* September 14, 1912, p. 129.
76. *Ibid.*
77. *IC*, December 20, 1913, p. 250.
78. *IC*, June 1, 1912, p. 9.
79. Day, *Amazing Philanthropists*, p. 235.
80. *IC*, May 25, 1912, p. 1.
81. *Ibid*, May 25, 1913, p. 48.
82. *Ibid*, May 25, 1913, p. 418.
83. *IC*, June 29, 1912, p. 48.
84. *Irishwomen's Suffrage Federation Report, First Annual Report 1911–1912*, p. 10.
85. *IC*, September 14, 1912, p. 130.
86. *Ibid.*
87. Day, *VFW*, April 14, p. 462.
88. *IC*, June 29, 1912, p. 47.
89. *IC*, May 17, 1913.
90. *IC*, July 11, 1914, p. 13.
91. *Ibid*, July 4, 1914, p. 51.
92. *Ibid*, June 15, 1912, p. 31.
93. *IC*, November 1, 1913, p. 192.
94. *The Vote*, December 19, 1913, p. 128.
95. *IC*, December 30, 1912, p. 255.
96. *VFW*, October 7, 1910, quotes *Cork Constitution*.
97. SSP April 1914, Ms 22,271.
98. Cousins, p. 167.
99. *Ibid*, p. 215.
100. *Ibid*, pp. 187–8.
101. Levenson, *op. cit.*, *passim*.
102. *Freeman's Journal*, April 1, 1912, p. 7.
103. *Cork Constitution*, May 15, 1912, p. 4.
104. *Amazing Philanthropists*.
105. *The Vote*, December, 1913, p. 85.
106. Tom Garvin, *The Evolution of Irish Nationalist Politics* (Gill and Macmillan, Dublin, 1981).
107. *VFW*, July 26, 1912.
108. *IC*, July 27, 1912.
109. C. P. Curran, *op. cit*, p. 177.
110. *VFW*, November 3, 1911, p. 68.
111. Frank Sheehy Skeffington, "The Prodigal Daughter", pamphlet reprinted from *Irish Citizen*, June 1915, NLI LO p. 74.

112. Tom Garvin, *op. cit.*, p. 98.
113. *Ibid.*
114. Margaret Ward, *Unmanageable Revolutionaries* (Brandon Press, Kerry, 1983), p. 92.
115. Brian Harrison, *op. cit.* p. 151.
116. See Chapter 6.
117. Harrison, *op. cit.*
118. *Anti Suffrage Review*, December 1912, p. 283.
119. *Ibid*, September 1912.
120. *Ibid*, February 1912.
121. *Ibid*, April 1914, p. 10.
122. *Irish Times*, January 11, 1910, p. 10.
123. *Ibid*, January 14, 1910.
124. *Anti Suffrage Review*, February 1911, p. 33.
125. *IC*, September 14, 1912, p. 129.
126. *IC*, September 14, 1912, p. 131.
127. *IC*, October 1912, p. 153.
128. *IC*, July 4, 1914, p. 50.
129. Harrison, *op. cit.* p. 118.

· 6 ·

"The Soul of Women's Suffrage"

As with many other social and political movements in early twentieth-century Ireland the women's suffrage movement did not and could not operate independently of the church's influence, approval or disapproval. Indeed Roman Catholic, Church of Ireland (Anglican), Methodist, Unitarian, Presbyterian and Quaker representatives all had some opinion to express on the Irish suffragists. These opinions ranged from hostile disapproval to rather benevolent support. However, concern among churchmen about the lives of Irish women was not a phenomenon peculiar to the Edwardian age. Throughout the nineteenth century the churches, particularly the Catholic Church, were conscious of and made declarations on the role of women in Irish society.

After the famine (1845–9) fewer and later marriages resulted in large numbers of single women in Ireland. The only opportunities available to the majority of these was celibate layhood, convent life or emigration. It has been argued that in Catholic dominated Ireland the convent system provided a safety valve for many women. It gave them an education and a career structure, served as a refuge from the inequalities of a male world and provided them with a respectable role in a society which was losing much of its male population to emigration. As one article on nuns in Ireland points out, by the end of the nineteenth century they had become the largest grouping, among Catholic women, in the census's category 'professional class'. Indeed the number of nuns in Ireland increased dramatically in the second half of the nineteenth century. Ironically enough, considering their secondary role, the number of nuns, at over 8000, was more than double the number of priests in Ireland.[1] However the number of nuns in the country helped perpetuate the church's idea that women should emulate the Virgin Mary.[2] Whether in the convent or in the home, women were guided by the clergy and with few exceptions they submitted to that guidance. According to one study of Irish nuns "The position of nuns in the church echoed the position of women in the home—essential but subordinate."[3]

Things changed in the late nineteenth century. The admittance of women into university, their advent into local politics with the Local Government Act of 1895 and the experience gained by women in the Ladies Land League all contributed to their gradual politicisation. Educated, political women were not necessarily going to be in awe of barely educated clergymen.

The proliferation of suffrage movements in the early twentieth century obliged Irish churches to reconsider or reinforce their beliefs on women's role in society. It was quite impossible for the clergy to ignore either the growing tide of women's meetings throughout the country or the publication of *The Irish Citizen*, which openly challenged their authority. They could not stand by while militants literally attacked their churches nor could they remain aloof while death lingered over the hungerstrikers in search of political status. They did not remain oblivious to women becoming more articulate, seeking further education, running meetings, going to demonstrations and in general questioning their traditional role. Increasingly the pulpit became a platform for the clergy's observations of the movement, its attendant lifestyles and overall effects on society.

This chapter is concerned with the dilemma faced by the churches (with an emphasis on the reaction of the Anglican[4] and Roman Catholic clergy) in Ireland when it became imperative to respond to the women's suffrage movements. It will survey their various reactions and question their motives. The statements made by the opponents and the fears behind them will be examined. Likewise the thoughts, beliefs and writings of the clergy who supported women's suffrage will be investigated. Here, too, motives will be under examination and the question will be posed whether or not they were truly feminist. It will be suggested that the views of womanhood, and its future, held by both the opponents and proponents of women's suffrage were basically the same. The claims of the author of *The Feminists*, Richard Evans, that feminism in Catholic countries was anti-clerical, weak and overwhelmingly Protestant, and that the Roman Catholic Church was "the most persistent and intractable of their enemies" will be tested against the Irish situation.[5]

The relationship between the churches and the suffragists was a two-way one. Many suffragists had very decided views on religion which did not conform with the views of the established churches in Ireland. There were those in the suffrage movement who rejected traditional or orthodox religion. This was not surprising considering they had already abandoned the traditional views on womanhood and it was widely held by suffragists in many countries that the church was the chief agent in women's suppression.[6] Some had abandoned religion altogether like Hanna Sheehy Skeffington[7] who believed "religion had a narrowing influence in Ireland."[8] She and her husband, unusually for that time in Ireland, decided not to have their son, Owen, baptised.[9] Others like the Cousinses[10] and Mrs Purser[11] were attracted to theosophy and the mysticism of the East.

Margaret Cousins on a number of occasions acted as a medium at seances.[12] She admitted that "I was not myself an enthusiastic church-goer."[13] While listening to, and heckling, a speech given by the Bishop of Liverpool she came to the conclusion "that the cause of womanhood was nothing to the established church, and that all organised religion would have to be dealt with, and not only on the matter of votes for women."[14] Another suffragist who acted as a medium, claimed to be psychic and wrote extensively on the subject was Cork suffragist, Geraldine Cummins.[15] James Cousins admitted "I was myself a bit of an atheist". At the same time he was convinced of the validity of reincarnation. The Cousinses were largely responsible for founding the Irish Theosophical Society.[16]

There appears to have been a reluctance by both church and state to accept the non-orthodox nature of these women's religious beliefs. When Hanna Sheehy Skeffington was in prison she was registered a Roman Catholic though declaring herself a pagan.[17] Margaret Cousins, a spiritualist and theosophist (and later founder of the Church of the New Ideal), found herself with a self-appointed Methodist pastor during her hunger strike in 1912.[18]

However, there were those in Ireland who very much wished to pursue their desire for suffrage within a religious framework.[19] Instead of pulling against their church in this matter they wished to obtain its patronage and blessing. Thus, in Ireland there was established a branch of the British Church League for Women's Suffrage for Anglican women. The Irish Catholic Women's Suffrage Society was later founded for Catholic women. Both of these had their own journals. The Irish branch of the CLWS was established in April 1913 when the English founder, the Rev. Hinscliff, came to visit Dublin. It was financially strong enough by June to be able to send a delegate to the International Congress at Budapest.[20] The Church League newspaper which had the same name as the organisation had a special Irish section.

The Irish Catholic Women's Suffrage Society was founded in 1915 during the war. It was an independent organisation but did have contact with the English suffragists. The women involved in its establishment were concerned that an organisation appealing specifically to Catholic women was necessary, for many Catholic women had not yet come forward—no doubt inhibited by declarations of their church and perhaps by the criticisms of the church emanating from suffrage circles. Two women involved in establishing it, however, were already convinced suffragists and members of the Irish Women's Franchise League. These were Mrs Stephen Gwynn and Prof. Mary Hayden. Mary Hayden had been instrumental in the founding of the Irish Women's Graduate Association in 1902 and had been appointed Professor of Irish History in 1908.[21] She also was an early women's history enthusiast and wrote about women in medieval Ireland.[22] Mary Hayden felt that there was a need to organise Catholic women as Catholics to fight for suffrage.[23]

A member of the Society, Catherine Mahon, believed that

the Catholic Women's Suffrage Society was the one society that "could win Catholic Irishmen, clerical and lay, to the support of Irishwomen in their demand for the franchise".[24] The movement was non-militant and aimed at involving working women. "In no country is there such devotion to the Mother of God as in Ireland. We hope to enlist Irishwomen to work for her honour, and helped by her good counsel, to establish in Ireland social conditions worthy of a Christian land."[25] Catholic women referred back to the sixth century saint Bridgid as the patroness of their movement[26] and on occasions articles appeared in the *Catholic Suffragist* on the saint.[27] They claimed that the movement would have had the approval of the late Pope Leo XIII who had urged Catholics to take an initiative in all true social reform.[28] Within four months of its formation it had seventy members. It had its own colours and published reports of its proceedings, which were written by Mrs Gwynn, in the journal of the English Catholic suffragists *The Catholic Suffragist*.

Even though these Catholic women wished to agitate for the vote within the sphere of their church it did not necessarily mean that the church automatically approved of their organisation or any other suffrage organisations. When the English Catholic suffragists approached the Archbishop of Westminster, later to become Cardinal Bourne, he replied "the matter of it is one on which the archbishop is precluded by his position from expressing any official position", which in effect said they could proceed but they were not that popular. Indeed the English Catholic suffragists felt that they were victims of a whispering campaign and at one point reports reached Rome that they were publishing immoral literature—reports that the suffragists demolished with ease.[29]

The Catholic Church in Ireland, as elsewhere, did not operate alone and had to take note of directions coming from Rome. Since the reign of Cardinal Cullen in the nineteenth century the ultramontanist movement had reached Ireland and utterings from the papal office had much more impact than before. Although Pope Pius X supported women's education he reputedly told an Austrian feminist in 1906 "Women electors, women deputies? Oh, no! . . . Women in Parliaments! That is all we need! The men have already caused enough confusion there!" /

In a papal audience with French politicians in 1909 he stated that it was an error for women to seek the same rights as men. This statement was widely reported and apparently did much damage to the French suffrage movement.[30]

There were those both within the English and Irish Catholic hierarchy who felt that the Church had done more than any other institution to raise the status of women: "to inculcate reverence for them and to give due honour and scope to those among them who possessed outstanding qualities as in the often quoted cases of St Hilda of Whitby, St Teresa of Avila and St Catherine of Sienna."[31]

An article appeared in the *Irish Ecclesiastical Record* which attempted to state the Catholic Church's position as regards women's suffrage in relation to the Church's history and teaching. A few points made in this article should be considered. Its author, David Barry, STL, began by claiming that the Catholic Church "had done so much to emancipate woman, to raise her status, and to dignify and enoble her position". It had done this by "emphasising the sublime function of one woman as mother of God, by the number of women placed on her calendar of saints, and by the vigilance and care that she lavished on the female communities that devoted themselves to God." He claimed that the Church was "the pioneer and will ever be the mainstay of the rights of women". He was expressing the old pedestal idea of womanhood. "On Catholic principles, at any rate, it is not explicitly defined that woman has the right to a living wage, or the duty of supporting herself at all. She is supposed to be shielded by her male relatives from most of the hardships and disabilities of citizenhood. As a wife, the efficient discharge of her duties under the fourth commandment renders it impossible for her to make her own way in the community, and hence there is no reason why she should have any direct part in the polity of the State." He concluded the article by saying "it would appear, then, that Catholic principles give no countenance to the movement for extending the franchise to women; not because they are inferior to men, for they are recognised as having peculiar aptitudes and endowments, that men do not possess, but because the movement is a retrograde one, tending to supplant their position of real superiority by one of nominal equality."[32] This reflects the Ruskinite view prevalent in the latter half of the nineteenth century that women were too 'good' to have the vote.

While many churchmen agreed with Fr. Barry they were at variance as to what caused this new unrest among women. Certain signs such as women attending boxing matches and smoking in private and public were seen as indications of women's rush towards downfall. Indeed the whole issue of women smoking was the subject of many letters to the *Irish Catholic*. To some it was an activity only pursued by English girls and not something to be undertaken by good, nationalist, Irish Catholic girls.[33] However, education for women, especially of the more academic type, was seen by some as responsible for women's discontent with their lot. Such an opinion was not entirely unfounded since the first generation of women graduates provided a number of suffragists. If women were less educated, or educated merely in home management, it was argued that there would no longer be a conflict of loyalties. Margaret MacCurtain has pointed out that the Church itself had a role to play in turning out the type of women it wanted in its own schools in the nineteenth century: "In the older schools founded in the 1830s and 1840s cultural and moral instruction was accompanied by the teaching of music, needlework, art and elocution in a curriculum that was not part of the state system. The task of turning young girls into young ladies was effectively accomplished through the teaching of Christian values and social aptitudes."[34]

Domestic training or what was called technical education for women, was according to the *Irish Catholic* essential for a successful marriage. It complained that "the value of technical education for girls is not sufficiently appreciated" and added if more girls concentrated upon this "there would be better wives and mothers, and, therefore, happier homes than there are."[35] A slightly less dramatic opinion was offered by the author of an article which appeared in the *Church of Ireland Gazette*. Referring to education the Rev. Edward John Harvey wrote ". . . we believe the more [education] healthy girls receive in art, literature and science the better, so long as they are trained at the same time in the domestic duties."[36]

However the reactionary Bishop O'Dwyer of Limerick, whose opinions were frequently quoted in favourable terms by the *Anti Suffrage Review*,[37] was not interested in making concessions. In a Confirmation sermon in May 1912 he said he believed the sexes should be educated separately.[38] Earlier that year he had expressed a worry about the growing assertiveness amongst girls at school:

> Even in our Catholic schools . . . one can perceive a spirit of publicity, a craving for notoriety, which is entirely new amongst us. For myself I am convinced that the annual publication of children's names and sometimes even of their photographs must, on educational grounds be injurious, and be fatal in the long run, to true scholarship and hard work, both for boys and girls, but for girls I regard it as the first step towards breaking down the delicacy and modesty which is their most precious possession.

Moreover he asserted, the problem was not confined to the primary and secondary sphere of education. The entrance of women into the universities produced further dilemmas. O'Dwyer regretted that no distinctions were made between women and their male colleagues "in their studies or social conditions". They were "thrown into large towns to rough it as best they can". Referring to the special colleges for women in England he observed that it was "an unpleasant commentary" that there were none in Ireland.[39] Still, as is evident from Mary Colum's account of hostels run for female students in Dublin by different orders of nuns, young women were well protected and segregated despite the fact that they may have attended similar lectures as the men.[40]

As early as 1902 in the compilation of the *Robinson Report* on women's higher education in Ireland O'Dwyer was asked for his opinions. He had no comprehensive proposals as to how a system that would meet with his approval could be set up. He had nothing to say about the position of women under any scheme except that "Some provision must be made, I have not thought that out." He admitted, "On the question of women I cannot give you any answer. They are admitted to degrees now. They must be admitted, but how that would be done, what relationship they would stand in—as to collegiate life and other things—to the new university I have not thought."[41]

Such ecclesiastical views that women should not receive the same higher education as men were not peculiar to O'Dwyer, but were further highlighted in the University of Dublin case which led to the resignation of Frank Sheehy Skeffington. While a registrar in University College Dublin Skeffington drafted a document which was circulated by the Women's Graduate Association. The document asked for women to be admitted on the same grounds as men. It pointed out that women who attended Trinity College Dublin could attend all lectures in Arts and Medicine as well as sit the examinations and take the degrees but Irish Catholics were barred from attending both Trinity and the Queens Colleges and had restrictions imposed on them in the Catholic University College Dublin. It urged that in continuance "of the policy initiated in 1899 by the admission of women to certain courses of lectures, steps should immediately be taken to admit women to all courses of lectures given in University College in preparation for the examinations."[42] Father William Delaney, president of the University, pointed out to Skeffington that as an officer of the college he really did not have the right to advocate opposition policy. Skeffington resigned in order to be free to express his opinion in the future.

In the years before and during the war there was such a feeling of bewilderment among the clergy with regard to women's actions and changing personality that any signs of hope for traditionalists were gratefully received. The reviewer of Mrs William O'Brien's book on religious women praised its appearance "at a time when the excessive zeal of a comparatively few unfeminine females is bringing discredit on the name of woman . . .". He wrote that the subjects of Mrs O'Brien's book accomplished splendid things "without any lowering of standards of conduct which, after all, made the difference between the true woman and the howling viragos".[43]

"Howling viragos" were not the only problem. Attention was drawn to false "female prophets".[44] These were the leaders

behind the organised suffrage movements. It was feared that
unless they and their followers were stopped traditional family
life was doomed. *The Irish Catholic* quoted a speech by Father
Day, on feminism, given in Manchester, in which he declared
". . . Woman is a member of the household not the world.
Feminism would fling her into the mire of degradation."[45]

This theme appears in the Lenten pastorals of Catholic
Bishops in 1912 and 1913. The *Catholic Bulletin* noted in
March 1912 that "Christian marriage, the responsibilities of
parents, the sphere of woman, education and kindred matters
received prominence from the Bishops of Derry, Clogher,
Down and Connor, Meath, Ross, Ardfert and Aghadoe."
The Bishop of Clonfert said in his pastoral

> A well regulated family is a small state; the family is in fact the model
> of the state. It is the family not the state, which is the unit of social
> life. In this little state the father is the head and the ruler. Though a
> wife sometimes has more brains and gifts of administration than her
> husband, yet she must recognise his position as head of the family . . .
> Subordinate to her husband, the wife should reign as queen in her
> home. Though woman is, in a sense, inferior to man, still her mission
> in life is not less noble than his . . .[46]

O'Dwyer of Limerick feared that the movement for women's
franchise had yet even more potential for doing harm than
the movement for equal education. In his pastoral letter of
1912 he pointed out that "there has been for some years a
movement to draw women from their homes and to engage
them in occupations which an older generation thought
entirely unsuited to them." He echoed an opinion voiced by
many anti-suffragists in Britain and elsewhere when he said
he had no objections to women being involved "in local
affairs such as workhouse administration" but he was against
their claim for the Parliamentary suffrage and to "sit equally
with men".[47] Public opinion in Ireland did not demand it
and unless people took care "the women of Ireland will be
placed in a position from which instinct and habits of thought
would shirk." He was against their participation in politics
because it would disrupt the domestic sphere. "A man comes
home at present from political turmoil and finds calm and
quietness which would be impossible if his wife was an active

participator in the same contest . . . ." He could hardly contemplate the thought of husband and wife taking opposite sides. He concluded that it must be the duty of Irishmen ". . . to stand at the threshold of their homes and keep them inviolate from such influences".[48] Three days after the *Irish Times* published O'Dwyer's observations a letter appeared in the newspaper from Margaret Cousins

> The whole of Dr O'Dwyer's diatribe against votes for women is based upon misrepresentation not facts. Those who will get the vote under our demands are women who have no men to represent them—widows and women who have to work for a living—and against these women getting the vote the Bishop makes no case . . . the Bishop is again wrong when he says there is no demand for it here. It should have come to his knowledge that the two most important representative bodies in his diocese, the Limerick County Council and the Limerick Corporation, have passed resolutions in favour of women's suffrage, and in Limerick city there are strong and active branches of three suffrage societies. Belief in the justice and commonsense of votes for qualified women has been expressed similarly all over Ireland, and we are cheered by hearing from the Bishop that the movement is so near to victory. If politics are so bad and so corrupt as the Bishops think them, then the sooner the women who have the public welfare at heart get an entry to them and start a spring cleaning the better.[49]

Neither O'Dwyer or any other of the anti-suffragist bishops took any notice of Cousins and would more than likely have answered that single women should do as their priests told them, and women were benefiting public welfare by their influence through the home.

A year later, in his pastoral letter, the Most Rev. Dr Mangan declared "To my way of thinking at any rate, instead of progress there is a decided decadence amongst the womanhood of our country from the old customs which were more in harmony with our circumstances and with the picture of the brave woman painted for us in the Scriptures (Proverbs xxxi. 10)."[50]

The Rev. McGrath chose Augustine's *Confessions* rather than the scriptures in his recommended text for wayward women. Indeed, in a sermon in May 1914, which was celebrating the festival of St Monica he advised his female congregation to emulate Augustine's mother, Monica. She had been the "simple instrument" which enabled the conversion of the "great Augustine". McGrath believed and probably correctly, that the "feminist movement created a tendency to withdraw woman from the home and plunge her into the glare and light of the world." Furthermore the movement was the "offspring of materialism". The Catholic Church could have no sympathy with such a movement. The home was "woman's rightful sphere". She should follow the example of St Monica who "had a pagan and rough husband and a wayward boy to contend with. Her home was set against her, yet by patience, by prayer she conquered all."[51] Clearly McGrath was giving a blessing to the long suffering Irish mother.

Fr. Downings S.J. of Galway summed up the feelings of a number of his colleagues when he asserted, on a visit to Dublin, "since the world began down to the present day woman has one grand mission to fulfil—to influence men for the good."[52] However his critics in the *Irish Citizen* were rather cynical about the influence his speech to the Children of Mary's Sodality would have: ". . . one thought will comfort suffragists that in the past it was nearly always dying or lost causes that sought sanctuary in the church."[53]

However nobody could mistake the vitality of the movement after 1910 when branches were being established all over the country. The movement received renewed impetus with the failure of various women's amendments to the Home Rule Bill between 1912 and 1914 and the defeat of a Women's Suffrage Bill.[54] As militancy became a feature of the suffrage movement in Ireland suffragists drew increased condemnation from the churches which was explained by Hanna Sheehy Skeffington thus: "the Church on the whole were opposed to the militant movement primarily because the revolt of women for their own emancipation is always frowned upon by organised males and partly because the Church is opposed to any change."[55] While many suffragists shied away from militancy and even condemned it openly in their annual reports, in the press and at public meetings the IWFL vigorously pursued it. On occasions members of the militant Pankhurst society, the WSPU, came to Ireland and clashed with the law. The much publicised incident of the English suffragettes Leigh and Evans did nothing to win over the clergy. They had followed Asquith on his visit to Ireland in 1912 and "sought to advance the cause of female suffrage by an attempt at murder and an effort to set fire to a place of public entertainment."[56]

Thus interpreting an incident where a missile was thrown and a match was struck in the Theatre Royal, the *Irish Catholic* supported Mr Justice Madden's sentence of five years penal servitude and declared "Happily no Irish women were involved." This sentence aroused widespread opposition and resulted in a number of petitions arriving at Dublin Castle. Despite the fact that the petitions contained the signatures of some English clergy, including the Bishop of Lincoln,[57] the *Irish Catholic* was adamant in its support of Madden. It did concede that "we, nevertheless, believe that the public of this country will feel a sense of relief when the wretched termagants now in penal servitude can be released to bear no other punishment than that inflicted by their own sense of shame and dishonour they have brought upon themselves."[58]

Militants, therefore, were seen as "acting contrary to God's law".[59] They were taking part in something which had been "invented by Satan".[60] *The Church of Ireland Gazette* noted that "while on the one hand they appeal to our moral sense for their cause on the other they outrage it with their militancy."[61] Outrage was indeed the emotion when the "criminal wing of the suffragette party had extended their nefarious campaign against churches in Ireland."[62] *The Church of Ireland Gazette* reported that a "vile attempt" to burn down Ballylession Church near Belfast had "been foiled by the timely arrival of the sexton". It added:

> Some people might find it impossible to understand the mental process of the perpetrators of these horrible outrages. Such dangerous anarchy is one of the ominous features of the present orgy. As yet no adequate measures are taken to inflict punishment deserved by these enemies of society or to protect the community.[63]

It is not surprising that members of the church disliked or even deplored violence. Even committed supporters of women's suffrage objected to any methods other than peaceful persuasion. This becomes clear in an article by the London correspondent of the *Irish Catholic* with regards to attacks on church property in England. In a report on the invasion of suffragists into Westminster Cathedral and Brompton Oratory in the summer of 1914 he expressed the hope that "they were merely misguided in their enthusiasm for the cause, which unfortunately, is suffering so much and is receiving such a setback owing to the militant tactics of the few whose actions show discredit when large numbers of distinguished and cultured women have the cause of women's suffrage at heart."[64] The Church League for Women's Suffrage and its leader the Bishop of London were condemned for failing to reprimand the suffragists involved in the church skirmishes. Readers of the *Church of Ireland Gazette* could not accept the Church League's desire to remain neutral by silence. It was insinuated that silence indicated support.[65]

Opposition to militancy was a point in common between the opponents and supporters of women's suffrage within the churches. However, it seemed to be the only point. One contributor to the *Irish Citizen* felt that the opponents were more vocal than the supporters of women's suffrage within the church. In an article on "The Clergy and Woman Suffrage" K. L. MacCarthy asked why were the clergy so quiet on suffrage since "they were always involving themselves in politics" and spoke on every issue "from landlordism to socialism". Certainly she had heard "suffragists denounced from the pulpit and called misguided, unwomanly creatures, lost to all sense of decency . . ." but, she argued, "there are many clergy in sympathy with the movement yet they remain silent."[66] This was not entirely true, clergy from different denominations spoke out publicly in favour of women's suffrage. A number of Irish clergy lectured on the topic, English and American clergy visited to show their approval of the cause in Ireland. Suffragist and non-suffragist papers, English and Irish, quoted supporters in the Irish churches. Indeed, another contributor to the *Irish Citizen*, a certain Miss Gladys, delighted in submitting lists of clergymen who were on the 'right side' to the paper.[67] In an article on 'Woman's Suffrage in Ireland' in the *Catholic Suffragist* Eily Esmonde wrote that he had asked a Dublin priest his opinion on "the vexed question of the suffrage".

The emphasis of his reply, I confess, almost surprised me, for we suffragists grow accustomed to discouragement. There was no mistaking his desire for the reform. "Morally, socially, from every point of view, women's influence is for every good, and how can it be exercised more potently than at the polling booths? Undoubtedly it is to be desired."[68]

The clergy themselves took up pen in support of the issue. A typical example was the Rev. O'Hannay who was more popularly known under his writing alias of George Birmingham. Birmingham sat on suffrage platforms, made speeches, and wrote to the press on behalf of the women.[69] His plays were a meeting place for suffragists and others. Indeed Hanna Sheehy Skeffington first saw Constance Markievicz acting as Eleanor in Birmingham's comedy *Eleanor's Enterprise*.[70] He told a meeting of the Conservative and Unionist Women's Franchise Association in February 1910 that he was a comparatively recent convert to women's suffrage. He had been "convinced that there must be sound arguments against women's suffrage, but when he examined them they actually turned him round the other way—they were so extraordinarily weak."[71] He wrote to the *Irish Citizen* in June 1912 that "The demand that the Parliamentary franchise should be based on the Local Government Register, and shall include women qualified to vote under the latter, seems to me most moderate."[72] He admitted he disliked violence but felt that in the last resort it was the only thing that worked. He abhorred the authorities' methods of dealing with the militancy and declared that the "Cat and Mouse Act strikes me as cruel and cruelty is as we know . . . the last resort of feeble men in a panic."[73]

Another Anglican "Sheebna the Scribe", had a weekly column in the *Church of Ireland Gazette*. He devoted a full article to questioning the arguments of those opposed to granting women the franchise. He believed "our personal support should be given to the women who are striving for enfranchisement." However, he too felt nothing could be gained by militancy and that "the public was rightly alienated by violence." He was of the opinion that women could no longer justifiably be denied their rights. "The advance of women as workers, as participants in the commercial and public life of the country, renders it more than ever necessary that she (sic) should be able to have a part in fashioning the legislation that affect her."[74]

In the *Irish Review*, there appeared an eccentric article by a Fr. Clery. It was based on a lecture he gave in 1911 called 'The Religious Aspect of Women's Suffrage'. He did not hold the view that women would be morally damaged by being involved in the voting process. After all "As to the moral effects of political practices other than voting, no question of course at present arises, since from the Ladies Land League to the Primrose League women have at all times been encouraged to indulge in political practices of all kinds, voting excepted." He approved of women's suffrage but not adult suffrage. He, like others, saw the former as a means of preventing the latter.[75]

In the *Cross*, the magazine of the Passionist Fathers, a letter from Father Raymond Saunders C.P. stated that there can be no doubt "that woman has a right to the franchise and in the present state of society we cannot see how it can be withheld without grave injustice."[76] At a meeting in Dublin in November 1911 the Rev. Father O'Ryan C.C. said he believed that every woman ought to have the vote.[77] He was echoed by the Rev. M. M. O'Kane who declared in a pamphlet published in 1913 "Women's franchise is recognised by the Church."[78]

A reviewer in the *Church of Ireland Gazette* wrote that if the general public desired to have a "sober and well balanced view of what the movement is, what it has accomplished and what it hopes to effect" he recommended they should read Zoë Fairfield's *Some Aspects of the Women's Movement*. They should also take note of the appendix which was made up of statements "prepared by responsible members of each of the denominations involved".[79]

Besides being prominent in print the clergy were also highly visible on suffrage platforms. The Rev. Barbor, 'a keen suffragist', took the chair at the first meeting in Castledermot.[80] The *Anti Suffrage Review* reported in April 1914 that the Rev. Carolin took part in a woman's suffrage debate in Rathmines representing the suffrage side.[81] The Rev. R. M. Gwynn gave a talk to the Irishwomen's Suffrage Federation on 'Industrial Law and Women' and the Rev. F.

Greer chaired a discussion on women's suffrage.[82] In an obituary to the Rev. Dean O'Brien of Limerick it was recalled "he had always been a supporter of women's suffrage. He presided over our first meeting in Synod week last year and joined our league . . .".[83]

Visiting clergy who were supporters of the movement came to speak to gatherings of Irish suffragists. The English secretary for the Church League for Women's Suffrage toured Ireland in October 1912. The League's newspaper reported that it was a complete success ". . . Mr Hinscliff preached in St George's, Belfast, . . . addressed a meeting of clergy, who gave an attentive and appreciative hearing to his statement of our cause."[84] One of the more notable visitors was the Rev. Hugh B. Chapman. He gave a talk to the Irish Women's Reform League in Aberdeen Hall in Dublin on the 'Soul of Women's Suffrage' which "sparkled with wise and witty observations". He told his listeners that "At the back of the desire for the vote lies this craving for freedom, and no words are needed to point out the barriers of prejudice, force and convention with which it has to contend." He begged them to "take your stand on the side of your poorer sisters, and preach this gospel of freedom throughout Ireland, until our politicians shall be compelled to grant your demands and the whole state shall be immensely improved."[85]

Colleagues of Fr. Chapman, and indeed many suffragists, believed that this "improvement to the state" could be brought about sooner with a little help from their deity. This was sought in prayer weeks, suffrage services and cathedral sermons. In effect, this put a seal on the relationship between the suffragists and their supporters in the church. Nevertheless there was some resistance among certain churchmen to allowing their churches to be used for these purposes. The Dean of St Patrick's (the Church of Ireland Cathedral) in Dublin provides such an example. He was presented with a petition by the suffragist doctor Kathleen Lynn which was signed by over 1,300 members of the Church of Ireland "among them 56 clergy". Despite this he refused to allow his church to be used for a service "which would pray for God's blessing and direction on the movement".[86] Perhaps he was influenced by the chairman of the Anti-Suffrage

League in Dublin, who happened to be his wife.[87] The
Irishwomen's Reform League annual report of 1913 reported
that plans were made to bring the question before the synod:
"However the Rev. Godfrey Day opened his church of
St Ann's to the Church League for Women's Suffrage."[88] In
the Church League's newspaper in November 1913 gratitude
was expressed to the Rev. Day who "has kindly offered his
church of St Ann's to us for the Celebration of the Holy
Communion. This is the first church in Ireland which has
opened its doors to us as a Church League."[89] And in January
1915 the Church League reported "on December 1st we
held our first cathedral service in Ireland with Corporate
Communion. Dean Hackett, assisted by two other clergy,
officiated and used Canon Scott Holland's service for 'the
Honour of Womanhood'." In the same issue it was reported
that in their half-yearly meeting on December 14th it was
"resolved that the bishops of Ireland be asked to authorise
that certain Suffrages for women (arranged by Canon Kernan)
and two prayers (adopted from our magazine) be used in the
Litany of Intercession for Soldiers and Sailors".[90]
    From the available evidence it would seem that services
specifically for women's suffrage were Anglican or Church of
Ireland rather than Roman Catholic. This could be explained
in a number of ways but it is clear that to some extent it
reflects the attitudes of different churches to women's
participation in church activity.[91] At this time there was
increased debate among Anglican and other Protestant
churches concerning the role of women in their church.
'Women as Deacons' was a frequent title of articles in church
newspapers.[92] The *Irish Catholic*, however, looked at this
debate rather contemptuously. When the Canton of Grisons
in Switzerland decided to allow all parishes in the Canton to
choose women 'clergymen' the *Irish Catholic* viewed this as
a "further light on the decadence of Protestantism."[93] Four
years later in 1916 it contained an article entitled 'The
Anglican Babel/Women as Parsons'. It quoted a resolution
which was passed at a meeting of 'The Council of the National
Mission' which declared "the aims and ideals of the woman's
movement . . . are in harmony with the teaching of Christ
and his Church as to equality of men and women in the sight

of God—equality in privilege, equality in calling—equality in opportunity of service." This was called "a somewhat ignorant and perverse pronouncement".[94] Two weeks later it conceded defensively "that in the Catholic Church women are frequently permitted to cite the rosary at gatherings of sodalities of their own sex . . .".[95] The following week it concluded ironically "There is of course, this to be said that seeing the manner of thing Anglicanism is, without validity of orders of succession—there can be no real heresy in claiming that a woman has as much right to appear in its pulpits as any mere man!"[96] Such statements once again reiterate the hypocritical view the Catholic church had with regard to women. On the one hand they were seen as special and superior but on the other they were not allowed to have any share in the running of the church—not to mind the state.

There were supporters of women's suffrage in both the main churches. However, the reasons behind their support need to be looked at in order to assess what it meant and how deep it went. How was this group different from the opponents? Did they have a different view of women's role in society in Ireland and of her future? Or did they too have an image of woman as the homemaker and man's helpmeet and decide to incorporate rather than reject her values into the system? Clearly the 'moral reform' issue, which one historian has noted as being an integral part of feminism in the nineteenth century, was carried over into the twentieth.[97] It becomes clear looking at a number of statements made by the clergy that they wished to see women enfranchised more from a belief in their 'goodness' than in their equality. Statements made in one study on women and the Irish Catholic church are certainly backed up by research done for this present volume:

> One could suggest that it was primarily as wife and mother that the Irish Catholic church drew on and utilised the support of the laywoman, and that the church in return propped up and glorified those roles . . . Within the home, however, she also appears as a moralising woman, going beyond passive acceptance of priestly direction to an active and highly effective reproduction of Catholic religious culture in her children, often in the face of her husband's indifference or remoteness. It was

in her role as moral and spiritual guide to her children, and to a lesser extent as moral influence on her husband, that she was the counterpart in the Catholic laity of the nineteenth century nun.[98]

The above observations are confirmed again and again in the statements of contemporary clergymen. For example, Fr. Clery believed if women had the vote they would introduce more religious feeling into the state. This was why, he said, the anti-clerical government in France was extremely anti woman's suffrage: "It is owing to the suppression of this influence in politics that the extraordinary phenomenon of the persecution of a national church becomes possible. The women pray and the men persecute."[99] The Rev. Hugh B. Chapman declared his agreement with the anti-suffragist Lord Salisbury when he said "woman is the soul of the state as she is of the home." However, Chapman asked why was it that men "do not welcome such a movement which would introduce more religion, more humaneness and more heart into what threatens to become a source of official tyranny."[100]

Women's work within the church was given certain recognition. The Mothers' Union "had the warm approval of the Bishop."[101] Referring to women's work in Sunday Schools and in parochial agencies, Sheebna the Scribe believed that it was imperative "the clergy should be in the forefront of the woman's struggle." After all, "they owe it to women, Christianity has done much for women but how much have women done for Christianity?"[102] If women got the vote perhaps they could perform the same valuable work for the state as they did for the parishes.

For similar reasons clergy were attracted to the suffrage movement because of its association with temperance.[103] In 1914 the *Citizen* reported that many priests were giving the Irish Women's Franchise League moral support because of its involvement with temperance.[104] The Rev. Hugh B. Chapman told his audience in Dublin "If your ambition is to cure the evil drink, you will boldly range yourself on its [suffrage movement's] side."[105] He was echoed by Sheebna the Scribe: "the curse of the drink traffic . . . would be more drastically dealt with if women had a share in legislation."[106] One writer to the *Irish Citizen* wrote "Ireland sober will be

Ireland free. Give her women the vote to attain the long desired ideal."[107] At a conference on temperance Elizabeth Mahon voiced the opinion that if women provided comfortable homes for their men they would not go out drinking.[108] In April 1915 suffrage societies in Ireland sent a petition to the government advocating the restriction of drink sales in Ireland.[109] However such a share in legislation was exactly what the brewing industry feared and when they saw the churches backing the women their worst fears were confirmed. The opposition of Guinness of Dublin[110] to women's suffrage was not peculiar in this; breweries in many countries feared the advent of women into the legislature.[111]

Likewise, clergy were attracted to the suffrage movement because of its opposition to prostitution. Fr. Clery paid tribute in the *Catholic Suffragist* in November 1915 to "the courage of women denouncing evil in the streets".[112] The opinion was voiced that should the suffragists eventually gain their place in the legislature "some of the vile traffickers in impurity would find more stern and effective methods applied."[113] Here too Hugh B. Chapman found cause to reinforce his support of the movement. Two events, he said, made an impression upon him. The first involved a suffragist who confessed to him that "since she had been one she had ceased to flirt, because she desired to be worthy of herself." The second of a woman engaged "in the White Slave Traffic who constantly attended suffrage meetings, and being asked the reason, answered with a callousness beyond words that her object was to entrap young girls in the audience because she felt that the movement would ruin her trade."[114] While the credibility of Fr. Chapman's examples are certainly subject to doubt, they illustrate the faith some clergy had in the suffrage movement as a moral force in society.

On the whole the suffragists tended to agree with the clergy that their sex would uplift the moral tone of political life. However they did not appear to see the similarity in the philosophy of the supporters and opponents among the clergy—a philosophy based on the belief in women's moral superiority. They should have been concerned about the reasons behind clerical support because, after all, their demand for the suffrage was based on a desire to be equal

not in a belief of superiority. If the suffrage movement was
to prevent prostitution some clergy hoped that it would foster
rather than destroy motherhood. *Votes for Women* reported
on the Bishop of Down's letter fo the London *Times* which
"makes a Fancy Franchise suggestion". According to him
the Parliamentary vote should be extended to "every married
woman or widow who is the mother of four children". *Votes
for Women* commented on how unfair this would be as it
would eliminate professional and other women "who render
a valuable service to the community" and more to the point
"votes for men are not narrowed down to fathers."[115]

This chapter has been concerned with the involvement of
the clergy with the suffrage movements in Ireland. As has
been indicated the relationship was complicated and not
always predictable. Reactions were varied and emotions
depended upon depth of conviction. There were predictably
enough a number of opponents to the idea of women's
franchise within the churches. Yet this opposition did not
kill the suffrage movement. At the same time there were
many supporters for the movement within the churches.
There were strong women's suffrage societies who wished to
work in cooperation with their churches thus belying Evans's
claims that the movement in Catholic countries was weak,
overwhelmingly Protestant and anti-clerical. It would seem
however that the friends of the suffrage movement in Irish
churches had not undergone a mental revolution with regard
to their view of womanhood but merely had rationalised their
previous conceptions about her attributes and modified them
to explain and cope with the new woman they were now
facing. What did all this mean from the suffragists' point of
view? Certainly in some respects it strengthened their
movement. When the women were being condemned by their
opponents in the church they could point to their supporters.
Declarations by clergy on women's moral right to have a part
in running their country gave a spiritual blessing to their
cause. The appearance of clergy on platforms gave an air of
respectability to their meetings and perhaps convinced the
more timid-minded to attend. The fact that clergy visited the
suffragists in gaol served as a moral reprimand to the
authorities and seemed to emphasise the goodness and

innocence of these women. By attending the public meetings, visiting prisoners and recording their support in print a respectable sector of society, the clergy, confirmed the respectability of another group, middle-class suffragists, and showed ultimately that neither group was revolutionary. /

Notes

1. Tony Fahey, "Nuns in the Catholic church in Ireland in the nineteenth century" in Cullen (ed.) *Girls Don't Do Honours: Irish Women in Education in the 19th and 20th Centuries* (Women's Education Bureau, Dublin, 1987), pp. 7–8. Margaret MacCurtain, "The Historical Image". *Irish Women: Image and Achievement. Women in Irish Culture from Earliest Times*, Eilean Ni Chuilleanain (ed.) (Arlen House, Dublin, 1985), pp. 37–50.
2. Eibhlin Breathnach, "Charting new waters: women's experience in higher education", *Girls Don't Do Honours, op. cit.*, pp. 55–78 esp. pp. 56 and 68.
3. Fahey, *op. cit.*, p. 26.
4. The Church of Ireland was the Anglican Church in Ireland.
5. Richard J. Evans, *The Feminists* (Croom Helm, London, 1977), pp. 30, 124.
6. Olive Banks, *On Becoming a Feminist* (Harvester Press, Brighton, 1987), p. 15.
7. Harrison Tapes, Fawcett Library, London. However Levenson and Natterstad (*Hanna Sheehy Skeffington*) point out that in her youth Hanna Sheehy Skeffington was quite religious and was received into the Association of the Children of Mary, pp. 6–7.
8. Sheehy Skeffington, A.D., *Votes for Women: Irish Women's Struggle for the Vote* (Gill and Macmillan, Dublin, 1975), p. 16.
9. SSP Ms 22,265.
10. Cousins, *We Two Together* (Ganesh, Madras, 1950), pp. 104–5.
11. Harrison Tapes, *op. cit.*
12. Cousins, *op. cit.*, p. 112.
13. *Ibid.*, p. 228.
14. *Ibid.*, p. 226.
15. "Geraldine Cummins: 'Psychic'", *Cork Examiner*, April 20, 1984.
16. Cousins, *op. cit.*, p. 75, p. 110.
17. GPB papers.
18. Cousins, *op. cit.*, pp. 228–31.
19. Banks, *op. cit.*, pp. 15, 88, 151.
20. *Church League for Women's Suffrage Annual Report*, 1913.
21. *International Women's News*, September 1942.
22. Mary Hayden, "Women in the Middle Ages", *Irish Review*, August 1913, pp. 282–95, September 1913, pp. 344–58.
23. *Catholic Suffragist*, March 15, 1915, p. 23.

24. *Ibid*, May 15, 1916, p. 46.
25. *Ibid*, December 15, 1915, p. 100.
26. *Ibid*, September 15, 1917, p. 72.
27. *Ibid*, Michael O'Mahony, "St Bridgid and Liberty", *The Catholic Suffragist*, June 15, 1917, p. 49.
28. *Ibid*, November 15, 1915, p. 95.
29. Nancy Stewart Parnell, *A Venture in Faith: A History of St Joan's Social and Political Alliance formerly the Catholic Women's Suffrage Society* (St Joan's Alliance, London, 1962).
30. Steven Hause and Anne Kenny, "The Development of the Catholic Women's Suffrage Movement in France 1896–1922", *Catholic Historical Review*, 1984, pp. 11–30.
31. Nancy Stewart Parnell, *op. cit.*
32. David Barry, "Female Suffrage from a Catholic Standpoint", *Irish Ecclesiastical Record*, Vol. XXVII, September 1909, pp. 295–303.
33. *Church of Ireland Gazette*, July 3, 1914, *Irish Catholic*, October 13, 1917, p. 6, *Ibid*, September 8, 1917, p. 1, *Ibid*, September 15, 1917, p. 5.
34. MacCurtain, "Towards an Appraisal of the Religious Image of Women", *Crane Bag*, Vol. 4, No. 1, 1980, pp. 26–53. Banks, *op. cit.*, Banks writes of ". . . the attractions of feminism to the girl who had been to college, as well as college to the girl who was already a feminist." p. 13.
35. *Irish Catholic*, July 28, 1917, p. 1. See Brian Titley, *Church, State and the Control of Schooling in Ireland 1900–1944* (1983).
36. *Church of Ireland Gazette*, July 24, 1914, p. 638.
37. *Anti Suffrage Review*, March 12, p. 51.
38. *Freeman's Journal*, May 14, 1912, p. 80. The colleges he was referring to were Girton College, Cambridge and Somerville College, Oxford.
39. *Irish Catholic*, February 17, 1912, p. 80.
40. Mary Colum, *Life and Dream* (Macmillan, New York, 1947).
41. SSP Ms 22,256 (i). See also Anne O'Connor, "The revolution in girls' secondary education in Ireland, 1860–1910", *Girls Don't Do Honours*, *op. cit.*, p. 51.
42. SSP Ms 21,641 (i).
43. *Irish Catholic*, September 28, 1912.
44. Fr. Boniface in *Irish Catholic*, December 4, 1910.
45. *Irish Catholic*, November 23, p. 8.
46. *Catholic Bulletin*, March 1912, Vol. 11, p. 125.
47. *Irish Catholic*, February 17, 1912, p. 8.
48. *Ibid*.
49. *Irish Times*, February 20, 1912, p. 8.
50. *Irish Catholic*, February 6, 1913, p. 9.
51. *Irish Catholic*, May 9, 1914, p. 53.
52. *IC*, July 4, 1914, p. 53.
53. *Ibid*.
54. See Chapter 6.
55. Hanna Sheehy Skeffington, "Reminiscences", in *Irishwomen's Struggle for the Vote*, A.D. Sheehy Skeffington and Rosemary Owens (Dublin, 1975).

56. *Irish Catholic*, August 10, 1912, p. 4.
57. GPB papers.
58. *Irish Catholic*, August 10, 1912, p. 4.
59. *Ibid*, September 28, 1912.
60. *Ibid*, November 23, 1912, p. 8.
61. *Church of Ireland Gazette*, June 26, 1914, p. 546.
62. *Ibid*, July 3, 1914, p. 560.
63. *Ibid*.
64. *Irish Catholic*, June 13, 1914.
65. *Church of Ireland Gazette*, June 26, 1914, p. 546.
66. *IC*, May 17, 1913, p. 412.
67. *IC*, July 1914, p. 59.
68. *Catholic Suffragist*, September 15, 1915, p. 72.
69. See Chapter 4.
70. *Prison Letters*, p. 11.
71. *Irish Times*, February 4, 1910.
72. *IC*, June 5, 1912, p. 29.
73. *IC*, January 1910, 1914, p. 226.
74. *Church of Ireland Gazette*, December 26, 1913, p. 132.
75. The lecture's "large and interested audience was noted" by *Votes for Women*, December 8, 1911, p. 166. The article appeared in *Irish Review*, November 1913, pp. 479–84.
76. *The Cross*, September 1913.
77. *VFW*, December 8, 1911, p. 166.
78. *IC*, July 11, 1914, p. 59.
79. *Church of Ireland Gazette*, December 3, 1915, p. 944.
80. *Catholic League for Women's Suffrage*, January 14, 1914, p. 18.
81. *Anti Suffrage Review*, April 1914, p. 53.
82. *VFW*, November 8, 1912, p. 84.
83. *Church League for Women's Suffrage Annual Report*, 1913, p. 41.
84. *Church League for Women's Suffrage*, November 1912, p. 116. See also *Irish Citizen*, May 17, 1913, p. 418.
85. *Church League for Women's Suffrage*, October 1913, p. 304.
86. *Church League for Women's Suffrage Annual Report* 1913, p. 41.
87. *Anti Suffrage Review*, April 1910, p. 8.
88. *The Irishwomen's Reform League Annual Report* 1913. See also *Church League for Women's Suffrage*, November 1913, p. 324.
89. *Ibid*.
90. *Ibid*, January 1915, pp. 5, 7.
91. Breathnach, *op. cit.*, p. 67.
92. Articles on this topic appeared in the *Church of Ireland Gazette* throughout August of 1913. They were written by L.A. Walkington and were entitled "The Position of Women in the Church". See also Sheila Fletcher, "Sailing to the Edge of the World", *History Today*, September 1987, pp. 10–11.
93. *Irish Catholic*, May 19, 1912, p. 4.
94. *Ibid*, August 12, 1916, p. 5.
95. *Ibid*, August 19, 1916, p. 1.

96. *Ibid*, August 29, 1916, p. 7.
97. Evans, *op. cit.*, p. 35.
98. Fahey, *op. cit.*, p. 28.
99. *Catholic Historical Review*, 1984.
100. Clery, *Irish Review*, November 1913, pp. 479–84.
101. *Church League for Women's Suffrage*, October 1913, p. 304.
102. *Church of Ireland Gazette*, November 20, 1914, p. 929.
103. *Ibid*. According to Evans "In coming to support the ideals of temperance in alcohol and self-restraint in sex which middle-class liberals advocated as the remedy for these two social 'evils', moderate feminists were of course representing the interests of their class . . .", *op. cit.*, p. 35.
104. *IC*, July 4, 1914.
105. Chapman, *Church League for Women's Suffrage Annual Report*, 1913, p. 41.
106. "Sheebna the Scribe", *Church of Ireland Gazette*, November 2, 1914, p. 929.
107. *IC*, November 2, 1912.
108. *Church of Ireland Gazette*, December 26, 1913, p. 113.
109. *Catholic Suffragist*, May 15, 1916.
110. *IC*, July 4, 1914, p. 49.
111. *Ibid*, November 23, 1912—Article on "The Women of Finland" claims that since women got the vote there had been anti-drink legislation.
112. *Catholic Suffragist*, November 1915.
113. *Ibid*.
114. *Church League for Women's Suffrage*, October 1913, p. 304.
115. *VFW*, May 29, 1914, p. 540.

· 7 ·

"Home Rule for All Ireland or No Home Rule"

The Relationship between the Suffragists and the Irish Party

Any study of the Irish women's struggle for suffrage must take into account their rather tempestuous relationship with the Irish Party. It was on the whole a one-sided relationship. The women needed the help of Irish representatives at Westminster to bring about their enfranchisement. Irish suffragists hoped to persuade the Constitutional Nationalists, for the main part the Irish Parliamentary Party, to help push a Woman's Suffrage Bill through Parliament or alternatively agree to an amendment to the Home Rule Bill or an Adult Suffrage Bill which would give Irish women the vote on the same terms as Irish men. Due to the combination of a number of circumstances the chances of this hope being realised seemed increasingly slight from the introduction of the first Conciliation Bill in 1910 to the final attempt to amend the Home Rule Bill in 1914. The relationship between the women and the Irish Party was one of false hopes, broken promises, bitterness and finally dismay. To appreciate why this was so it is necessary to examine what exactly was at stake for the Irish Party.

Since the Act of Union in 1801 Irish MPs sat at Westminster, the Irish Parliament having been abolished. From that time on there was a desire among Irish Nationalists to re-establish their Parliament and at the very least gain Home Rule (a control of Irish affairs) and for some to gain complete independence. The Irish found two paths open to them: there was the legitimate path of persuasion through the medium of their MPs at Westminster and there was the coercionist path as followed by the Young Irelanders, the Fenians, the Irish Republican Brotherhood and Sinn Fein and witnessed in the risings of 1848, 1867 and 1916. Irish women interested in suffrage hoped to get the aid of the Constitutionalists. In the words of one they realised "though the House of Commons was still the arbiter of Irishwomen's as well as Irishmen's destinies, we should have to . . . begin at once on our own MPs pressing to have a clause embodying Votes for Women in our measure of Home Rule."[1]

For a long period the Constitutional Nationalists gained little sympathy from their English masters for self-government. Catholic Emancipation in 1829, though certainly an advance for the representation of the Irish, did not signal the advent of self-rule. The struggle for Catholic Emancipation has been compared to the later women's struggle,[2] and Daniel O'Connell did make sympathetic noises on the oppression of women.[3] Anna Wheeler has been credited for bringing the notion of women's equality to Daniel O'Connell and his circle.[4] One of the reasons for the slow headway must be the disorganised nature and the disunity of Nationalist MPs at Westminster, as well as the reluctance of successive British governments to loosen the leash. An attempt to make them a force to be reckoned with in the 1850s failed.[5] It was not until the arrival of Charles Stewart Parnell that it seemed possible to mould these rather disparate MPs into a political party. Through his introduction of obstructionism he wielded them into a force so strong that they split the Liberal Party in 1886.[6] Gladstone's ministries saw an attempt to deal fairly with the Irish. "My mission is to pacify Ireland" declared the Grand Old Man and his introduction of the two Home Rule Bills in 1886 and 1893 illustrated how he believed this could be done. He failed because his opponents outnumbered him. Besides ninety-three members of his own party these included the Conservatives who wished to 'kill Home Rule with kindness', and the House of Lords whose veto proved to be an insurmountable obstacle in getting the Bill beyond its first stages, not to mention the Northern Unionists who had no desire to break with their mother country.[7]

It was not until twelve years after Gladstone's death that
a certain number of events combined to make the demand
for Home Rule realistic. The abolition of the veto of the
House of Lords (a consequence of their refusal to pass Lloyd
George's budget) under the Parliament Act of 1911 signalled
the realisation of a Home Rule Bill.[8] The success of the Irish
Party in the elections of 1910, but most particularly in the
December election in which they gained eighty-four seats
and ended up holding the balance of power, meant that they
were in a strong negotiating position and they opted for
supporting the Liberals with the understanding that a Home
Rule Bill would be forthcoming. It is here that the suffragists
reappear on the scene. For the abolition of the Lords veto
in 1911 also eliminated the biggest obstacle to woman suffrage.
English women felt that they must now push even harder
for a Woman's Suffrage Bill, Irish women felt likewise, and
they had an added chance of being enfranchised under a
Home Rule Bill (with the possibility of being enfranchised
before the English women).

However the Irish Party was unwilling to have anything
to do with the women's suffrage question. This was ironic
since the aims of both were rather similar in that they were
concerned with the right to achieve self-determination. Both,
by this stage, were well established and had gradually
politicised sections of the public into accepting their views
and both had built up followers outside and inside Parliament.
The difference was of course that the Nationalists were
represented in Westminster—all eighty-four of them, while
the women remained clamouring at its gates. The Nationalists'
demand was in the process of going through Parliament while
the women's never got past a tentative suggestion. One writer
to the *Irish Times* asked (referring to the struggle for Catholic
Emancipation) "Have Catholic Irishmen lost their sense of
chivalry? Because they suffered so recently from political
disabilities, should not their imaginations be fired by the
passionate struggle women today are making to win what
they won?"[9] Hanna Sheehy Skeffington declared in her
reminiscences that:

the MPs' minds were virgin ground mostly—unreceptive to any feminist ideas . . . Here were good Irish rebels, many of them broken in to national revolt, with all the slogans of Irish revolution and its arsenal of weapons—Boycott, Plan of Campaign, Land for the People, and so forth, the creators of obstruction in Parliament—yet at the whisper of Votes for Women many changed to extreme Tories . . .[10]

Rose Lavery wrote in 1908 in the *Irish Review* that "Irishmen do not need to have indicated to them the hardship of being governed by those alien to them in temperament, ideals, and traditions. An Englishman, they say, can never understand the needs of a country like Ireland. How strange then that all men should be considered gifted with the wonderful power of sympathetic interest which enables them to so easily understand the needs of women."[11]

Things did not seem so straightforward to the Nationalist MPs and certainly the dilemma was more complex than it was for their English colleagues. It was not just a matter of agreeing or disagreeing to the principle of women's suffrage. It involved much more than that. This was so because of their attempt to manœuvre the rather delicate Home Rule Bill through its final stages, and some feared that if they had anything to do with another controversial question they might damage their first priority—Home Rule. Thus, a number of Irish Nationalists claimed to be women's suffragists but consistently voted against it. While seeing nationalism as profoundly important and Home Rule as their first priority, they told the women that their turn would come. When Ireland had achieved Home Rule the men would give women the vote, or at least think about it. "Ireland should decide for herself whether she deserves woman's suffrage or not."[12] But one of the flaws of this argument was that Ireland was really 'himself'! In the meantime women were supposed to bide their time and support the men.

However, dedicated suffragists were not persuaded by this argument. They were suspicious of the men's promises and wanted immediate gratification. Too much was in the balance: perhaps Home Rule would not be achieved. Perhaps it would and women would not be enfranchised. They feared a provision in the Home Rule Bill whereby the Irish Parliament would for a term of three years be debarred from making any change in the franchise. Along with this was the provision that any decision of the Irish Parliament would be subject to the veto of the Imperial Parliament.[13] The suffragists wanted to get women's suffrage out of a British Parliament before an Irish Parliament could refuse it or delay it. They had waited long enough.

Thus began a debate which was carried out with vigour by both sides though it must be admitted that in most cases the women were the initiators of the debate. Some of the MPs (using the same argument that was also used by the revolutionary nationalists) accused the women of being anti-nationalistic and selfish. They accused them of belonging to an English movement and of being 'unIrish'. It was stated that the suffragist movement in Ireland was being run in opposition to the nationalist movement. For the most part this was untrue, there being a number of independent Irish suffrage organisations and the IWFL made it clear on a number of occasions that their movement and goals were quite separate from the English organisations.

In her autobiography Margaret Cousins denied the accusation ". . . the Nationalist Party who had been taught by the press to regard us as opponents to Irish freedom, which we certainly were not, but opponents to the opposite of freedom in Ireland as anywhere else . . .". She added "We were as keen as the men on the freedom of Ireland, but we saw the men clamouring for amendments which soiled their own interests and made no recognition of the existence of women as fellow citizens. We women were convinced that anything which improved the status of women would improve not hinder, the coming of Home Rule."[14] Nevertheless she felt that

> No self-respecting woman can be satisfied with any self-government Bill which makes her sex a disqualification for citizenship . . . the Irish Women's Franchise League is not working to wreck Home Rule, as Nationalists believe, but is upholding the demand of all patriots of the past to the right of the people to govern themselves. If we do not see to it that "people" included women as well as men, we are only perpetuating the idea that woman is only property and not a person in her own right.[15]

However, suffragists like Dora Mellone gave fuel to the

Nationalists' accusations with statements like ". . . As
suffragists we have no concern with Home Rule . . .". The
fact that she was a member of the English WSPU as well as
belonging to Irish suffrage organisations gave even more
weight to the Nationalist recriminations.[16]

The Irish party did not want to do anything which would
upset or humiliate Asquith, the pilot of Home Rule and, at
this stage, still as anti-suffragist. Any reorganisation of the
franchise might have disastrous consequences for Irish
representation at Westminster. It was reckoned that they
were more than doubly represented compared to British
constituencies with forty more seats than they should have
had.[17] If their representation had been cut it would have
meant the end of the Irish Party holding the balance of
power, thus the fall of the Liberals, a new Conservative
government and the loss of Home Rule. Similarly if women's
suffrage was passed the Unionists could call for an election
to see if the new electorate approved of either the Liberal
government or Home Rule in accordance "with the constitutional convention whereby the enfranchisement of new
voters must at once be followed by a general election".[18]
However the inevitability of such an event was disputed.[19]
Since women were believed to be more conservative, the Irish
MPs felt that this would also mean the downfall of their
allies and again the loss of Home Rule. To sum up, Irish
MPs were either anti-suffragist, ambivalent or if pro-suffrage
unwilling to risk supporting it for the above reasons.

Be this as it may the Irish suffragists were not going to let
matters rest and they were determined to get their message
across that women in Ireland wanted the vote. From the
founding of the first Irish suffragist organisation in 1876, the
Irish Women's Suffrage and Local Government Association,
the suffragists endeavoured to bring their plight to the
attention of Irish MPs both Nationalist and Unionist. Thus
from an early stage some sympathetic MPs appeared on their
platforms. When John Stuart Mill brought the first women's
suffrage bill before Parliament among his supporters were
some Irish.[20] Helen Blackburn in her early suffrage history
of the British Isles reports Irish MPs attending suffrage
meetings in the late nineteenth century including Parnell's

associate Joseph Biggar.[21] Parnell himself presented a petition
for women's suffrage from the citizens of Dublin to the
House of Commons in 1887.[22] The founder of the Irish
cooperative movement, Sir Horace Plunkett, gave a speech
in Parliament in 1892 on women's suffrage based on his
observations in Wyoming.[23] But basically women's suffrage
was not of great (or minor!) concern to the Irish Party, who
were more preoccupied with the Land and Home Rule
Questions. /

Therefore the IWSLGA and the later organisations had as
a major aim the attraction of the support of the MPs. They
were invited to meetings, asked to give talks, to chair
discussion, engage in debates and give opinions. One would
imagine in the early period this type of gathering of middle
class ladies in drawing-room meetings and 'at homes' must
have appealed to some as a pleasant way of passing an evening
and it was easy to make promises which they saw no hope
of being fulfilled. After all the women were moderate and
only wanted the vote on very limited terms, namely on the
same terms that men had it (and some were prepared to
accept less than this). Perhaps, too, for some there seemed
little difference between these organisations and the women's
branches of the Liberal and Conservative parties—the Primrose League and the Conservative and Unionist Women's
Association. Certainly the women appeared to be of the same
social composition. But as the women grew increasingly
impatient and more revolutionary groups were formed (mainly
due to the ineffectiveness of the IWSLGA and the sluggish,
not to say static, nature of parliamentary cooperation), the
MPs' cosy gatherings were over. Vague mumblings were no
longer acceptable and definite commitments were sought
after.

In her article on Nationalism and Feminism McKillen has
argued that the suffragists devoted too much attention to
pursuing the Constitutional Nationalists and that they were
wasting their time.[24] Her point is clearly made from hindsight
and does not take into account the immediacy that the Home
Rule Bill had in the period 1912–14. After all, a revolution
was not at all inevitable. And should it happen was it
necessarily going to succeed and if it succeeded who was to

say, at this stage, that the revolutionaries would introduce women's suffrage? For the suffragists those with seats in Parliament were the only ones with the power of introducing women's franchise and thus had to be pursued with vigour.

In 1910 the IWFL issued queries to all Irish candidates contesting the first of the 1910 elections in January on their attitudes to votes for women. They were asked the following questions:

1. Are you in favour of the extension of the Parliamentary franchise to women on the same terms as men?
2. If elected would you secure inclusion of Irish women in any woman suffrage measure introduced in the House of Commons?
3a. Are you prepared to bring in a bill conferring the franchise on Irish women on the same terms as Irish men?
3b. In event of a legislative assembly being established in Ireland would you endeavour to secure that women would have the franchise on the same terms as Irish men?
4. Will you extend your influence in Parliament to secure that all women who may be imprisoned for political offences in connection with the suffrage agitation shall be treated as political prisoners?

There were twenty-one replies, seventeen were in favour of the extension of the franchise. One or two felt that women should be concerned with other issues such as housing and education. Thirteen gave affirmative answers to all the questions.[25] In the December election the IWFL circulated a manifesto at polling stations "calling upon Irishmen to question all candidates and to vote only for those who give satisfactory pledges . . .".[26] It would seem at this stage that the women had reason enough to be optimistic. Even with only a dozen MPs pushing their cause in the Commons they could perhaps influence legislation. However this was to be the last election before the Reform Act of 1918 and the women had little chance to repeat such election pressure. And Irish MPs could justifiably say, as they so often did, women's suffrage had never been an election issue.

As the women began to insist on more steadfast commitment they found that superficial promises were difficult to turn into Parliamentary proposals. Margaret Cousins recalled the growing tension in her autobiography. "I lobbied Tim Healy, Hugh Law, John Redmond, and five or six others, all of whom were cross with Irish women for trying to gate crash their sacrosanct politics."[27] She told a meeting in London in 1911 "We must catch the bull by the horns, 'John Bull', I mean . . . We hear a good deal about a wedding present to Ireland [Home Rule], but whoever heard of a wedding without a woman in it?"[28] The IWFL extracted written pledges from MPs who found themselves being heckled at meetings, waylaid in strange places and generally being annoyed.

The suffragists examined carefully the MPs' public statements with regards to suffrage and they kept a record of when and where the politicians were approached, challenged and heckled. The women made sure that the MPs could not use the excuse that they were not aware of a demand among Irish women for the suffrage. In 1913 the IWFL reported that "The League has been represented at practically every political demonstration held in Ireland throughout the year", and "the reality of Irishwomen's demand for enfranchisement has been insistently brought under the attention of the Irish members, who never again can say with truth that the matter has never been raised in their constituencies."[29] Some of the Irish suffrage organisations sent members to London during Parliamentary sessions in order to be closer to the MPs and thus remind them of their duty to Irish women.[30]

The focus of suffragist attention was of course John Redmond, the leader of the Irish Party. He epitomised what they were up against. He was the man of empty promises, the man who went back on his word. When he was accused of anti-feminist leanings he replied scornfully: "Feminist! I'm not sure that I know what a feminist is!"[31] He was the person who at first met their deputations and failed to allow any discussion to be reported in the press[32] and later when things got too uncomfortable for him he would neither meet their deputations as they "would only lead to unpleasantness"[33] nor allow them into the Irish Party's National Convention.

He was the one who in 1909 said he agreed with political status but when the matter became a serious issue for the women between 1912 and 1914, refused to back them.[34] His statement in Wicklow in October 1911 that "I understand the Home Rule Ireland needs" was scoffed at. "If this be

true", wrote Christabel Pankhurst in *Votes for Women*, "then
he understands that Ireland wants and needs that her women
should have full protection of the vote. . . . In short
Mr Redmond has the knowledge which should prompt him
to demand Home Rule for Irish women as well as Irish men,
and he has according to his own statement of the case, the
power to enforce this demand."[35] He told a deputation from
the IWFL in April 1912 that

> With regard to a clause in the Home Rule Bill to give votes to women;
> I am entirely and absolutely opposed to it. I consider that there is no
> question more essentially a local question, an Irish question to be
> decided by an Irish Parliament, than the question of the franchise . . .
> No I am not going to say that you will get the measure straight away,
> or that I will introduce a Bill. At any rate I would resent intensely the
> English Parliament deciding any domestic question of this kind over
> our heads. It is a purely domestic thing that we must settle for
> ourselves.[36]

The women pointed out that he had allowed other domestic
issues like insurance be decided by Westminster. He was
among the forty-nine Irish MPs who voted for forcefeeding[37]
and he supported the introduction of the Cat and Mouse
Act.[38]

For the suffragists he was altogether the villain with no
redeeming features. It was he who said that there was no
demand for women's suffrage in Ireland and who also declared
the individual members of the Irish Party were free to vote
as they wished but almost certainly exercised the party Whip
on them. The women saw him trying to reassure Ulster
Unionists that concessions would be made towards them
under Home Rule, "Mr Redmond is not to be trusted. He
will yield only to pressure. He slobbers over Ulster, because
Ulster has fought him and remains the Lion in his path. He
ignores women and treats them as outlaws because up to the
present women have not fought him, but have treated him
and his party with the greatest consideration. The moral is
obvious."[39] They argued that he was prepared to make
concessions towards religion but not sex.[40]

In a rather bizarre way the women, though asserting their
nationalism, felt their situation similar to that of the Unionists
as two groups who were getting a raw deal from the proposed

Home Rule Bill. *Votes for Women* declared in June 1912 "The fiction that all Ireland apart from the dissentient Ulsterman is satisfied with the Home Rule Bill as it stands at present, is destroyed. Irish women have begun to express their discontent at the great injustice which the Home Rule Bill would inflict upon their sex . . . ."[41] Obviously any comparisons drawn by them between their situation and that of the Unionists can not have reinforced their argument of being independent and Irish in Nationalist eyes.

Since John Redmond embodied the evil of the Irish Party, the women never let him out of their sight. As one of the suffragists put it "We early recognised the necessity for interviewing Ireland's political leader, John Redmond."[42] He was followed around from meeting to meeting. He was surprised in corridors of hotels. Even at the bridge opening ceremony in Waterford he could not get away from them. He was asked, by a Mrs Bryan and a Miss Hayes, "When do you mean to open a bridge for the women of Ireland?"[43] The most notorious confrontation he had with suffragists was with English suffragists who fired a missile at him and the visiting English prime minister Mr Asquith. However he refused to press charges since it would probably have drawn more unnecessary attention to him as an anti-suffragist.[44]

Following Parnellite tactics, the IWFL women intended to make their voices heard and force Redmond to listen to them by attempting to influence the results of elections.[45] Interestingly enough, as one study of elections in Ireland in the nineteenth century notes, women had played a part in the outcome of elections before by negotiating bribes for their husbands, taking part in election demonstrations and riots and by becoming unofficial election agents.[46] Now they intended to use more legitimate politically shrewd methods and imitated the actions of Parnellites at the general election of 1885 when:

> The Irish Party were in a position not unlike that occupied by the suffragists today [1910–12]. Neither Liberal nor Conservative leader would promise Home Rule. How was the Irish vote to be given? The bold and effective policy was adopted of voting against every Liberal candidate irrespective of his personal convictions on the subject of Home Rule. Had the Irish voters supported the Liberal policy at the

election Mr Gladstone would have been independent of the Irish members, and a Home Rule Bill would never have been introduced . . .[47]

Likewise during elections and by-elections the suffragists canvassed for pro-suffragist candidates—and if these were rather sparse, they campaigned to keep out members who would support the government. The most famous case was the Derry by-election where a Liberal candidate was standing. The situation arose where a Unionist, Colonel Pakenham, and a Nationalist, Mr Hogg, were contesting a vacant Parliamentary seat. The IWFL sent Mrs Palmer and the IWSS of Belfast sent Mrs McCoubrey to canvass the voters. Their object was to 'Keep the Liberal out' (referring to Mr Hogg's party's alliance with the Liberals). Such action could not have endeared the IWFL to the Nationalists and as was seen in an earlier chapter incurred the wrath of some nationalist women.[48]

It was not in Ireland alone that Redmond was made to feel the disapproval of suffragists. On visits to Australia and the United States suffragists informed him of funds being contributed to his party and warned they would be stopped unless he supported a pro-suffragist view. In 1912 the Women's Political Association of Victoria reminded Redmond that Australian women "have always subscribed liberally to Home Rule funds" and asked that he "pay the debt that Ireland owes to Anna Parnell and the Land league".[49]

During Redmond's visit to the United States in September 1910 he was told by Irish women there that they could not provide him with funds unless the Irish Party at Westminster would press forward on votes for women. Despite this he still returned to Ireland with $100,000 in election funds.[50] Letters appeared periodically in suffrage journals reminding Redmond that votes for Irish women was certainly not another domestic issue but caused grave concern across the Atlantic. Had Redmond read Mr Henry Moskowitz's (of the Down Town Ethical Society, New York) letter to *Votes for Women* perhaps he would have realised that this was not just another domestic issue. Mr Moskowitz wrote

We Americans are intensely interested in the prospect of Irish Home Rule. With us State and local autonomy is no longer a conviction; it is a political instinct . . . To a believer in democracy Irish Home Rule is as inevitable as votes for women . . . there is no logic in answering the democratic demands of the Irish people by an undemocratic Home Rule Bill. For to deprive the women of Ireland of the privilege of active participation in the political life of their country is not only undemocratic but it is unjust to Ireland and its manhood and womanhood.[51] /

In the same year the *Irish Citizen* also endeavoured to bring home to Mr Redmond the pressure of Irish-American public opinion:

On the 4th of May an immense demonstration of American women, numbering 10,000 at least, took place in New York, and amongst the demands they put forward was one for the extension of the vote to Irishwomen in the Home Rule Bill. We trust the Irish Party will not be blind to the significance of the action of the American women and will learn in time the moral danger of a position which claims Home Rule for the Irish men and denies it to Irish women.[52]

Although there was much support for Irish women's demand for suffrage it was clearly not as powerful a force as the Irish suffragists believed and did not significantly affect funds to political groups in Ireland.

Across the Irish Sea the English suffragists were never very far from Redmond's shadow since he was not only preventing Irish women getting the vote but English women as well. Christabel Pankhurst of the WSPU wrote that her organisation would do everything in its power to oppose the Home Rule Bill "unless we convince Mr Redmond of our power to destroy his cause he will persist in his policy of destroying ours." She added that the Bill was an insult to Irish women. "Nothing more reactionary could be conceived than to establish a brand new constitution which gives political rights to men only . . . We are determined that Irishmen shall wait for ever for Home Rule unless women are to have it too."[53] She believed that "it is now too late in the world's history to create parliaments and grant constitutions without giving equal franchise rights to women. This wrong was done for the last time so far as the Empire is concerned in South Africa. It cannot be done in Ireland."[54] //

The determination of the English suffragists to make Redmond listen was impressed upon him on his visits to

Britain. In December 1912 *Votes for Women* reported on 'The Irish Betrayer at Dalstow' and recorded him being shouted down at the meeting,[55] something which he had become quite familiar with in Ireland. He seemed particularly susceptible to attacks on trains. After the Irish Party Convention in 1912 one Irish suffragist met Redmond travelling back on the boat-train to London. She entered his compartment and asked him "What about Votes for Irishwomen? Irishwomen have helped you in the past, and in return you refuse to admit five of your countrywomen to your Convention, though that five included the granddaughter of Daniel O'Connell and the daughter of Gavan Duffy."[56] The following year Redmond and his wife were greeted with bags of flour while travelling on a train to Newcastle.[57]

Back at home there was to be no respite. When the Irish Party had its annual conventions in 1910 and 1911 the suffragists and their supporters asked embarrassing questions and generally made a scene. Redmond decided to ban women from the 1912 convention and the IWFL complained about it bitterly. In a letter to the *Freeman's Journal* Margaret Cousins argued that a precedent "for the admission of our deputation has been created by the permission accorded to Dr Douglas Hyde to plead on behalf of the Gaelic League for Compulsory Irish in the National University. We trust that a similar courtesy will now be extended to Irish women pleading for the emancipation of their sex."[58] In another letter published the same day in London she wrote "It is possible that official prejudice may deny us even this measure of justice, but the spectacle of a 'National' Convention excluding the representations of more than half the nation will cause many to fear for the future of Ireland."[59] It is clear by this stage Redmond and the majority of his Party were no longer prepared to listen.

One Nationalist who did little to disguise the fact that he was not open to persuasion was John Dillon, the deputy leader of the Irish Parliamentary Party. He told a deputation of suffragists "Women's suffrage will, I believe, be the ruin of our Western civilisation. It will destroy the home, challenging the headship of man, laid down by God. It may come in your time—I hope not in mine."[60] When he declared the Irish Party would accept Home Rule for all Ireland or no Home Rule (referring to the Unionists' reluctance to separate from the United Kingdom) the women said they hoped by that he included their sex.[61] When he gave an // address at University College Dublin on 'The Healing Power of Freedom' he was prevented from speaking at various points.[62] Women attending his meetings to remind him of their existence in Ireland usually got thrown out after the first call of 'Mr Dillon!'[63]

In June 1912 John Dillon in a speech on Home Rule said that one of the blessings "Ireland will bring to the British Empire will be that its people will endeavour to make that what it ought to be, a messenger to the free world." This was greeted by *Votes for Women* as "good news" and it expressed the hope that "you will begin this great work for the Empire by seeing to it that freedom is given as part of the Home Rule Bill to your own countrywomen in Ireland."[64] Dillon was a witness in a court case where women were on trial for breaking his windows and the windows of the United Irish League. During the trial he admitted "All my life I have been against giving the Parliamentary vote to women", though he did point out that he had never actually voted against it until militancy had begun.[65]

However, not all Irish Nationalists were like Redmond and Dillon. There were individuals who for time at least believed themselves to be suffragist and in some cases voted bravely on the issue against the grain of opinion of their fellow Nationalists. These men were torn between the two issues and if they succumbed to the nationalist one they immediately acquired the label of traitor from the suffragists. Likewise they were not too much admired by their colleagues for their flirtation with the women's cause.

It has been claimed by the historian Constance Rover that the Irish Party was the biggest pro-suffrage group in Parliament, bigger even than Labour.[66] This was also the view of some suffragists at the time, thus explaining their initial optimism and faith that they could be helped by the Parliamentarians. This might superficially have been the case if one counted all the MPs who believed themselves to be suffragists or those who told the suffragists that they were willing to help them. However, on a closer examination of their statements and actual voting practices this assertion while containing grains of truth does not amount to much. In October 1911 the IWFL carried a resolution stating that Irish women should be included in the provisions of the Home Rule Bill. It was claimed that this demand had received the wide support of Nationalists in Ireland.[67] Why then did not Irish women get the vote until 1918 when the political situation was entirely different? It would appear that there was a limit to the Nationalists' feelings of obligation to the women.

Certainly a number of Nationalists, for a time at least, were of practical assistance to the women and did lend credibility to the belief that they were supporters of extending the suffrage. Indeed when the Irish women joined the English suffragists in a deputation to the House of Commons in December 1910, they were rescued from scuffles by some of the Irish MPs who were present.[68] Members of the Irish Party like Stephen Gwynn, Hugh Law and Tom Kettle were drawn to the issue because of its similarity to the Home Rule demand. They were also related to women in the movement in one way or other. Kettle married Hanna Sheehy Skeffington's sister and Stephen Gwynn's wife was a founder member of the Irish Catholic Women's Suffrage Society. As will be seen it was their association with women in the movement which initially attracted but ultimately could not sustain their support.

These MPs made Parliamentary speeches on matters pertaining to Irish women. Gwynn, MP for Galway, said he supported women's suffrage as a matter of justice[69] and supported women in their claim against the unfairness of the Intermediate Education Bill (Ireland) with regards to its pay for women teachers and endeavoured to amend the measure.[70] He attended some of the IWFL meetings. In 1913 he presented a petition to the House of Commons calling for a government measure on women's suffrage.[71] He supported Snowden's introduction of a women's suffrage amendment to the Home Rule Bill.[72] However he disappointed the women with his inconsistent voting on the Conciliation Bills.[73]

The Nationalist MP for Galway, Mr Hazleton, asked

questions in the Commons on the difference between the treatment of Irish and English suffragist prisoners.[74] However his concern may be misleading. Perhaps, it could be argued it did not arise out of suffragist conviction but rather from misplaced chivalry?[75]

A rather unexpected supporter of the women who spoke up for them many times in the House was John Redmond's younger brother William. He attended their meetings and was castigated by the Ancient Order of Hibernians for supporting the suffragists.[76] Time and time again he referred to the success of women's franchise in other countries, particularly Australia.[77] He had visited that country on a number of occasions and felt that many fears of the Anti-suffragists were dispelled by the evidence there. ". . . It is conceded all round that the enfranchisement of women in the Commonwealth of Australia has done much for public welfare, and has served the community immensely." He disagreed with those who believed that women, if enfranchised, would make up a powerful lobby: "It is absurd to assume that the women would act entirely together and would strengthen one party or the other. They would take sides just as men take sides, and some of them would be Liberals and some Conservatives, some would be strong supporters of the Labour party, and I believe a great many women would be in favour of doing justice to Irish people." Referring to the division in Ireland on the question he told the House of Commons

> A great many of my colleagues here will either oppose this measure or
> abstain from supporting it, but it is equally true that a great number
> of us are enthusiastically in favour of it, and have always been so . . .
> We see in Ireland as you see here in the local life of the country most
> wonderful service given to the local community by women in matters
> of local government and everything appertaining to the interests of the
> people, such as education, health, and other things affecting their daily
> lives.

The measure in question was the second reading of the Conciliation Bill. Redmond disliked the fact that it did not propose to enfranchise women on the same terms as men and disagreed with those who argued that full franchise would eventually logically follow. He felt it would be argued that they would have to wait and see "how the women who had already received the franchise will exercise it before granting it generally to the whole sex."[78] However he was to vote against the third reading and vote against a women's suffrage amendment to the Home Rule Bill, probably on the grounds that it only allowed for a limited franchise.[79] Certainly he was eloquent on the women question, but its important shrank for him when Home Rule seemed to be at stake.

Another Nationalist MP, Hugh Law, had held great hope for the Irish women. He made several statements supporting them and appeared on their platforms. At a meeting in February 1910 he told his audience that they "had adopted a system of government in which appeal was made by everybody, even in the House of Lords, to some wonderful person called 'The Will of the People'. It had this disadvantage—it was not a reality. They appealed to the people and the people was carefully defined so as to exclude rather more than half of the population."[80] That same year he was the sponsor of the Local Authorities (Ireland) (Qualification of Women) Bill which when passed in 1911 gave Irish women the same eligibility to sit on local bodies as was conferred on women of Great Britain under the act of 1907.[81] However when he made a statement in the House of Commons that there was no "noisy demand" for women's suffrage in Ireland the *Irish Citizen* produced the Suffrage Map of Ireland as a reply.[82] The IWFL contradicted this statement, shattering Law's silence by breaking windows in the Customs House.[83] Like the others, though considering himself a suffragist, his first priority lay with nationalism. However he was more pompous about it.

Everyone must realise that Irish nationalist members are sent here primarily to win Home Rule for Ireland, and that, if we had good reason to believe that the carrying of a women's suffrage amendment would prejudice that cause we should be bound as loyal representatives of our constituents, however painful such a course might be to us as individuals, to abstain from supporting or even if need be, to vote against such an amendment. This attitude has been described as selfish. For my part I think it is the only one consistent with the duty we owe to those who sent us to represent them in the House . . .[84]

This explanation was seen by the women as woefully

inadequate in view of the fact that they had no say in his electoral success. It was, however, to be very prophetic of his future action. He further strained the relationship when he wrote to the English suffrage organisation the NUWSS that Irish MPs must not damage the Home Rule cause. He went on to say that the hostility of some suffragists to Home Rule, the outrages attending Asquith's visit to Ireland and attacks upon Redmond "have, I fear, irretrievably alienated some who were formerly friendly and have imposed a severe strain even upon those of us who are most convinced of the innate justice of the suffrage claim."[85]

Professor Tom Kettle, a brother-in-law of Hanna Sheehy Skeffington and a member of the Irish Party, represented East Tyrone until 1910 when he resigned his seat for academic reasons. He was a close friend of the Cousinses and the Sheehy Skeffingtons and was a founding member of the IWFL.

The resignation of his parliamentary seat was regretted by the IWFL as it meant one articulate supporter fewer in the House of Commons.[86] Ironically his resignation was the result of protests by a woman colleague over his being involved with politics while holding a full-time professorship.[87] In his last speech in the Commons he pleaded with Asquith to meet a deputation of women. After his resignation he was to continue to be a spokesman for their cause, for a time at least, within the Irish Party.[88] At a meeting in the Mansion House in October 1911 he stated that unless the Home Rule Bill included a clause giving votes to women, he, speaking as a Nationalist and a politician, would not be able to regard such a Bill as a real measure of self-government for Ireland.[89] The reason he was first attracted "to the struggle for the enfranchisement of women was the similarity between their position and that of Ireland. For all practical purposes, he said, Ireland was a country without a vote; it had no power to make laws under which the people of the country lived."[90] He supported the cause of women's suffrage "on the very simple ground that a woman living in an organised state, should have a vote, otherwise she is an alien, an inferior, an outlaw!"[91] He put forward the women's cause at Party meetings and spoke on the subject at the Convention of 1911.

However all this verbosity seemed rather shallow when in the controversial Irish Party Convention of 1912 he failed to put forward a proposal as promised that women should be included in the Home Rule Bill. This non-action invoked the wrath of the IWFL.[92] He further enraged them when he wrote in a letter to the *Freeman's Journal* in April 1912 that the IWFL was becoming "a mere copyist of the English organisation"[WSPU]. He continued, rather self-righteously, ". . . As one who was a supporter of the woman suffrage before any of the Leagues began, and will remain a supporter of it after all the Leagues have committed suicide, I feel it my duty to say for all Irish Nationalists men and women, Home Rule comes first and everything else second . . . ."[93] This was termed by Frank Sheehy Skeffington as Mr Kettle's first "breach of faith with the women's suffrage party".[94]

From now on he was a traitor to be seen in the ranks of the enemy. He had raised hopes of the suffragists only to have them dashed. The strained relationship between Kettle and the IWFL was confirmed when he resigned from the suffrage organisation in 1912 because "they had declared war on the Irish Party." While he admitted that he disapproved of the "bewildering action" of the Irish Party when they defeated the Conciliation Bill, he nevertheless saw the Party as the "indispensable instrument of the political redemption of Ireland . . .".[95] Frank Sheehy Skeffington wrote bitterly of Kettle "Every time the woman's suffrage movement in Ireland has relied on Mr Kettle at a crisis, he has betrayed it."[96]

Despite the hostility Kettle evoked he did attend the Mansion House meeting the following year which met to condemn the Cat and Mouse Act.[97] However the good intentions of this action were somewhat spoilt by his statement that he was "prepared not to sacrifice, but to postpone, any social or franchise reform for the sake of seeing Ireland mistress of her own household." (Again, it is ironic how the female personification and symbolism of Ireland was constantly used by males denying women a share in its government.) This statement was met with cries of "you're not a woman" and "that's not a woman's view".[98]

An important point to note is that some Irish Nationalists who were seen as the suffragists' strongest supporters had already broken from the Irish Party on other points of disagreement and were known as Independent Nationalists. As mavericks they were more likely to be open-minded on issues such as women's suffrage. However, though they supported the women they only had the political pressure of individuals and not of a whole party. Three of the six Independent Nationalists particularly are of interest. These were William O'Brien, T. M. Healy and Laurence Ginnell.

T. M. Healy was a barrister-at-law and an MP. He wrote to the IWFL in 1911 ". . . my conviction as to the essential justice of the claim of women to the vote strengthens with years . . .".[99] He achieved acclaim in English suffrage circles when he defended three militant suffragettes at a trial in Bow Street.[100] At the close of the trial he declared "it is very convenient, when you have able and active political opponents, to be able to prosecute them for 'conspiracy'. It is a method that has been repeatedly adopted by English Governments against the Irish Nationalist Party, when that Party was a dangerous opposition force. Yet we find the Irish Party's organ, 'The Freeman's Journal', in its London correspondence, gloating over the condemnation of Mrs Pankhurst and Mr and Mrs Pethick Lawrence . . . ."[101] Along with a minority of Irish MPs who voted against force-feeding.[102] Unlike many Nationalists he was known to receive women's suffrage deputations 'with sympathy'.[103] It is interesting that figures in Irish nationalist history are often viewed just from one perspective—yet viewed from another perspective the villain becomes a champion. Thus Healy in the perspective of suffragists was quite different from the stock nationalist image of the scheming, unprincipled clericalist.[104]

Veteran parliamentarian William O'Brien believed that the members of the Irish Party were "more or less respectable mediocrities, hard up for a career, who were elected to their snug treasury salaries either by the influence of a 'long-tailed family' or by the questionable arts of a local 'Molly' Convention."[105] He always voted pro-suffrage in Parliament[106] and supported equal pay for teachers.[107] He was a friend of the Skeffingtons and attended suffrage meetings with them.[108] Comparisons were later to be drawn between O'Brien and the suffragists because of his demand during the land struggle to be recognised as a political prisoner.[109] //

Slightly more lukewarm of these suffragists was Mr Ginnell, MP for Westmeath (North). His cattle-running in 1907 and consequent imprisonment had often been pointed out by the militant suffragists. He had broken the law for political purposes. He questioned Mr Birrell (Ireland's Chief Secretary) in the House on the treatment of Irish suffragist prisoners after he had received requests from the IWFL and Frank Sheehy Skeffington to do so. Frank Sheehy Skeffington hoped that "you will be able to interest yourself in this matter, in accordance with that old Nationalist tradition which the members of Mr Redmond's Party have so largely forgotten."[110]

These then were the main members of the cast who were involved in the women's suffrage side-show of the Home Rule drama. There were others who played more than a walk-on part. Asquith was obviously an important player. He was not a supporter of women's suffrage until 1915[111] (when the position of the Irish Party was different in that they no longer held the balance and the priorities of the government had changed) and he was a backer of the Home Rule Bill.[112] However he did concede to the formation of a Conciliation Committee in 1910 which was composed of a number of members from each party and whose task was to come up with an acceptable women's suffrage bill. The Committee had Lord Lytton as its chairman, and H.N. Brailsford as its Secretary. Its membership was composed of twenty-five Liberal MPs, seventeen Conservative MPs, six Irish Nationalist MPs, and six Labour MPs. The committee sponsored a private members' Bill framed in such a way that it could receive support from MPs of all parties.[113] The Conciliation Bill came before Parliament a few times between 1910 and 1912. In the words of one of its backers the bill had to reconcile two extreme sections of the supporters of woman suffrage. "It has to conciliate the Radical who will not vote for an increase of power to the propertied classes, and it has had to conciliate the moderate Liberal and the

Unionist who want to move with great caution. It satisfies both, and at the same time it does nothing to prevent future movement just as rapidly as the democratic sense of the country shall desire."[114] The Bill in its 1912 form was sometimes termed as the 'Widows and Spinsters' Bill because of its bias towards propertied women.[115]

While it was in the process of being drawn up the Irish women made sure that their desire for its passage, despite some reservations at its limited nature, was made known to their political representatives. Their efforts partly bore fruit if one considers the resolutions that were taken around the country. It was reported by the *Men's League for Women's Suffrage* that "at least 65 City and Town Councils have passed resolutions in favour of the Bill and not a single council condemned it!"[116] In November 1910 *Votes for Women* rather grandly declared that 'Cork Demands the Bill' as Cork Council passed a resolution in favour of the Bill.[117] This was followed by a spate of resolutions around the country. In 1911 a resolution was passed by Dublin Corporation that "a petition be adopted, sealed with the City seal, and presented to Parliament, to pass into law this present session the Women's Suffrage Bill now before Parliament," it was further resolved that the Lord Mayor of Dublin and "as many members as may accompany him", invoking an ancient law, go to the Bar of the House of Commons and present a petition favouring the Bill. The resolution concluded that "the reasonable expenses of the Lord Mayor and said officers be defrayed out of the borough fund". According to Christabel Pankhurst "The news from Dublin comes as a clarion call to all the supporters of the Bill to be up and doing."[118] The Lord Mayor, Tom Kelly, a spokesman for the Irish suffragists on a number of occasions[119] duly went to London and was given a rather rapturous welcome reception by the English suffrage organisations.[120]

Before the third reading of the Bill in 1912 canvassing was intensified. Anna Haslam, the elderly and anti-militant founder of the IWSLGA wrote to Cabinet members and all Irish MPs asking them "to ensure that our Conciliation Bill, or some reasonable extension of it, will be enacted during the present session". She added that had this demand been conceded earlier "the lamentable events which have just occurred in London, and elsewhere, would never have taken place. The responsibility for those lawless acts, in our judgement, must largely rest with those who have so long persistently denied our women any measure of enfranchisement."[121] Despite all this effort at publicising their demand John Redmond in April 1912 was still able to declare "I have never met anybody—man or woman—who was in favour of the Conciliation Bill." He voted against it because "I considered it my duty."[122]

The voting pattern of the Irish Party members from the first to the third Conciliation Bill showed a dramatic turnabout. An identical Bill to the 1912 Bill had received a majority of 167 on the second reading in May 1911, thirty-one Irish members had voted in favour of the Bill. Not one of Redmond's Party voted in favour of it in 1912. Their change of mind was described by one observer thus: "Without a word said on their behalf, without any explanation vouchsafed, those members of the Party who had previously voted in favour of political freedom swung round, and either abstained from a critical division or actually reversed their previous votes . . . ."[123] This revolution in attitudes was more than likely due to the nearing proximity of a Home Rule Bill. Even though other reasons for the defeat of the Bill have been suggested, such as thirteen suffragist Labour MPs being absent because of strikes in their constituencies and the alienation of MPs in general by the window-smashing campaign carried out in London in March, it was admitted that "the absence of Irish Nationalist support alone was sufficient to turn the balance."[124]

In their defence supporters of the Nationalists argued that had the Conciliation Bill passed its second reading its subsequent stages would have taken up time which could have been allocated to Home Rule discussions. "This plea comes well from a faction which thrust aside the Home Rule for the Insurance Bill, and have already assisted in passing the second reading of a Scotch Temperance Bill and the Single Schools Area Bill."[125] The *Irish Times* asked "What does it profit him [Redmond] that he has gained a week of

Parliamentary time and alienated the sympathies of every woman suffragist in Ireland?"[126] However as Rosen points out time wasting may have been the least important consideration in the matter. He argues that "Redmond had urged his followers to oppose the Bill in order to avoid any possibility of Asquith's resigning and the cabinet breaking up, such an occurrence being viewed as detrimental to the prospects of independence for Ireland."[127]

When the Conciliation Bill was defeated with all the Irish Party voting against it or abstaining the suffragists' outrage and bitterness knew no limits.[128] The WSPU issued a statement after its defeat that they knew for many months of Redmond's intention to defeat the Bill in the supposed interests of Home Rule.[129] In Ireland Mrs Palmer spoke of the "dastardly trickery" of the Irish Nationalists.[130] Redmond, not surprisingly, was seen as the culprit. His manœuverings behind the scenes were held responsible for the defeat. His promise made before the voting on the Bill that the Irish Party were free to vote as they wished now seemed treacherous and empty and was focused upon in the post-mortem discussions on the Bill. He told a deputation from the IWFL "I am not inclined to discuss the action of the Irish Party on the matter; the action of the Irish Party was the action of individuals—as a Party we took no action."[131] Hanna Sheehy Skeffington wrote to the *Irish Times* that "if this were true the action of so many 'stalwarts' in 'ratting' on the question would indeed be inexplicable. Not one of them has attempted publicly to justify it." She stated that Mr Brailsford had written that at a meeting of the Irish Party Mr Redmond gave an order that "none of his followers should support women's suffrage this year." This statement was denied by Redmond as being "utterly untrue".[132] Sheehy Skeffington asked

> . . . if this be true why is Mr Redmond ashamed to avow it? If, in the supposed interests of Home Rule, the Irish Party managers thought it wise to declare war on women the public is entitled to know why. A statement from Mr Redmond of the reasons for the action is necessary, and should be insisted on. Those members of the Irish Party who feel keenly the disgrace of their recent "ratting" (and I know that there are

some such) should insist on their leaders shouldering the responsibility which clearly belongs to them.[133]

However to the further disappointment of Skeffington nobody made such a demand. Her husband, Frank, wrote "Had the Irish Party abstained the Con Bill would have passed: it was only by throwing overboard personal convictions and written pledges of a lifetime on the part of the Irish Nationalists that the killing of the measure was secured."[134] Other members of the IWFL also expressed their outrage. Professor Oldham wrote to Redmond

> From Daniel O'Connell all the way down to the Boer war and English labour movement—how clean was the record of Irish Nationalists! That is our moral strength. You are the first Irish leader to smirch our record—when you threw the party vote to kill the Women's Bill. It is not a case of your personal opinions. John Mitchell supported negro slavery as a private person; had he done it as Irish leader his action would have been suicidal to movement for Irish liberty.[135]

A letter appeared in the *Freeman's Journal* supporting Redmond's action but which inadvertently let slip a confirmation of the women's accusations that there had been a Party Whip.[136] Some time later T. P. O'Connor, with what Millicent Fawcett called "a *naivete* for which we thank him", wrote in a letter to the *Chicago Tribune* that Redmond's followers were 'detached' from supporting the Conciliation Bill with the implication that the government would break up if the Bill were passed. This was the reason why he felt there was such a swing in the Irish vote.[137]

The assumption that militancy was an important factor in swinging the vote was met with scepticism in suffrage circles. Even the anti-militant English suffragist Millicent Fawcett felt this was not convincing. She was commenting on Lloyd George's speech to a women's suffrage deputation at Swindon where he told them to face facts:

> He says that the friends of women's suffrage in Ireland were alienated and anti-suffrage feeling created there by attempts to murder Mr Redmond by throwing a hatchet at him . . . The date of this assault was July 1912. The Irish vote was wholly detached from the support of women's suffrage, and the Conciliation Bill consequently defeated, in the previous March almost four months earlier. Unless the Irish

members have the Celtic gift of insight in a very remarkable degree the whole body of Mr Redmond's followers could not have known on March 28 that Mrs Leigh would scratch him with a hatchet in the following July . . .[138]

From the time of the defeat of the third Conciliation Bill the relationship between the suffragists and the Irish Party was almost one of war. According to the *Irish Citizen*

Until the Irish Party killed the Conciliation Bill without a word of explanation or regret, the militant movement in Ireland treated the Party with excessive respect, carefully discriminating between it and the Government. Not till a peaceful parade of suffragists was wantonly assaulted in Dawson Street on Home Rule Sunday, by a mob of Hibernians did the IWFL declare war on the Irish Party. The official Nationalists, not the suffragists were the aggressors. And even yet as the correspondence columns of this paper show, the non-militant suffragists in Ireland are treating the Irish Party with extreme leniency.[139]

After the disappointment of the Conciliation Bills there were a few more Parliamentary straws for the women to grasp at. An amendment to the Home Rule Bill which proposed that the franchise under some circumstances should be extended to Irish women was proposed by Snowden and supported by Lord Robert Cecil and others. Philip Snowden, a member of the English Labour Party, had declared his support of women's suffrage both within the Labour party and in the House of Commons.[140] According to Olive Banks he had been indifferent, if not hostile, to feminism until he was converted by his wife Ethel and her friends Isabella and Bessie Ford.[141] He had been an ardent defender of the Conciliation Bill.[142] He was vice-president for the Men's League for Women's Suffrage and in its handbook of 1912 he advocated women should be enfranchised under the 'Government of Ireland Bill'. His amendment was concerned with the ninth clause of the Home Rule Bill.[143] In the April issue of the *Christian Commonwealth* (a journal to which he contributed regularly) Snowden wrote that the Irish Party in their wisdom "have decided that the cause of Home Rule can best be served by refusing the right of self-government to the women of Ireland and Great Britain." He continued warning that

It will no longer be possible for Mr Redmond and Mr T. P. O'Connor to claim as they have so often claimed, that the labouring classes in Great Britain have always found the Irish classes supporting their demand . . . The Irish members, of course, have a right to shape their own policy and to follow their own course, but if they think they are going to retain their sympathy and support of the British democracy by using Irish votes in Parliament to defeat proposals for which the British democracy were fighting before the present Irish members were born, they are pursuing a line of action which experience will show them to be fatal to their own aims.[144]

His amendment proposed to give the vote to Irish women on the basis of the Local Government register. This would enfranchise 100,000 Irish women, 70,000 of whom owned and managed their own farms. Snowden pointed out that under the proposed Irish Councils Bill for Ireland in 1907 the vote had been offered to women who already had the vote for Town and County Councils. This bill had been refused by the Irish because it had been too restrictive, but not on the grounds that women would get the vote. In the *Men's League Handbook*, 1912 he argued that there was now all-party support for women taking part in Local Government. The proposed Irish Parliament would be a subordinate legislature, therefore there should be no objection to women voting.[145] However there were objections and plenty of them. There was an attempt to have the amendment dropped in exchange for Redmond using his influence to get a women's amendment to the Manhood Suffrage Bill. Hanna Sheehy Skeffington declared that "A deal with these notorious promise-breakers is unthinkable."[146] It was realised from the beginning that it would be difficult getting an unofficial amendment through. Nevertheless an organisation known as the 'Irish Women's Committee for Securing Votes under the Home Rule Bill' was set up in London with the purpose of securing "from Members of Parliament representing constituencies in Great Britain a pledge that they will vote for Mr Philip Snowden's amendment to the Home Rule Bill."[147] During the debate Mr Snowden said he had no hostility to the Bill as such but he felt it was impossible to let the opportunity pass without trying to get representation for women in the new Parliament.[148] The amendment was defeated on 5 November 1912 with an overall vote of two to one to exclude women from the Irish electorate.[149] Seventy-two members of the Irish Party voted against it and eleven for it. Once again the voting of Irish members was not so much on the issue itself but rather on the possible consequences arising from it.[150] After its defeat an article in *Men's League for Women's Suffrage* commented:

> While three of the United States were admitting women to citizenship as an incident in the General Election, our House of Commons was occupying itself in refusing the franchise to the women of Ireland . . . Listening to these three speeches by the two Redmonds and Mr Law, one realised what is at the centre of the situation. The Irish Party is resolved at all costs that the Home Rule Parliament shall not start with women electors. They dread the disruptive effect of the suffrage on the Liberal Cabinet, but even more, it seems to me, they dread the experiment of enfranchising their own sisters and wives . . . In order to perpetuate the votelessness of their own women, they must also enforce the subjection of our own.[151]

In 1913 there was a Woman Suffrage Amendment to the Reform (Suffrage) Bill. This was proposed by Willoughby Dickinson. For a while there was a rumour of a 'plot' that Irish women would not be included in this amendment (as a result of a 'deal' between Lloyd George and the Irish Party) but this turned out not to be the case.[152] It proposed to grant votes to women over twenty-five, women householders and to the wives of voters. It was similar to the situation in Norway and thus was sometimes called the Norwegian Franchise Bill. It was drafted by a group of Liberal MPs. Irish women were not happy with it since it did not give them the vote on the same terms as men but in the words of Hanna Sheehy Skeffington, they felt "'twould serve."[153] The IWFL again hoped that perhaps this time some women would get the franchise, but they were confronted with realities. "Limited and unsatisfactory as this Bill is, we expect the 5 pledged suffragists in the Irish Party to cast their votes in favour of the principle of women's enfranchisement. If the vote is a truly free one, as has been promised, the majority of the Irish Party being suffragist, will give it their support."

However the *Freeman's Journal*'s London correspondent made them wary of being too enthusiastic about the outcome when he wrote that an urgent whip summoning the Irish

Party's full attendance on the Woman Suffrage Bill, when "critical divisions will take place". Kathleen Houston of the IWFL asked why was it 'critical' if the vote was to be an absolutely 'free' one. She asked "Does this mean that the Irish Party are again preparing to throw the women's claim overboard, inspite of their repeated pledges to the contrary . . . ?"[154] Hanna Sheehy Skeffington wrote on the eve of the voting of the Bill "the ways of politicians are devious and dark and the wary suffragist no longer attaches much importance to lip service and election 'pledges'."[155] Irish Members voted against the Dickinson Bill. Twenty-nine of these had been pledged suffragists.[156] The disappointment with its defeat was expressed by the shattering of glass of the United Irish League and the broken windows of Mr John Dillon's house.[157]

A final attempt to enfranchise English and Irish women before the war was the Home Rule amending bill which was to be introduced into the House of Lords after the summer holidays in 1914. It, too, was concerned with giving women who were on the Local Government Register the Parliamentary franchise. The chief obstacle to this again was seen to be Redmond. The Irish suffragists wished to go on deputation to him and to Asquith. Both men refused to see the women—an indication of how they felt the amendment would go.[158] However the Bill did not materialise because of a changed situation as a result of the war.

The role of the Irish Party as a group who could swing legislation on women's suffrage either way in the period discussed above 1910–14 disappeared with the advent of the war. Asquith's decision to form a national government in 1915 meant the Irish lost their powerful position of holding the balance. With the Home Rule Bill gone through all its stages, but deferred because of the war, they now no longer had any reason to have strong objections to a Women's Suffrage Bill. However women's suffrage was brushed aside until 1917 when there was the introduction of a Representation of the People Bill.[159] A women's suffrage amendment to this Bill was proposed and a majority of Irish members voted for it. One historian has written thus of the final achievement of the suffragists' aims.

On the evening of 28 March 1917, after a debate remarkably lacking in acrimony, the Commons approved the introduction of legislation based on the report of the Electoral Conference by an overwhelming majority of 341 to 62. This division marked the real turning point in the Parliamentary progress of women's suffrage—thereafter, the outcome was never seriously in doubt. Just as before the war the passage of women's suffrage legislation had been blocked by a combination of factors—the Liberals' fear of too narrow a franchise, the Tories' fear of too "broad" a franchise, Asquith's premiership, and the desire of Nationalists to keep him in office—so, now, a number of war wrought factors—the decreased importance of party divisions under the Coalition, the remarkably lessened fear of adult suffrage, the entry into the government of several conspicuously fervid suffragists, the replacement of Asquith by Lloyd George . . . combined to create a political climate highly favourable to the enfranchisement of women.[160]

However at this stage to many in Ireland it was now a non-issue. The Republicans had promised a vote to all women over twenty-one (and not over thirty as the English Bill stipulated) and a number of people were now no longer concerned with English legislation. //

The relationship between the Irish Party and the suffragists up to the summer of 1914 can be seen as the struggle between two groups endeavouring to make the other recognise the importance and priority of their cause. Although this applied more in the case of the suffragists, it became so for the Party when they felt their cause was being held back by the women. Each feared the other damaging their goal. The women feared that the Irish Party would bring them into a new Ireland which still had the old problem of unrepresented women, but the Party feared that supporting the women might waste time for their own urgent cause by bringing about legislation which would damage their representation in the Commons, and, worse, cause the collapse of a pro-Home Rule Government. They also felt that another principle was involved—that of having autonomy over what they felt to be a domestic decision, although they were somewhat hypocritical in this. It is clear also that they were traditionalist in that they did not wish their hand to be forced by women. However on a number of occasions a majority of the Irish Party promised the women they would vote in favour of women's suffrage legislation, only time and time again to renege on these promises. It is difficult to assess whether or not these promises were sincerely meant and failed to stand up to the power of the Party Whip or whether they were a mere decoy to distract the women elsewhere. It is true that the MPs felt that legitimate damage could be done to Home Rule if they did not watch their step, but certain inconsistencies in their arguments would lead one to the conclusion that all but a very few cared not a whit for women's suffrage. For them nationalism did not only win over suffragism, it was the only issue. //

Notes

1. Hanna Sheehy Skeffington, "Reminiscences of an Irish Suffragette" in A.D. Sheehy Skeffington and R. Owens, *Irish Women's Struggle for the Vote* (Arlen House, Dublin, 1975), p. 2.
2. Theresa Muir MacKenzie, *Irish Times*, April 1912.
3. According to a correspondent of the *Freeman's Journal* Daniel O'Connell was "a great supporter of human as opposed to masculine rights. He did not ask for Emancipation for men only. He fought for women, too, and in national affairs." *Freeman's Journals*, Nov. 20 1911, p. 6. See valued the opinion of women on political questions and their cooperation in national affairs." *Freeman's Journasl*, Nov. 20 1911, p. 6. See K. Theodore Hoppen, *Elections, Politics and Society in Ireland 1832–1885* (Clarendon Press, Oxford, 1984), pp. 406–8 on women attending his rallies.
4. Margaret MacCurtain, "The Historical Image", *Irishwomen: Image and Achievement*, Eilean Ni Chuilleanain, (ed.) (Arlen House, Dublin, 1985), p. 46.
5. J. H. Whyte, *The Independent Irish Party, 1850–1859* (Oxford University Press, 1958), F. S. L. Lyons, *Ireland Since the Famine* (Weidenfeld and Nicolson, London, 1971), pp. 112–22.
6. F. S. L. Lyons, *Charles Stewart Parnell* (Suffolk, 1977).
7. A. C. Hepburn, *The Conflict of Nationality in Modern Ireland* (Arnold, London, 1980), pp. 48–50.
8. Brian M. Walker (ed.), *Parliamentary Election Results in Ireland, 1861–1922* (Royal Irish Academy, Dublin, 1978).
9. *Irish Times*, April 18, 1912, p. 8.
10. Hanna Sheehy Skeffington, *op. cit.*, p. 13.
11. Rose Lavery, "The Future of Irish Women", *New Ireland Review*, 1908, pp. 193–8.
12. *IC*, June 13, 1914.
13. *VFW*, April 19, 192, p. 456.
14. Cousins, *We Two Together* (Ganesh, Madras, 1950), p. 86.

15. *VFW*, April, 1912.
16. *The Vote*, September 26, 1913, p. 350.
17. Martin Pugh, *Women's Suffrage in Britain 1867–1928* (The Historical Association, London, 1980), p. 28.
18. Les Garner, *Stepping Stones to Women's Liberty: Feminist Ideas in the Women's Suffrage Movement 1900–1918* (Heinemann Educational Books, London, 1984), p. 96.
19. *VFW*, June 28, 1912.
20. *Catholic Suffragist*, December 15, 1915, p. 100.
21. Helen Blackburn, *A Record of the Women's Suffrage Movement in the British Isles* (Williams and Norgate, 14 Henrietta Street, Covent Garden, London, 1902), p. 127. See also *English Women's Review*, February 15, 1877.
22. *Catholic Suffragist*, December 15, 1915, p. 100.
23. Margaret Digby, *Sir Horace Plunkett: An Anglo American Irishman* (Basil Blackwell, Oxford, 1949).
24. See Chapter 6.
25. *Irish Times*, January 15, 1910.
26. *VFW*, December 9, 1910, p. 174.
27. Cousins, *op. cit.*, p. 185.
28. *VFW*, November 3, 1911, p. 68.
29. *Report of the Executive Committee of the Irish Women's Franchise League*, Dublin, 1913, p. 5.
30. Archival Material about the setting up of a London Branch. "Irish Women's Franchise League—London", *Votes for Women*, March 10, 1911, p. 278, *Ibid*, March 31, 1911, p. 434, *Ibid*, May 12, 1911, p. 539. Hanna Sheehy Skeffington, *Irish Review*, July 1912, pp. 225–7.
31. SSP, Ms 21,639 (i).
32. *Ibid*.
33. *IC*, June 13, 1914.
34. Redmond "in December 1909 assured the IWFL deputation that he was 'heart and soul with them' with regard to the treatment of political prisoners." *Irish Citizen*, June 22, 1912, p. 34.
35. *VFW*, October 27, 1911, p. 5.
36. SSP, Ms 21,639 (i).
37. *IC*, June 22, 1912.
38. *Ibid*, July 18, 1913.
39. *Ibid*, June 1, 1912, p. 10.
40. "Not one of them in the Nationalist ranks would remain if they thought there was the slightest possibility of injustice to Protestants. Were not the rights of the women of Ireland equal to the rights of the Protestants of Ireland?" *VFW*, Nov. 3, 1911, p. 68.
41. *VFW*, June 21, 1912, p. 610.
42. Cousins, *op. cit.*, p. 68.
43. *Executive Report*, *op. cit*, p. 6.
44. *VFW*, July 26, 1912, p. 696.
45. Hanna Sheehy Skeffington, *op. cit.*, p. 13.
46. K. Theodore Hoppen, *op. cit.*, pp. 406–8.

47. *Executive Report, op. cit.*, p. 8.
48. *VFW*, June 7, 1912, p. 589.
49. *Ibid*, January 13, 1911, p. 246.
50. F. M. Caroll, *American Opinion and the Irish Question 1910–23*, (Gill and Macmillan, Dublin, 1978).
51. *VFW*, June 7, 1912, p. 589.
52. *IC*, May 25, 1912, p. 2.
53. *Ibid*, April 19, 1912. *Men's League for Women's Suffrage*, July 1912, p. 136.
54. *VFW*, October 20, 1911, p. 41.
55. *Ibid*, Nov 21, 1913, p. 118.
56. *VFW*, May 3, 1912, p. 491.
57. *Ibid*, April 1913, p. 161.
58. *The Freeman's Journal*, April 19, 1912, p. 5.
59. *VFW*, April 19, 1912, p. 45.
60. Hanna Sheehy Skeffington, *op.cit.*, p. 18.
61. *Irish Citizen*, June 22, 1912, p. 36.
62. *Executive Report, op. cit*, p. 6.
63. *VFW*, March 6, 1914, p. 344.
64. *Ibid*, June 7, 1912, p. 577.
65. *Ibid*, May 30, 1913, p. 519.
66. Constance Rover, *Women's Suffrage and Party Politics in Britain 1866–1914* (Routledge and Kegan Paul, London, 1967), p. 155).
67. *Ibid*, October 27, 1911, p. 53.
68. *IC*, December 30, 1910.
69. *Cork Constitution*, June 25, 1913.
70. *Irishwomen's Suffrage Federation, Third Annual Report 1913–1914*, p. 6.
71. *Irishwomen's Suffrage Federation Third Annual Report 1913–1914*, p. 8.
72. *Irishwomen's Suffrage Federation. First Annual Report for 1911–1912*, South Ann Street, Dublin (National Library, Dublin, I3996314) 1911–1912, p. 24.
73. Rover, *op. cit.*, p. 146.
74. GPB Papers.
75. "War in Europe, House of Commons Oral Answers, Women Suffragist Prisoners (Amnesty)", SSP, National Library of Ireland.
76. *VFW*, May 16, 1913, p. 479.
77. As early as 1904 William Redmond was pointing to the success of women's suffrage in Australia. *The Englishwoman*, April 1, 1904, pp. 87–90.
78. *VFW*, April 20, 1912, p. 8.
79. *Ibid*, November 8, 1912, p. 84.
80. *Men's League for Women's Suffrage*, March 1910, p. 22.
81. *VFW*, December 15, 1911, p. 170.
82. *IC*, August 23, 1913, p. 109.
83. *IC*, August 23, 1913, p. 109.
84. *Executive Report, op. cit.*, p. 4.
85. Hugh Law, House of Commons, December 11, 1912.
86. C. P. Curran, *Under the Receding Wave*, (Gill and Macmillan, Dublin,

1970), p. 190.
87. *Ibid*, p. 148.
88. J. B. Lyons, *The Enigma of Tom Kettle—Irish Patriot, Essayist, Poet, British Soldier 1880–1916* (The Glendale Press, Dublin, 1983).
89. *Ibid*, October 27, 1911, p. 53.
90. Leah Levenson, *With Wooden Sword* (Gill and Macmillan, Dublin, 1983), p. 106.
91. *VFW*, October 27, 1911, p. 50.
92. *Anti Suffrage Review*, May 1912, p. 103.
93. *Freeman's Journal*, April 20, 1912, p. 10.
94. Levenson, *op. cit.*, p. 10.
95. *VFW*, April 19, 1912, p. 10.
96. Levenson, *op. cit.*, p. 137.
97. *Votes for Women*, July 4, 1913, p. 590.
98. *Votes for Women*, July 4, 1913, p. 57 and General Prison Board Papers, *op. cit.*
99. *Votes for Women*, July 6, 1912.
100. T. M. Healy, KC MP, *Right of Petition, The Defence at Bow Street* Suffrage box, Personal Authors D–K 396 11B, undated.
101. *IC*, June 13, 1912, p. 9.
102. *IC*, July 6, 1912, p. 49.
103. *Irishwomen's Suffrage Federation, Annual Report, 1912–1913*, p. 6.
104. Tom Garvin, *The Evolution of Irish Nationalist Politics* (Gill and Macmillan, Dublin, 1981), pp. 89–90.
105. Joseph V. O'Brien, *William O'Brien and the Course of Irish Politics 1881–1918* (University of California Press, Berkeley, 1976). William O'Brien, *The Party, Who They Are and What They have Done* (Maunsel, Dublin and London, 1917). "Molly" refers to the Molly Maguires, a violent agrarian secret society with origins in the late eighteenth century.
106. *VFW*, November 8, 1912, p. 85.
107. *IC*, July 25, 1914, p. 78.
108. William O'Brien Diaries, Trinity College, Dublin. Levenson, *op. cit.*, p. 98.
109. *The Catholic Suffragist*, August 15, 1916, p. 76.
110. June 23, 1912, *Sheehy Skeffington Papers*, National Library, Dublin, Ireland.
111. Kenneth O. Morgan, *Suffragists and Liberals* (Oxford, 1975), *passim*.
112. Ronan Fanning, "The Irish Policy of Asquith's Government and the Cabinet Crisis", *Studies in Irish History* (Dublin, 1979), pp. 279–303.
113. Andrew Rosen, *Rise Up Women!* (Routledge and Kegan Paul, London and Boston, 1974), p. 134.
114. Philip Snowden, *In Defence of the Conciliation Bill* (Wandsworth, The Rydal Press, Keighley, undated), Fawcett Library, 396 11B.
115. *Ibid*.
116. *Men's League for Women's Suffrage*, May 1911, p. 77.
117. *VFW*, November 18, 1910, p. 101.
118. *Ibid*, April 17, 1911, p. 444.
119. *Ibid*, August 9, 1912, p. 737.

120. *Men's League for Women's Suffrage*, 1911, p. 77.
121. March 16, 1912, Archival Material Box 295, Fawcett Library, City of London Polytechnic, London, England.
122. SSP Ms 21,639 (i).
123. *VFW*, April 19, 1912, p. 458.
124. Rover, *op. cit.*, p. 95.
125. *VFW*, April 12, 1912, p. 440.
126. *Irish Times* (Votes for Women, April 12, 1912, p. 440).
127. Rosen, *op. cit.*, p. 163.
128. Forty-one Irish Nationalist MPs voted against the Bill. Ten abstained.
129. Rosen, *op. cit.*, p. 163.
130. *Freeman's Journal*, May 1912.
131. SSP Ms 21,639 (i).
132. *Ibid.*
133. *Irish Times*, April 8, 1912, p. 7, col. 6.
134. Undated pencil written letter, SSP Ms 21,639.
135. *Freeman's Journal*, April 2, 1912.
136. *Ibid*, April 3, 1912.
137. *VFW*, February 21, 1913, p. 294.
138. Suffrage Box, Fawcett Library 1905–1914, Personal Authors D–K, 396. 11B.
139. *IC*, May 17, 1913, p. 11.
140. Rover, *op. cit.*, p. 155.
141. Olive Banks, *On Becoming a Feminist* (Harvester Press, Brighton, 1987), p. 120.
142. Philip Snowden, *In Defence of the Conciliation Bill*, *op. cit.*
143. *Men's League for Women's Suffrage Handbook*, 1912.
144. *Christian Commonwealth*, April 1912. See also *Irish Worker*, April 13, 1912, p. 1.
145. Rover, *op. cit.*, p. 155.
146. *VFW*, September 6, 1912, p. 792.
147. *Ibid*, August 30, 1912, p. 769.
148. *Ibid*, November 8, 1912, p. 84.
149. *Ibid.*
150. Rover, *op. cit.*, p. 144.
151. *Men's League for Women's Suffrage*, November 1912, p. 153.
152. Executive Report, *op. cit.*, pp. 3–6.
153. SSP Ms 21,639.
154. Kathleen Houston, Irish Women's Franchise League, May 3, 1913. SSP Ms 21,639.
155. SSP Ms 21,639.
156. *IC*, May 17, 1913, p. 410.
157. *Report of the Executive Committee*, *op. cit.*, p. 5.
158. *VFW*, June 5, 1914, p. 545.
159. Martin D. Pugh, "Politicians and the Women's Vote 1914–1918", *History*, 59 No. 197, 1974, Les Garner, *Stepping Stones to Women's Liberty: Feminist Ideas in the Women's Suffrage Movement 1900–1918* (Heinemann, London, 1984) p. 97, Morgan, *op. cit.*, pp. 47–8.
160. Rosen, *op. cit.*, p. 262.

Conclusion

During the early twentieth century the suffrage movement was a significant force in Irish society. Far from being a fringe movement it crossed into all areas of mainstream Irish life. The very fact that there were so many different groups indicate that the suffrage movement did not draw its members from one limited sector of society. Nationalist, Unionist, Protestant, Catholic, Socialist, Liberal and Conservative were all to be found within its ranks. These women ranged from ladies of leisure to serious young graduates with degrees in law, medicine and the humanities. All agreed on one thing, that women should not be excluded from the electorate because of their gender.

Suffragists were not intellectually impermeable, existing apart from the society around them. They could not ignore outside forces and fight their cause in a vacuum. There were some casualties. A study of these years has shown that the suffrage movement existed almost independently of the dominant nationalist movement and that Irish society was not unidimensional—concerned only with nationalism. However in two ways the suffragists found it impossible to ignore the nationalist cause. It threatened to deplete their numbers. At the same time the women needed the help of Nationalist politicians to get women's suffrage legislation through Parliament. Nationalism was the dominant emotion in Ireland at this time and politicised women were forced to make a decision between their sex and their nation. As has been illustrated some felt obliged to choose the latter. Yet the movement survived.

The suffragists' determination and persistence can be seen in their moving out of meeting rooms to open fields, public squares and town halls in order to reach as wide an audience as possible. Judging from contemporary sources it was not unusual for them to address a crowd numbering between one and two thousand. They were not only active vocally but in print also—publishing an Irish suffrage newspaper and writing letters to the Irish and English press.

The Irish people gave them a mixed reaction but considering the novelty of the idea to many, in a nation that had long been disenfranchised itself, there was a surprising amount of support. There were a number of people in the society interested enough, one way or another, to put pen to paper and express their views on the topic. Comment came from such disparate areas of Irish society as the churches, the press, the intellectuals and a minority of politicians. Support did not always arise out of genuine feminist feeling but rather out of a belief that woman's goodness should be enshrined in the state. Nevertheless such support gave the women backing and encouragement.

Irish suffragists were not just important in an Irish context but in a world context also; and this gives them a rightful claim to a place in world suffrage history which has been denied to them until now. They were clearly very much influenced by international feminism. Yet this was not a one-way process. As well as foreign women coming to Ireland, the Irish women went abroad and were represented at important demonstrations and conferences. They saw that their particular Irish situation applied in the outside world. However they were not just imitationists copying the foreign movements, despite their size they were prepared to take an individual stand and stress their independence as an Irish movement.

That individual stand was reflected at home. There were a number of active suffragists prepared to put in time, money, travel and sometimes personal freedom for the suffrage cause. Their imprisonment, claims for political status and subsequent hungerstriking are testament to a strong central core in the Irish movement. It was not a hobby for these women but a philosophy—a way of life. The terms of their imprisonment evoked debate. They claimed to be in a direct line of Irish political prisoners. They were no different because their concern was with women's suffrage and not with nationalism.

However, much as this study has indicated and to some extent filled a missing gap, it should serve not as a conclusion—but rather as an indicator of what as yet has to be done. A number of questions suggest themselves in the preceding chapters that require detailed investigation by both this writer and others. Among these firstly are the main components of this dissertation, the women themselves. Little is known about many of their lives or the forces that produced them. Even the more well-documented women have been scantily studied. The recent biography of Hanna Sheehy Skeffington has been very welcome but it hopefully is only the beginning.[1] Margaret Cousins, a fascinating woman, has been almost untouched. When she left Ireland in 1913 she went to India and spent a number of decades campaigning for Indian women. Her papers are in the Connemara Library in Madras and should provide the basis of a fascinating biography. Fox's biography of Louie Bennett while commendable could be replaced by a more rigorous work in the light of recent scholarship on women and trade unions.

Apart from women and trade unions the suffragists fall into a number of other interesting categories which could form the basis for a number of thematical studies. There were the suffragist doctors, Dr Kathleen Lynn and Dr Kathleen Maguire. Was there some common feature in their pursuit of a medical education that turned them towards suffragism? Did breaking into an almost entirely male profession equip them with a determination that other spheres such as suffrage should not be denied to them? There were also a number of women writers in the movement. This is especially the case when one looks at the Munster Women's Franchise League. Susan Day, the writing team Somerville and Ross, and Geraldine Cummins were the main women in that organisation. Did it have something to do with their common experiences as writers?

The MWFL and other suffragist groups apart from the IWFL have little or nothing written about them. Is the militant woman more attractive to the woman's historian?

Are the non-militants to be ignored? Part of the answer in the Irish case is that there are more documents left by the IWFL. Many documents disappeared or were destroyed during the Irish War of Independence 1919–21 and thus make in-depth research in a lot of areas impossible. It is difficult enough to find out about those who wished to be visible but what about those women not involved in the movement? How did they feel about women's suffrage? To what extent were they influenced by vocal opposition in their society? Were they inhibited by the Lenten Pastorals and church sermons? Were they nervous at being thought unnationalistic? Or were they conditioned enough not to care? These silent women are almost invisible and it is difficult to recapture what their lives must have been like.

Therefore in conclusion this book has shown that in the early twentieth century the suffrage movement in Ireland involved a significant number of women and was not only reacted to by Irish society but was an integral part of that society. However while this point has been made it is clear that much more work will have to be undertaken before a more balanced picture of Irish history will emerge in the history books. Referring back to the *Irish Citizen*'s claim that the suffrage movement in Ireland was proportionately comparable with that in England, the same cannot be said of scholarly work done in both countries. Unlike England, the last two decades in Ireland have not witnessed a flood of scholarly books on the subject. This should not be so considering the number of potential thesis topics thrown up by the years considered in this book.

Note

1. Levenson, Leah and Jerry H. Natterstad, *Hanna Sheehy Skeffington, Irish Feminist* (Syracuse University Press, Syracuse, 1986).

Note on Primary Sources

The primary sources used in this volume can be found in Dublin, Ireland and London, England. The main Irish suffrage papers are in the National Library of Ireland in Dublin. The sizeable collection of Sheehy Skeffington Papers cover nearly twenty years and contain hundreds of letters including some from well-known foreign suffragists. Another interesting collection is the diaries of Professor Mary Hayden. Also in the National Library are the annual reports of the main suffrage organisations and a number of their publications.

In the State Paper Office, Dublin, there are three untidy, unclassified boxes containing the papers of the General Prisons Board. These papers are almost exclusively concerned with Irish suffragist prisoners. In Trinity College are the papers of Irish Nationalist William O'Brien and also materials from the 1975 Women's Suffrage Exhibition which was held in Dublin. The Fawcett Library, London has a fund of useful sources. It has a vast collection of women's journals and newspapers, feminist and otherwise, as well as other contemporary publications. The Harrison tapes have been very valuable to this work and to my knowledge the interviews with Irish women have not been utilised by an Irish historian before. The Police Records in the Public Records Office, Kew, London, contain very little comment on women's suffrage meetings which is rather interesting. The British Library's newspaper library at Colindale has a marvellous collection of newspapers which include the *Irish Citizen* and provincial Irish newspapers. Other useful libraries and archives include the British Library, Public Records Office, Dublin, Senate House Library, London.

Bibliography

Primary Sources

Archival Material

Sheehy Skeffington Papers in National Library of Ireland.
Mary Hayden's Diaries in National Library of Ireland.
William O'Brien Papers, Trinity College, Dublin.
Shaw Papers, British Library, London.
Haslam Papers, British Library, London.
Irish Women's Workers Union minutes 1913–1960, No. 1060 Public Records Office, Ireland.
Police Records Co. 904, Public Records Office, Kew, London.
Hunger Strike and Political Status of Irish Prisoners CO906/18/3 (sets out conditions for treatment of political prisoners in Ireland refers back to Temporary Discharge for Ill-Health Act, 1913), Public Records Office, Kew, London.
Suffrage boxes numbers 76, 89, 303, 147, 148, 149, 298, 396 Fawcett Library, City of London Polytechnic, London.
Tape recordings with Irish suffragists, their friends and relations by Brian Harrison made in 1977, in Fawcett Library, London.
Recording made at The White House, Albany Street, March 1960. Lady Sheet conducts interview with Mary Leigh, Fawcett Library 396 11B.

Annual Reports

Irish Women's Suffrage and Local Government Association 1896–1918, National Library of Ireland.
Annual Reports of the Irish Women's Franchise League, National Library of Ireland.
Report of the Executive Committee of the IWFL 1913, National

Library of Ireland.
Annual Reports of the Irishwomen's Suffrage Federation, National Library of Ireland.
Annual Reports of the Church League for Women's Suffrage, Fawcett Library, London.
Annual Reports of Catholic Women's Suffrage Society, Fawcett Library, London.

Newspapers
Anti Suffrage Review
Bean na hEireann
The Catholic Suffragist
The Catholic Review
The Church of Ireland Gazette
Common Cause
The Cork Constitution
The Cork Examiner
Cork Free Press
Daily Express
The Evening Standard
The Freeman's Journal
The Irish Catholic
Irish Citizen
The Irish Independent
The Irish Times
The Irish Worker
Men's League for Women's Suffrage
The Nation
The National Democrat
United Ireland
The Vote
Votes for Women
The Women's Dreadnought

Journals
Alexandra Magazine
Catholic Bulletin
The Catholic Suffragist 1915–1918 monthly
Church League for Women's Suffrage 1912–1917 monthly
The Conservative and Unionist Women's Franchise Review
Coming Day/Free Church League for Women's Suffrage 1916–1920 weekly
The Cross
The Englishwoman

The Englishwoman's Review
English Woman's Journal
The Irish Homestead
The Irish Nation
The Irish Review 1911–1914
The Irish Ecclesiastical Record
Men's League for Women's Suffrage
Monthly News of the Conservative and Unionist Women's Franchise Association 1914–1918
New Ireland Review

Plays
Frank Sheehy Skeffington, "The Prodigal Daughter" A Comedy in One Act published by *Irish Citizen* 1915.

Short Stories
Nellie O'Connor "Kitty's Fight for Freedom", *The Catholic Bulletin*, pp. 290–301.

Articles
Anon., "Some Further Reasons Why An Irishwoman Would Like 'The Suffrage', *The Englishwoman's Review*, April 15, 1898, pp. 99–102.
Barry, Rev. D., "Female Suffrage from a Catholic Standpoint", *Irish Ecclesiastical Record*, Vol. xxv, pp. 293–303, Sept 1909.
Boyd, Ernest A., "Feminism and Women's Struggle", *Irish Review*, May 1913.
Clery, Arthur E., "The Religious Aspect of Women's Suffrage", *Irish Review*, November 1913, pp. 479–84.
Colum, Padraic, "Francis Sheehy Skeffington", *The Irish Rebellion of 1916 and its Tragic Martyrs*, Maurice Jay (ed.) (New York: Devin-Adair, 1916), pp. 380–92.
Duffy, Patrick J., "The Education of Catholic Girls", *Catholic Bulletin*, March 1912, pp. 162–7.
Editorial, *Irish Review*, May 1911 (on subject of growing female emigration), pp. 105–8.
Esmond, Eily, "Woman's Suffrage in Ireland", *The Catholic Suffragist*, September 15, 1915, p. 72.
Gonne, Maud, "Responsibility", *Irish Review*, December 1911, pp. 483–5.
Gore Booth, Eve, "The Women's Suffrage Movement Amongst Trade Unionists" in Brougham Villers *The Case for Women's Suffrage* (London, 1907).
Hayden, Mary, "Women in the Middle Ages", *Irish Review*, August

1913, pp. 282–95, September 1913, pp. 344–58.

Kettle, Thomas, "The Amending Bill", *Dublin Review*, July 29, 1914.

Lavery, Rose, "The Future of Irish Women", *New Ireland Review*, December 1908, pp. 193–8.

Mellone, Dora, "Women's Suffrage in Ireland", *The Englishwoman*, October 1913, p. 1.

Mitchell, Susan, "The Petticoat in Politics", *The Voice of Ireland*, William G. Fitzgerald (ed.) (Dublin, John Heywood, 1924), pp. 64–6.

O'Delaney, Barry, "Cumann na mBan", *The Voice of Ireland, Ibid*, p. 62.

Reynier, Madeline, "La Mentalité Féminine Française", *Irish Review*, June 1913, pp. 191–4.

Russell, George, "Ideals of the New Rural Society", *The United Irishwomen, Their Place, Work and Ideal*, Horace Plunkett (ed.) (Dublin, Maunsel and Co., 1911), pp. 36–50.

Ryan, Frederick, "The Suffrage Tangle", *Irish Review*, September 1912, pp. 346–51.

Sheehy Skeffington, "Irish Secondary Teachers", *Irish Review*, October 1912, pp. 393–8.

―――― "The Women's Movement—Ireland", *Irish Review*, July 1912, pp. 225–7.

―――― "Women in Politics", *The Bell*, November 1943, pp. 143–8.

Snowden, Philip, "The Dominant Issue", *Christian Commonwealth*, February 5, 1913.

"Suffrage Plays in Dublin", *Sinn Fein*, April 23, 1910, p. vii.

Tod, Isabella, "Temperance and Women's Suffrage", *Englishwoman's Review*, March 15, 1888, pp. 103–7.

Tynan, Katherine, "A Trumpet Call to Irish Women", *The Voice of Ireland*, William G. Fitzgerald (ed.) (Dublin, John Heywood, 1924), pp. 70–4.

Wyse Power, Mrs, "The Political Influence of Women in Modern Ireland", *The Voice of Ireland, ibid*, pp. 158–61.

Pamphlets

Aberdeen, Countess (ed.), *Women in Politics, The International Congress of Women 1899* (London, T. Fisher Unwin, 1900).

Byers, Mrs (Principal of Victoria College, Belfast) *Girls' Education in Ireland, Hopes and Fears* (Belfast, 1889).

Clayton, Joseph, *Votes for Women, The Appeal to Catholics* (published by Catholic Women's Suffrage Society, London, undated).

Christie, Elizabeth, *A Word on Woman Suffrage*, published by The

Catholic Women's Suffrage Society (undated, Fawcett Library).

Cousins, Margaret, *The Awakening of Asian Womanhood*, Madras 1912.

Cumann na mBan Manifesto (Dublin, 1914).

Cumann na mBan, Constitution and Rules (Dublin, 1915).

Day, S. R., *Women in the New Ireland* (Cork, published by Munster Women's Franchise League, 1912).

Despard, Charlotte, *Theosophy and the Women's Movement* (London, 1913).

—— *Women in the New Era* (London, The Suffrage Shop, 1910).

Deuchar, Maude L., *The Sheehy Skeffington Case* (London, The National Labour Press Limited, 1916).

Elliott, Rev. J., *An American Priest on Votes for Women* (Dublin, published by Irish Catholic Women's Suffrage Association, 1915).

Ephedros, *The Economic Aspect of Women's Suffrage* (Irish Women's Reform League) (Dublin, Corrigan and Wilson, undated).

Gordon, Helen, *The Prison, A Sketch: An Experience of Forcible Feeding* (Manchester Strangeways Prison, 1909).

Handbook of the National Union of Women Workers of Great Britain and Ireland, Constitutions, Bye-Laws, List of Committees, Affiliated Societies and other Information. (London, published by NUWW at the Office, 59 Berners Street, 1898).

Haslam, Thomas, *Women's Suffrage from a Masculine Standpoint* (Dublin, 1906).

—— *Some Last Words on Women's Suffrage* (Dublin, 1916).

Healy, T. M., *Right of Petition The Defence at Bow Street*, Box D–K 396 11B, Fawcett Library.

Holloway, Joseph, *Some Impressions of a Dublin Playgoer* (Dublin, 1910).

Irish Women's Franchise League Programme of Public Meetings (National Library of Ireland ILB 94109).

Leigh, Mary, *Fed by Force, a statement by Mrs Mary Leigh Who is still in Birmingham Gaol 1909* (London 1909).

Markievicz, Countess, *Women, Ideals and the Nation* (Dublin, 1900).

Men's League for Women's Suffrage Annual Report (London, 1912).

Pankhurst, Mrs, *Why We Are Militant, A Speech delivered in New York Oct 21 1913* (London, The Woman's Press, 1914).

Pethick Lawrence, Emmeline, *The Faith that is in Us* (London, Women's Press, Strand, undated).

Pethick Lawrence, F.W., *Treatment of the Suffragettes in Prison* (undated 2 page pamphlet Fawcett Library Box 396 11).

—— *The Trial of the Suffragette Leaders* (London, undated).

Shaw, George Bernard, '*The Unmentionable Case for Women's*

Suffrage', Fawcett Library Suffrage Box S–Z 396.113 taken from *Englishwoman* (undated), pp. 112–13.

Sheehy Skeffington, Francis, *War and Feminism*, republished in Leah Levenson, *With Wooden Sword* (Dublin, Gill and Macmillan, 1983), pp. 241–59.

Sheehy Skeffington, Hanna, *Sinn Fein in America* (Dublin, The Davis Publishing Co., 1919).

——— *British Militarism as I have known it* (New York, Donnelly Press, 1917).

Snowden, Philip, *In Defence of the Conciliation Bill* (The Rydal Press, Keighley undated Fawcett Library).

Registration of Women Electors under the Local Government Act (Cork, 1904).

The Treatment of the Women's Deputation by the Metropolitan Police, Copy of Evidence collected by Dr Jessie Murray and Mr H. N. Brailsford, and forwarded to the Home Office by the Conciliation Committee in Support of its demand for a Public Enquiry (London, The Woman's Press, 1912).

Women's Suffrage in Practice (London, published by The International Woman Suffrage Alliance, 1913) (Available in Fawcett Library—a few references to Ireland).

Books

Blackburn, Helen (ed.), *A Handy Book of Reference for Irishwomen* (London, published at The Irish Exhibition, Olympia, London, 1888).

——— *A Record of the Women's Suffrage Movement in the British Isles* (Messrs Williams and Norgate, London, 1902).

Bradshaw, Myrrha, *Open Door for Irish Women* (issued by Irish Central Bureau for the Employment of Women, 30 Molesworth Street, Dublin, 1907).

Colquhoun, Mrs Archibald, *The Vocation of Woman* (Macmillan, London, 1913).

Connolly, James, *The Reconquest of Ireland* (Published at Liberty Hall and printed by Trade Union Labour on Irish paper, Dublin, 1915).

Day, Susan, *The Amazing Philanthropists* (Sidgwick and Jackson, London, 1916).

Fairfield, Zoë (ed.), *Some Aspects of the Woman's Suffrage Movement* (published by Student Christian Movement, London, 1915).

Fawcett, M. G., *The Women's Victory and After* (London, 1920).

Harvey, Rev. Edward John, *The Five Talents of Woman, A Book for Girls and Woman* (Fisher Unwin, London, 1888).

O'Brien, William, *The Party Who They Are and What They Have Done* (Maunsel and Co. Ltd., Dublin and London, 1917).

Owens Blackburne, Elizabeth, *Illustrious Irish Women* (Tinsely, London, 1887).

Pankhurst, Christabel, *The Great Scourge and How to end it* (London, 1913).

Pankhurst Emmeline, *My Own Story* (London, 1914).

Pankhurst, Sylvia, *The Suffragette Movement. An Intimate Account of Persons and Ideals* (Longman's, London, 1931).

Plunkett, Sir Horace, *United Irishwomen* (Maunsel and Co., Dublin, 1911).

The Polite Lady: or, a course of Female Education. In a series of letters from a mother to her daughter (Dublin, printed for J. Exshaw [edc] 1763).

Roberts, Katherine, *Pages From the Diary of a Militant Suffragette* (Garden City Press, London, 1910).

Tynan, Katherine, *Twenty-Five Years: Reminiscences* (Smith Elder, London, 1913).

Wells, H. G., *Ann Veronica* (Fisher Unwin, London, 1909).

Zimmerman, Alice, *Women's Suffrage in Many Lands* (Chancery Lane, London, 1909).

Secondary Sources

Unpublished Theses

Collins, Finola, *The Ladies Land League*, MA (University College Cork, 1973).

Feeney, Mary, *Alexandra College and the Higher Education of Women 1886* (Dublin, 1977).

Hannigan, Ken, *Francis Sheehy Skeffington*, Dissertation, (University College Dublin, 1975).

Articles

Boyle, Emily, "The Linen Strike of 1872, *Saothar 2* (Journal of Irish Labour History Society), 1976, pp. 12–22.

Breathnach, Eileen, "Women and Higher Education in Ireland (1879–1914)", *Crane Bag*, v, 1, 1968, pp. 47–54.

Breathnach, Eibhlin, "Charting new waters: women's experience in higher education, 1879–1908", *Girls Don't Do Honours: Irish women in education in the 19th and 20th centuries*", Mary Cullen, ed. (Women's Education Bureau, Argus Press, Dublin, 1987), pp. 55–78.

Campbell Ross, Ian, "The Triumph of Prudence over Passion: Nationalism and Feminism in an Eighteenth Century Irish Novel", *Irish University Review*, pp. 132–240.

Caine, B., "John Stuart Mill and the English Women's Movement", *Historical Studies*, Vol. 18 (1978) pp. 52–67.

Cullen, Mary, "Some Aspects of Feminist Studies", *Educational Matters*, No. 1, December 1978.

—— "How Radical was Irish Feminism between 1860 and 1920?", *Radicals, Rebels and Establishments, Historical Studies* xv (Dublin, Appletree Press, 1985), pp. 185–201.

—— "Women in History", *Maynooth Review*, 1980.

—— "Telling it Our Way", *Personally Speaking*, Steiner-Scott, Liz, ed. (Attic Press, Dublin, 1985), pp. 254–66.

Daly, Mary E., "Women in the Irish Workforce from Pre-Industrial to Modern Times", *Saothar* 7, 1981, pp. 74–82.

—— "The Development of the National School System 1831–40", *Studies in Irish History*, Cosgrove and MacCartney (eds) (University College, Dublin, 1979), pp. 150–163.

Devine, Francis, "Women in the Irish Movement: A Note", *Oibre* 2 (Journal of the Irish Labour History Society), 1975.

Fahey, Tony, "Nuns in the Catholic Church in Ireland in the nineteeth century", *Girls Don't Do Honours: Irish Women in Education in the 19th and 20th Centuries*, Mary Cullen, ed. (Women's Education Bureau, Argus Press, 1987), pp. 7–30.

Fanning, Ronan, "The Irish Policy of Asquith's Government and the Cabinet Crisis", *Studies in Irish History*, pp. 279–303.

Farrell, Brian, "Markievicz and the Women of the Revolution", *Leaders and Men of the Easter Rising Dublin 1916*, F. X. Martin (ed.) (Cornell University Press 1967), pp. 227–38.

Fletcher, Sheila, "Sailing to the Edge of the World", *History Today*, September 1987, pp. 10–11.

Gwynn, Denis, "Thomas M. Kettle 1880–1916", *Studies*, 55, 1966, pp. 384–91.

Hause, Steven C. and Kenny, Anne R., "The Development of the Catholic Women's Suffrage Movement in France 1896–1922", *Catholic Historical Review*, 1984, pp. 11–30.

Hughes, Marie, "The Parnell Sisters", *Dublin Historical Record*, Vol. 20, No. 1, March 1966, pp. 14–27.

International Women's News, Obituary to Dr Mary Hayden, September 1942.

Jordan, Ellen, "The Christening of the New Woman: May 1894", *The Victorian Newsletter*, Spring 1983, No. 63, pp. 19–21.

Kime Scott, Bonnie, "Emma Clery in *Stephen Hero*" in Henke,

Women in Joyce (Brighton: Harvester Press, 1982).

Lee, Joseph, "Women and the Church since the Famine", *Women in Irish Society, The Historical Dimension*, MacCurtain and O'Corrain, eds (Arlen House, Dublin, 1978).

McHugh, Roger, "Tom Kettle and Francis Sheehy Skeffington", *University Review*, 1, 9, 1956, pp. 6–18.

McKillen, Beth, "Irish Feminism and National Separatism 1914–1923", *Eire/Ireland* xvii: 3, Fall 1981, pp. 2–67; xvii: 4, Winter 1982, pp. 72–90.

MacCurtain, Margaret, "Towards An Appraisal of the Religious Image of Women", *Crane Bag*, Vol. 4, No. 1, 1980, pp. 26–53.

———— "The Historical Image", *Irishwomen: Image and Achievement. Women in Irish Culture from Earliest Times*, Eilean Ni Chuilleanain, (ed.) (Arlen House, Dublin, 1985), pp. 37–50.

Madden-Simpson, Janet, "Womanwriting", *Personally Speaking*, Steiner-Scott, Liz (ed.) (Attic Press, Dublin, 1985) pp. 177–88.

Malcolm, Elizabeth, "Temperance and Irish Nationalism", *Ireland Under the Union Varieties of Tension*, F. S. L. Lyons and R. A. J. Hawkins (eds) (Oxford: Clarendon Press, 1980).

Moloney, Helena, "James Connolly and Women", *Dublin Labour Year Book* 1930.

Moriarity, Theresa, "No vote, no information", *Irish Times*, April 3 1981 p. 12.

New York Times, "Mrs Skeffington, Irish Patriot Dies", *New York Times*, April 21 1946.

O'Connor, Anne V., "The Revolution in girls' secondary education in Ireland, 1860–1910", *Girls Don't Do Honours: Irish women in Education in the 19th and 20th Centuries*, Mary Cullen, ed. (Women's Education Bureau, Argus Press, Dublin, 1987), pp. 31–54.

Owens, Rosemary, "Votes for Ladies, Votes for Women; Organised Labour and the Suffrage Movement 1876–1922", *Saothar 9, Journal of the Irish Labour History Society*, 1983.

Pankhurst, Richard, "Anna Wheeler—A Pioneer Socialist", *Political Quarterly*, Vol. 25 (1954), pp. 132–43.

Prelinger, C., "Religious Dissent and Women's Rights and the Hamburger Hochschule für das weibliche Geschlecht in mid-nineteenth century", *Church History*, March 1976, V, Col. 45, pp. 42–5.

Pugh, Martin, "Politicians and the Women's Vote 1914–1918", *History*, 59, No. 197, 1974, pp. 358–75.

Rimo, Patricia, A., "Mollie Colum and Her Circle", *Irish Literary Supplement*, Fall 1985, pp. 26–7.

Rowan, Caroline, "Women in the Labour Party 1906–1920", *Feminist Review*, Vol. 12 (1982), pp. 74–91.

Smyth, Ailbhe, "Feminism in the South of Ireland", *The Honest Ulsterman*, No. 83, Summer 1987, pp. 41–58.

——— "Voices of Feminism", *Irish Review*, Summer 1987, pp. 116–19.

Van Voris, Jacqueline, "Daniel O'Connell and Women's Rights, One Letter", *Eire/Ireland*, xvii:3, pp. 35–9.

Walzi, Florence, "Dubliners: Women in Irish Society", *Women in Joyce*, Henke and Unkeless (eds) (Brighton, Harvester Press, 1982).

Ward, Margaret, "Feminism in the North of Ireland", *The Honest Ulsterman*, No. 83, Summer 1987, pp. 59–70.

——— "Suffrage First Above All Else: An Account of the Irish Suffrage Movement", *Feminist Review*, No. 10, London, Pluto Press, 1982.

——— and McMinn, Joanna, "Belfast Women Against All the Odds", *Personally Speaking* (Dublin, Attic Press, 1985), pp. 189–200.

Pamphlets

Pugh, Martin, Women's Suffrage in Britain 1867–1928 (London, 1980).

Sheehy Skeffington, A.D. and Owens, R., *Votes for Women: Irish Women's Struggle for the Vote* (Dublin, 1975).

A Venture in Faith: A History of St Joan's Social and Political Alliance, formerly the Catholic Women's Suffrage Society 1911–1961 (London, published by St Joan's Alliance, 1962).

Books

Akenson, D. H., *The Irish Education Experiment: The National System of Education in the Nineteenth Century* (London, 1970).

Banks, Olive, *The Biographical Dictionary of British Feminists Vol. 1 1800–1930* (Harvester Press, Brighton, 1987).

——— *Faces of Feminism* (Martin Robertson, Oxford, 1981).

——— *Becoming a Feminist: The Social Origins of "First Wave" Feminism* (Harvester Press, Brighton, 1987).

Barash, Carol (ed.), *An Olive Schreiner Reader* (Pandora, 1987).

Beale, Jenny, *Women in Ireland—Voices of Change* (Gill and Macmillan, Dublin, 1986).

Berresford, Ellis P. (ed.), *James Connolly: Select Writings* (Penguin, London, 1973).

—————— A History of the Irish Working Class (Victor Gollancz, London, 1972).

Bew, Paul, Conflict and Conciliation in Ireland 1890–1910: Parnellites and Radical Agrarians (Clarendon Press, Oxford, 1986).

Bolger, Patrick, The Irish Cooperative Movement: Its History and Development (Dublin, 1977) (Chapter on William Thompson and Anna Wheeler).

Boumelha, Penny and Foley, Tadgh, In the Shadow of his Language: Gender and Nationality in Nineteenth Century Irish Fiction (Harvester Press, forthcoming).

Bowen, Desmond, Paul Cardinal Cullen and the Shaping of Modern Irish Catholicism (Gill and Macmillan, Dublin, 1980).

Boylan, H. A Dictionary of Irish Biography (Gill and Macmillan, Dublin, 1978).

Brailsford, H. N., Shelley, Godwin and their Circle (London, 1912).

Breathnach, Eibhlin, Staking our Claim: The Women's Movement for Higher Education in Ireland (Arlen House, Dublin, 1988).

Bright, Esther, Old Letters and Memories of Annie Besant (Theosophical Publishing House, London, 1936).

Burke, Helen, The People and the Poor Law in Ireland (Arlen House, Dublin, 1987).

Byrne, J. F., Silent Years: An Autobiography (Farrar, Straus and Young, New York, 1953).

Cardoza, Nancy, Maud Gonne: Lucky Eyes and a High Heart (Victor Gollancz, London, 1979).

Carroll, F. M., American Opinion and the Irish Question 1910–23 (Gill and Macmillan, Dublin, 1978).

Collis, Maurice, Somerville and Ross: A Biography (Faber, London, 1968).

Colum, Mary, Life and Dream (Macmillan and Co., New York, 1947).

Comerford, R. V., The Fenians in Context (Wolfhound Press, Dublin, 1985).

Concannon, Helena, Women of '98 (Gill, Dublin, 1919).

—————— Daughters of Banba (Gill, Dublin, 1930).

Conlon, Lil, Cumann na mBan and the Women of Ireland 1913–25 (Kilkenny People Ltd, 1969).

Cousins, James and Margaret, We Two Together (Ganesh, Madras, 1950).

Coxhead, Elizabeth, Daughters of Erin: Five Women of the Irish Renaissance (Secker and Warburg, London, 1969).

Craig, Patricia, Elizabeth Bowen (Penguin, 1987).

Cronin, John, *Somerville and Ross* (Bucknell University Press Irish, Writers series, 1972).

Cronin, Sean, *Irish Nationalism: A History of its Roots and Ideology* (Academy Press, Dublin, 1980).

Cullen, Mary (ed.), *Girls Don't Do Honours: Irish women in Education in the 19th and 20th Centuries* (Women's Education Bureau, Argus Press, Dublin, 1987).

Cullen Owens, Rosemary, *Smashing Times* (Attic Press, Dublin, 1984).

Curran, C. P., *Under the Receding Wave* (Gill and Macmillan, Dublin, 1970).

Denson, Alan, *James H. Cousins and Margaret E. Cousins. A Bio-Bibliographical Survey* (Kendal, Alan Denson, 1967, National Library of Ireland, IR 92C152).

Digby, Margaret, *Sir Horace Plunkett: An Anglo American Irishman* (Basil Blackwell, Oxford, 1949).

Diner, Hasia, *Erin's Daughters in America: Irish Immigrant Women in the Nineteenth Century* (Johns Hopkins UP, Baltimore and London).

Doughan, David and Sanchez, Denise, *Feminist Periodicals 1855–1984: An Annotated Critical Bibliography of British, Irish, Commonwealth and International Titles* (Harvester Press, Brighton, 1987).

Edwards, Ruth Dudley, *James Connolly*, (Gill and Macmillan, Dublin, 1981).

Ellmann, Richard, *Four Dubliners* (Hamish Hamilton, 1987).

Ellsworth, Edward, *Literature of the Female Mind. Educational Reform and the Women's Movement* (Greenwood Press, London, 1979).

Evans, R. J., *The Feminists: Women's Emancipation Movements in Europe, America and Australasia 1840–1920* (Croom Helm, London, 1977).

Evans, Richard, *Comrades and Sisters: Feminism Socialism and Pacifism in Europe 1870–1945* (Harvester Press, Brighton, 1987).

Fallon, Charlotte, *Soul of Fire* (The Mercier Press, Cork and Dublin, 1986).

Ffrench Eager, *Irene Margaret Anna Cusak: One Woman's Campaign for Women's Rights; A Biography* (Arlen House, Dublin, 1980).

Fitz-Gerald, William G., *The Voice of Ireland: A Survey of the Race and Nation from all Angles By the Foremost Leaders at Home and Abroad* (John Heywood Ltd, Dublin, 1924).

Fox, R. M., *Louie Bennett* (Talbot Press, Dublin, 1957).

———— *Rebel Irish Women* (Talbot Press, Dublin, 1935).

Fulford, Roger, *Votes for Women. The Story of a Struggle* (Faber and Faber, London, 1956).

Gaddis, Rose Marily, *Katherine Tynan* (Bucknell University Press, Irish Writers series, 1974).

Gallagher, S. F. (ed.), *Women in Irish Legend, Life and Literature* (Colin Smythe, Bucks, 1983).

Garner, Les, *Stepping Stones to Women's Liberty: Feminist Ideas in the Women's Suffrage Movement 1900–1918* (Heinemann Educational Books, London 1984).

Garvin, Tom, *The Evolution of Irish Nationalist Politics* (Gill and Macmillan, Dublin, 1981).

Gawthorpe, Mary, *Uphill to Holloway* (Traversity Press, Penobscot, Maine, 1962).

Gwynn, Stephen Lucius, *John Redmond's Last Years* (E. Arnold, London, 1919).

—— *The Life of John Redmond* (London, 1932).

Harrison, Brian, *Separate Spheres: Opposition to Women's Suffrage 1867–1928* (London, 1978).

Hearne, Dana (ed.), *The Tale of a Great Sham* (Arlen House, Dublin, 1987).

Henderson, Leslie M., *The Goldstein Story* (Stockland Press, Melbourne, 1973).

Henke and Unkeless (eds), *Women in Joyce* (Harvester Press, Brighton, 1982).

Hepburn, A. C., *The Conflict of Nationality in Modern Ireland* (London, 1980).

Hickey, D. J. and Doherty, J. E., *A Dictionary of Irish History since 1800* (Gill and Macmillan, Dublin, 1980).

Hoppen, K. Theodore, *Elections, Politics and Society in Ireland 1832–1885*, (Clarendon Press, Oxford, 1984).

Jalland, Pat, *Women from Birth to Death: The Female Life Cycle in Britain 1830–1914* (Harvester Press, Brighton, 1987).

Johnson, Josephine, *Bernard Shaw's New Women* (Colin Smythe, Gerrards Cross, 1975).

Kime Scott, Bonnie, *Joyce and Feminism* (Harvester Press, Brighton, 1984).

—— *James Joyce* (Harvester Press, Brighton, 1987).

Kohfeldt, Mary Lou, *Lady Gregory, The Woman Behind the Irish Renaissance* (Athenaeum, London, 1985).

Kraditor, Aileen S., *The Ideas of the Woman Suffrage Movement/ 1890–1920* (W.W. Norton, New York, 1981).

Levenson, Leah, *With Wooden Sword* (Gill and Macmillan, Dublin, 1983).

———— and Jerry Naderstad, *Hanna Sheehy Skeffington: A Pioneering Irish Feminist* (Syracuse University Press, 1986).

Levenson, Samuel, *Maud Gonne* (Cassell, London, 1977).

Linklater, Andro, *An Unhusbanded Life. Charlotte Despard, Suffragette, Socialist and Sinn Feiner* (Hutchinson, London, 1980).

Lyons, F. S. L., *Ireland Since the Famine* (Weidenfeld and Nicolson, London, 1971).

Lyons, F. S. L., *Charles Stewart Parnell* (Fontana, London, 1977).

Lyons, J. B., *The Enigma of Tom Kettle—Irish Patriot, Essayist, Poet, British Soldier 1880–1916* (The Glendale Press, Dublin, 1983).

MacCurtain, Margaret and O'Corrain, Donnacha (eds), *Women in Irish Society: The Historical Dimension* (Arlen House, Dublin, 1978).

McDowell, P. B., *Alice Stopford Green* (Allen Figgs, Dublin, 1969).

MacKenzie, Midge, *Shoulder to Shoulder. A Documentary* (Allen Lane, London, 1975).

Madden Simpson, Janet, *Woman's Part: An Anthology of Short Fiction by and about Irishwomen 1890–1960* (Arlen House, Dublin, 1984).

Marreco, A., *Rebel Countess: The Life and Times of Countess Markievicz* (London, 1967).

Mitchell, David, *Women on the War Path* (London, 1967).

Mitchell, David, *The Fighting Pankhursts* (Jonathen Cape, London, 1967).

Morgan, David, *Suffragists and Liberals* (Blackwell, Oxford, 1975).

Nethercote, Arthur H., *The Last Four Lives of Annie Besant* (Hart Davis, London, 1963).

Ni Chuilleanain, Eilean (ed.), *Irishwomen: Image and Achievement* (Arlen House, Dublin, 1985).

Ni Dhubhghaill, C. Maire, *Women in Ancient and Modern Ireland* (Kenny Press, Dublin, 1971).

Ni Eireamhon, Eibhlin, *Two Great Irish Women, Maud Gonne MacBride and Countess Markievicz* (Fallon, Dublin, 1971).

O'Brien, Joseph, *William O'Brien and the Course of Irish Politics 1881–1918* (University of California Press, Berkeley, 1976).

O'Broin, Leon, *Protestant Nationalists in Revolutionary Ireland. The Stopford Connection* (Gill and Macmillan, Dublin, 1985).

Pankhurst, R. K. P., *William Thomson, 1775–1883* (Watts, London, 1954).

Pethick Lawrence, Emmeline, *My Part in Changing the World* (Victor Gollancz, London, 1938).

Pethick Lawrence, Frederick, *My Fate has been Kind* (Hutchinson, London, 1943).

Raeburn, Antonia, *The Militant Suffragettes* (London, 1973).

Rendell, Jane, *The Origins of Modern Feminism* (Macmillan, Basingstoke, 1985).

Romero, Patricia, *Sylvia Pankhurst: Portrait of a Radical* (Yale University Press, 1987).

Rose, Catherine, *The Female Experience: The Story of the Woman Movement in Ireland* (Arlen House, Dublin, 1975).

Rosen, Andrew, *Rise Up Women!* (Routledge and Kegan Paul, London and Boston, 1974).

Rover, Constance, *Woman's Suffrage and Party Politics in Britain 1866–1914* (Routlege and Kegan Paul, London, 1967).

Rubinstein, David, *Before the Suffragettes: Women's Emancipation in the 1890s* (Harvester Press, Brighton, 1987).

Russell, G. W., *Selections from the Contributions to the Irish Homestead*, Henry Summerfield, ed. (Humanities Press, Atlantic Highlands, NJ, 1978).

Somerfield, Henry, *That Myriad Minded Man: A Biography of George Russell (AE)* (Colin Smythe, Bucks, 1975).

Snowden, Philip, *An Autobiography* (Nicholson and Watson, London, 1934).

Strachey, Ray, *Millicent Garrett Fawcett* (John Murray, London, 1931).

Tomalin, Claire, *The Life and Death of Mary Wollstonecraft* (Penguin, Harmondsworth, 1977).

Townshend, Charles, *Political Violence in Ireland Government and Resistance since 1848* (Clarendon Press, Oxford, 1983).

Van Vorris, Jacqueline, *Constance Markievicz: In the Cause of Ireland* (Massachusetts University Press, Amherst, 1967).

Walker, Brian M. (ed.), *Parliamentary Election Results in Ireland 1861–1922* (Royal Irish Academy, Dublin, 1978).

Ward, Margaret, *Unmanageable Revolutionaries: Women and Irish Nationalism* (Brandon Books, Dingle, 1983).

Weintraub, Rodelle, *Fabian Feminist: Bernard Shaw and Women* (Pennsylvania State University Press, 1984).

West, Trevor, *Horace Plunkett: Co-operation and Politics* (Colin Smythe, Gerrards Cross, The Catholic University Press, 1986).

Whyte, J. H., *The Independent Irish Party, 1850–1859* (Oxford University Press, Oxford, 1958).

Appendix 1

(The following is a list put together by the IWFL in an attempt to assess which MPs were favourable to their cause.)

Class 1. Reliable Supporters

Irish Nationalist Party
Abraham, Wm
Boland, J. P.
Cotton, W. F.
Devlin, Joseph
Esmond, Sir T. G.
Ffrench, Wm
Gwynn, Stephen
Hayden, J. P.
Hazleton, Richard
Joyce, M.
Kennedy, U. P.
Lardner, J. C. R.
Law, Hugh
MacNeil, Michael
Meehan, F.C.
Nanetti, J. P.
O'Malley, W. M.
O'Shea, J. J.
Redmond, Wm
Scanlan, T.
White, Patrick

Independent Nationalists
Healy, Maurice
Healy, T. M.
O'Brien, William
Sheehan, D. D.

Irish Unionists
Barrie, H. T.
Craig, Captain J.
Kerr-Smiley, P.
Mitchell-Thompson, W.
Thompson, Robert

Class 2. Less Reliable Supporters

Irish Nationalist Party
Brady, P. J.
Clancy, J. J.
Condon, T. J.
Delany, Joseph
Ginnell, Laurence
McKean, John
Molloy, M.
O'Kelly, E. P.
O'Kelly, J. J.
O'Donnell, Thomas
O'Neill, Dr C.
Sheehy, David
Roche, Augustine

Independent Nationalists
Guiney, P.

Irish Unionists
Campbell, J. H. M.
Chambers, J.
Horner, A. L.

Class 3. Adult Suffragists

Irish National Party
Dillon, John
O'Connor, T.P. (Practically these are opponents)

Class 4. Neutrals

Irish Nationalist Party
Boyle, Daniel
Esmonde, Dr. J.
Farrell, J. P.
Fitzgibbon, J.
Flavin, M. J.
McShee, R.
Meehan, P. J. dead [?]
Nolan, Joseph
O'Doherty, Philip
O'Sullivan, T.
Phillips, Jon

Independent Nationalists
Gilhooly, James
Walsh, J.

Liberals
Hogg, David
Russell, T. W. ["Some of these may have decided convictions but they are not on record" – IWFL]

Class 5. Anti-Suffragists

Irish Nationalist Party
Cullinan, John
Donelan, Capt. A. J. G.
Doris, W.
Duff, W. J.

Hackett, J.
Haviland Burke, E.
Kelly, Edward
Kilbride, D.
Lundon, Thomas
Mooney, J. J.
McVeagh, J.
Muldoon, John
Nugent, Sir Walter
O'Brien, Patrick,
O'Dowd, John
O'Shaughnessy, P. J.
Reddy, M.
Roche, John
Smyth, Thos. J.
Young, Samuel
Murphy, Martin
Redmond, John

Independent Nationalists
Crean, Eugene

Class 6. Very Decided Opponents

Carson, Sir E.
Craig, C. C.
Featherstonhaugh, G.
Gordon, J.
MacCaw, W. J. M.
McCalmon, Capt.
McMordie, R. J.
Moore, Wm
O'Neill, Hon. A.

Source: Sheehy Skeffington Papers, National Library, Dublin

Appendix II

Voting pattern of Irish Parliamentary Party on Suffrage Bills or Amendments

Voting on Second Reading of the Conciliation Bill, May 5, 1911

Voting for the Bill   *Voting against the Bill*
31 Nationalists   9 Nationalists
Total   310   Total   143

A large proportion of the absent Nationalists were opposed to Women's Suffrage

1912 Conciliation Bill
Voting for the Bill   *Voting against the Bill*
3 Nationalists   35 Nationalists
Total   208   Total   222

1913 Dickinson's Representation of the People Bill
Voting for the Bill   *Voting against the Bill*
13 Nationalists   54 Nationalists
Total   211   Total   268

1917 Representation of the People Bill
Voting for the Bill   *Voting against the Bill*
33 Nationalists   —————
Total   387   Total   57

Index